Anonymous

**The Mystery of Living**

Cheap, Good and Healthy Cooking, Health, Wealth, Time and Morals

Anonymous

**The Mystery of Living**
*Cheap, Good and Healthy Cooking, Health, Wealth, Time and Morals*

ISBN/EAN: 9783744792134

Printed in Europe, USA, Canada, Australia, Japan

Cover: Foto ©Andreas Hilbeck / pixelio.de

More available books at **www.hansebooks.com**

# THE MYSTERY OF LIVING

AND

## BERNEY'S PATENT

Tea Kettle Boilers, Family Coffee Cones, Tea Kettle Steamers, and other Household Wares,

CAN BE PURCHASED AT

DUTTON & CAMPBELL'S Wholesale Depot of Household Wares, 87 Cornhill, Boston, Mass.
DUTTON & LUNDY, Wholesale Depot of Household Wares, Market Street, Phila., Pa.
S. PICKENS, Albany and Troy, New-York,

And all the CONDENSED MILK COMPANIES in the United States.

### NEW-YORK CITY.

A. BERNEY, 116 John Street.
A. MAYER, 488 Grand Street.
C. M. SMITH, 490 Grand Street.
DANFORTH & CO., 70 Murray Street.
D. SHAW, 380 Bowery.
FRAZER, BELL & LOUGHRAN, 213 Pearl St
JOSEPH GEATIEN, 203 Hester Street.
C. GILBERT, 403 West 18th Street.
L. GEARATY, 511 East 13th Street.

### BROOKLYN, N. Y.

J. T. VAN SLYCKE, 380 Court Street.
C. JACQUES, 126 Myrtle Avenue.
WM. F. TATE, 560 Myrtle Avenue.
EVANS & DOWDESDALE, 727 Myrtle Ave.
JOHN S. OLIVER, 593 Myrtle Avenue.
D. K. VAN DERLIP, 20 Cheever Street.
M. B. & L. RAY, 375 Myrtle Avenue.
RAY, FORDER & CO., 63 Fulton Street.

### WILLIAMSBURGH, N. Y.

M. CLARK, 69 Broadway.
G. W. COGER, 89 Broadway.
B. SCHAFFER, 221 Grand Street.
J. HORN, BROTHERS, 253 Grand St.
LEONARD & DALY, 181 Grand Street.

### JERSEY CITY, N. J.

TERHUNE BROTHERS, 71 & 73 Newark Av.
R. B. EARLE & CO., 54 & 56 Montg'y St.
L. D. LANDRINE, 225 Grove Street.
J. W. HARRISON, 16 Exchange Place.

And any person wanting the Books or Wares, can get them by calling at any Household, Tinware, or Hardware Store in the Country. The Dealers will order them of us, (if they do not write to the nearest Agent on this list,) and we will send them.

In the hurry of going to press, we omit several dealers, but in the next edition will give a complete list of them, with others as soon as arrangements are made.

## FIFTY CENTS TO FIFTY DOLLARS,

AND A MAGAZINE,

### GIVEN FOR ANY ORIGINAL COOKING OR USEFUL HOUSEHOLD RECIPES.

The publisher, desirous of printing, in this magazine, only economical, useful, and good recipes, *will pay from fifty cents to fifty dollars* for every recipe sent that we deem worth publishing, in the other editions of this work. We shall pay not less than fifty cents for every one used, and as much more as they are worth, and a copy of the magazine, free of charge, to every one whose recipes we use, with the recipes in it.

MANY FAMILIES HAVE EXCELLENT recipes for cooking, that are used only by them. Every day new ones are sent to us, one of which we paid twenty dollars for.

We also solicit the various Companies and individuals manufacturing CORN STARCH, MAIZENA, HOMINY, SAMP, MEAL, FARINA, VERMICELLI, MACCARONI, SAGO, FLOUR, RICE FLOUR, PREPARED COCOANUT, CASSAVA, MANIOCA, CONDENSED MILK, ARROW ROOT, or other Foods, to send us their recipes, which we will cheerfully insert *(giving them credit for them)*, *free of charge.*

$100 REWARD will be paid to any person who will furnish the evidence necessary to convict any party or parties of infringing my PATENTS, COPYRIGHTS, TRADE MARK or COPYRIGHTED TITLES, to my goods. The money paid to the informant upon conviction of the guilty party.
The infringers shall suffer the full penalty of the law, I shall show no mercy to patent pirates.

Address all communications to

A. BERNEY,

*New York City.*

# To Those who Wish to Purchase
## "THE MYSTERY OF LIVING."

If the book-stores or newsdealers do not have them on hand, and will not get them for you, enclose *Twenty-five Cents* and you will receive the First Part of No. 1, Vol. I., which relates to Cooking Instructions and Recipes;

Or *Thirty-five Cents*, and receive the First and Second Part of No. 1, Vol. I., together. The Second Part has hundreds of Household Recipes and useful information for the household;

Or *Fifty Cents*, and receive Part First, Second, and Third of No. 1, Vol. I. The Third Part contains full instructions for preserving the beauty, how to grow fat or lean, and increasing the strength. Recipes for the Skin, Hair, Teeth, Eyes, Feet, Hands, Nails, &c., with much other useful information that is of great importance to both sexes.

Each Part has many more pages than the other, and is printed upon better paper, has stronger, handsomer covers, according to the price.

Send the price for one, two, or three Parts, and we will mail it free of postage. Address

*A. BERNEY,*
116 John St., New York.

---

### To Purchasers of the Tea-Kettle Boilers, Coffee Cones, Hand Gas-Lamps, Non-Explosive Cans, or any of our Patent Goods.

When you can not purchase them in the place where you are, mail us the amount stated below, and we will send them by express or freight, as desired.

Recollect we deal only in patent articles, of which we have sole control, and they can be bought only of our agents or at the depot.

---

## A New Chance to Make Money.

**$2 to $12 a Day is now made**
by persons selling our books and wares, not only in New York City, but in every place where sold—Jersey City, Newark, Trenton, Princeton, N. J.; Williamsburgh, Brooklyn, Albany, Troy, N. Y.; Philadelphia, Pa.; Boston, Mass.

S. Pickens, O. Dutton, D. Lunday, E. Falcone, M. Bedell, S. Sparks, and twenty others, are making from four to twenty dollars a day. Mr. Falcone has made more than that; he is a smart, active man.

---

## Not less than Fifty Cents and a Magazine
### GIVEN FOR ANY ORIGINAL COOKING OR USEFUL HOUSEHOLD RECIPE.

The publisher, desirous of printing in this magazine only economical, useful, and good recipes, *will pay Fifty Cents and upward* for every recipe sent that we deem worth publishing, in the other editions of this work. We shall not pay less than fifty cents for every one used, and as much more as they are worth, and a copy of the magazine, free of charge, to every one whose recipes we use, with the recipes in it.

Many families have excellent recipes for cooking, that are used only by them. Every day new ones are sent to us.

We also solicit the various Companies and individuals manufacturing Corn Starch, Maizena, Hominy, Samp, Meal, Farina, Vermicelli, Maccaroni, Sago, Flour, Rice Flour, Prepared Cocoanut, Cassava, Manioca, Condensed Milk, Arrow Root, *or other foods, to send us their recipes, which we will cheerfully insert* (giving them credit for them) *free of charge*.

*$100 reward will be paid to any person who will furnish the evidence necessary to convict any party or parties of infringing my PATENTS, COPYRIGHTS, TRADE MARK or COPYRIGHTED TITLES, to my goods. The money paid to the informant upon conviction of the guilty party.*

*The infringers shall suffer the full penalty of the law. I shall show no mercy to patent pirates.*

### THE MYSTERY OF LIVING.
#### E. FALCONE.

A. Berney is now selling a book,
To learn all good wives how to cook;
In this magazine are a thousand receipts
For roasting and baking all kinds of meats;
Also for making all kinds of cakes,
And no fear of making any mistaker;
All kinds of puddings and pastry, too,
That any good housewife has to do;—
In fact, this is the book that all can inspect,
So as to have every thing good and correct.
This will show you all kinds of pickling and preserving,
Which any prudent housekeeper will think worth reserving.
If you go by the receipts which are laid down in this book,
They will make you laugh and grow fat, also a good cook.
They will also tell you how to retain good health,
Which is better in this world than a mine of wealth.
There is no receipt about a house worth giving,
Unless you find it in the "Mystery of Living."

---

ADDRESS ALL COMMUNICATIONS TO
## A. BERNEY, 116 John Street, New York City.

# LUBIN'S
# Flavoring Extracts

### For Cooking Purposes.

## THE BEST IN THE WORLD!
### ALL FLAVORS..

| | |
|---|---|
| Extract Lemon, | Custards, |
| Extract Bitter Almond, | Jellies, |
| Extract Peach, | Blanc Mange, |
| Extract Ginger, | Charlotte Russe, |
| Extract Nutmeg, | Cakes, |
| Extract Orange, | Puddings, |
| Extract Cinnamon, | Pies, |
| Extract Cloves, | Ice Creams, |
| Extract Celery, | Water Ices, |
| Extract Raspberry, | Frozen Custards, |
| Extract Strawberry, | Corn Starch, |
| Extract Nectarine, | Maizena, |
| Extract Pineapple, | Cocoanut, |
| Extract Vanilla, | Farina, |
| Extract Rose, | Rice, |
| Extract Coffee, | Syrups, |
| Extract Chocolate, | Drinks, |

(center: **FOR FLAVORING**)

and every preparation of food and drink where a delicious flavor is desired.

Prepared from Fruits of the choicest and best quality, and so highly concentrated that a much smaller quantity than that of any other manufactured need be used. Their great excellence consists in their strength, purity, and rare delicacy of flavor to be found in no other. They are entirely free from the poisonous oils and acids which enter into the composition of many of the factitious fruit flavors now in the market.

## LUBIN'S "BLUSH,"

A Purely Vegetable Preparation for Tinting Ice Creams, Jellies, Custards, Corn Starch, Maizena, etc., etc.

Ask for **LUBIN'S FLAVORING EXTRACTS**, insist on having them, and take no other; they are the cheapest because the best.

The genuine bear the *fac simile* signature plainly written across the label of each bottle, that you may always get the genuine.

Sold by Druggists and Grocers everywhere.

### HALL & RUCKEL,
*WHOLESALE DRUGGISTS,*
No. 218 Greenwich Street.

LUBIN'S EXTRACTS are sold in BOSTON by

M. S. BURR & Co.,
26 Tremont Street,

STEPHEN WEEKS & Co.,
234 Tremont Street.

## THE EDITOR'S ADDRESS TO THE PUBLIC.

| | PAGE | | PAGE | | PAGE |
|---|---|---|---|---|---|
| The Mystery of Living | 1 | How to make and save Money | 2 | Wholesale Flour Dealer | 4 |
| The Mystery of our Being | 1 | The Tricks of Trade | 2 | Wholesale Butcher | 4 |
| Of the Health we enjoy | 1 | The Adulterations of Food | 2 | Wholesale Vegetable Dealer | 4 |
| Of Sickness and Pain | 1 | New Inventions | 2 | | |
| Of Food by which we sustain our Bodies | 1 | Practical Receipts | 2 | How to select Goods | 4 |
| | | OUR RECIPES. | | Provisions | 4 |
| Of Liquid we drink | 1 | | | Sugars | 4 |
| Of Medicines | 1 | Mrs. Prudence Winslow's Anti-burning Tea Kettle Boiler | 2 | Coffee | 4 |
| Of the Air we breathe | 1 | | | Tea | 4 |
| Of Heat | 1 | | | Soap | 4 |
| Of Clothing | 1 | Preserve the Mystery for Binding | 2 | Starch | 4 |
| Of Exercise | 2 | | | Syrups and Molasses | 4 |
| Of Bathing | 2 | Mrs. Prudence Winslow's Rules for Trading Economically | 3 | Flour and Meal | 4 |
| Of Amusements | 2 | | | Fruits and Vegetables | 4 |
| Of Labor | 2 | | | Druggists' Articles | 4 |
| Of Love | 2 | Wholesale Druggist | 4 | Fish | 4 |
| Of Tobacco | 2 | Wholesale Provision Dealer | 4 | Meats, Poultry, Game, etc. | 5 |
| The Vices of Mankind | 2 | Wholesale Grocer | 4 | Franklin's Maxims | 5 |

## MRS. PRUDENCE WINSLOW'S ECONOMICAL COOKING RECEIPTS.

| | PAGE | COCOANUT. | NO. | | NO. |
|---|---|---|---|---|---|
| Classification | 6 | Cocoanut Bread Pudding | 39 | Pineapple | 74 |
| Time | 6 | Plain Cocoanut Pudding and Pies | 40 | Apple | 75 |
| Articles and Quantity | 6 | | | Pear | 76 |
| Directions | 6 | Cocoanut and Corn Starch Pudding | 41 | Quince | 77 |
| Remarks | 5 | | | Peach | 78 |
| | | A very rich Pudding | 42 | Cherry | 79 |
| MILK. | NO. | Rich Cocoanut Custard | 43 | Grape | 80 |
| Milk | 1 | Cocoanut Pie | 44 | Orange | 81 |
| Boiled Milk | 2 | Rich Cocoanut Pie | 45 | Lemon | 82 |
| Skim Milk | 3 | Cocoanut Gingerbread | 46 | Ginger | 83 |
| Condensed Milk | 4 | Cocoanut Pound Cake | 47 | Nutmeg | 84 |
| To prepare Milk | 5 | Cocoanut Cake | 48 | Cinnamon | 85 |
| Cocoa Milk | 6 | | | Vanilla | 86 |
| Cocoa or Chocolate | 7 | JELLIES. | | Clove and Allspice | 87 |
| Rice Milk | 8 | Gelatine and Isinglass | 49 | Ice Cream Freezers | 88 |
| Coffee Milk | 9 | Plain Jelly Stock | 50 | Directions for Freezing | 89 |
| French Coffee | 10 | To clarify Plain Jelly Stock | 51 | | |
| Tea Milk | 11 | Lemon Jelly | 52 | MAIZENA. | |
| Tea | 12 | Orange Jelly | 53 | Maizena Custard | 90 |
| Suet Milk | 13 | French Jelly | 54 | Maizena Blanc Mange | 91 |
| Bread and Milk | 14 | To make Twenty Kinds of Jelly | 55 | Maizena Lemon Pudding | 92 |
| Real Cream | 15 | | | Maizena Plain Pudding | 93 |
| Cream Toast | 16 | | | Maizena Baked Pudding | 94 |
| Mock Cream | 17 | ICE CREAMS, WATER ICES, FROZEN CUSTARDS. | | Floating Island | 95 |
| Milk Porridge | 18 | | | Cream Cake | 96 |
| Wheys | 19 | How to make Ice Cream | 56 | To make the Cake | 97 |
| Curds | 20 | Frozen Custards | 57 | Sponge Cake | 98 |
| Plain Custard | 21 | Water Ices | 58 | | |
| English Custard | 22 | Fruit Creams, Ices and Custards | 59 | CORN STARCH. | |
| French Custard | 23 | | | Thin Corn Starch Custard | 99 |
| Condensed Milk Custard | 24 | Spice Creams, etc. | 60 | Muffled Cake | 100 |
| Fruit Custard | 25 | Essence Creams, etc. | 61 | Apple Souffle | 101 |
| | | | | Orange Corn Starch | 102 |
| RICE. | | TO COLOR ICE CREAMS, Etc. | | Corn Starch Fruit Blanc Manges | 103 |
| Rice Water | 26 | Red | 62 | | |
| Rice Gruel | 27 | Purple | 63 | Coffee Corn Starch | 104 |
| Rice Boiled | 28 | Yellow | 64 | Corn Starch and Cocoanut Jelly | 105 |
| Rice for Children | 29 | White | 65 | | |
| Rice Pudding | 30 | Pink | 66 | Corn Starch Omelets | 106 |
| Rice Boiled whole | 31 | Brown | 67 | Cake of Corn Starch | 107 |
| Rice and Apples | 32 | | | General Recipe for making Creams of Corn Starch | 108 |
| Rice Fritters | 33 | TO FLAVOR ICE CREAMS, Etc. | | | |
| | | Strawberry | 68 | General Recipe for making Corn Starch Jellies | 109 |
| FARINA. | | Raspberry | 69 | | |
| Boiled Farina plain | 34 | Blackberry | 70 | General Recipe for making Corn Starch Custards | 110 |
| Ice Farina Pudding | 35 | Whortleberry | 71 | | |
| Boiled Plum Farina Pudding | 36 | Gooseberry | 72 | General Recipe for making Corn Starch Puddings | 111 |
| Baked Farina Pudding | 37 | Red Currant | 73 | | |
| Wheaten Grits | 38 | | | | |

## CONTENTS.

| | NO. |
|---|---|
| To Color Corn Starch Creams, Custards, Jellies, Puddings and Sauces | 112 |
| Corn Starch Sauces | 113 |
| Corn Starch and Cocoanut Pies | 114 |
| Milk or Cream in Corn Starch | 115 |
| Condensed Milk | 116 |
| Corn Starch Snow | 117 |
| Corn Starch Charlotte Russe Cake | 118 |

### EGGS.

| | |
|---|---|
| To Preserve Eggs | 119 |
| To Preserve with Mucilage | 120 |
| To Preserve with Mutton Fat | 121 |
| To Preserve with Lime | 122 |
| Poached Eggs | 123 |
| To Bake Eggs | 124 |
| To Boil Eggs | 125 |
| Dropped Eggs | 126 |
| To Fry Eggs | 127 |
| Scrambled Eggs | 128 |
| Fricasseed Eggs | 129 |
| Plain Omelets | 130 |
| Herb, or Ham, or Meat Omelet | 131 |

### TOMATOES.

| | |
|---|---|
| Raw Tomatoes | 132 |
| To Stew Tomatoes | 133 |
| Baked Whole Tomatoes | 134 |
| Baked Tomatoes | 135 |
| Tomato Fritters | 136 |
| Boiled Tomatoes | 137 |
| Tomato Paste | 138 |
| Tomato Leather | 139 |
| Tomato Sauce | 140 |
| Preserved Tomatoes | 141 |
| Tomato Figs | 142 |

### CHEESE.

| | |
|---|---|
| Improved Welsh Rarebit | 143 |
| Stewed Cheese | 144 |
| Cheese Sandwich | 145 |
| French Macaroni | 146 |
| Cheese Custard and Maccaroni | 147 |
| Cheese Fingers | 148 |
| Pastry Remakins | 149 |
| Macaroroni | 150 |
| Maccaroni and Fish | 151 |
| Mock Crab—Sailor Fashion | 152 |

### SALT FISH.

| | |
|---|---|
| The Best way to soak Salt Fish | 153 |
| To cook Salt Fish | 154 |
| Fish Sauce | 155 |
| A Downeast Fish Dinner | 156 |
| Fish Balls | 157 |
| Croquettes of Fish | 158 |
| Fish Fritters | 159 |
| Spiced Soused Fish | 160 |
| Lobster Fish | 161 |
| Oyster Fish | 162 |
| Stewed Fish | 163 |
| Fricasseed Fish | 164 |
| English Baked Fish | 165 |
| French Stew of Fish | 166 |
| Parisian Style | 167 |
| East India Style | 168 |
| Italian Style | 169 |

### HOMINY.

| | |
|---|---|
| Hominy Plain Boiled | 170 |
| Hominy Fried | 171 |
| Hominy Cakes | 172 |
| Hominy Bread | 173 |
| Hominy Muffins | 174 |
| Samp Boiled | 175 |
| Hominy Gruel | 176 |
| Hominy Cakes | 177 |

### POTATOES.

| | NO. |
|---|---|
| Steam Potatoes | 178 |
| To Boil old Potatoes | 179 |
| To Boil new Potatoes | 180 |
| To Bake Potatoes | 181 |
| Mashed Potatoes | 182 |
| Browned Mashed Potatoes | 183 |
| Potato Cakes | 184 |
| Stewed Potatoes | 185 |
| Baked Chopped Potatoes | 186 |
| Fried Cold Potatoes | 187 |
| Fried Raw Potatoes | 188 |
| Potato Ribbons | 189 |
| To Fry them light or swelled | 190 |
| To Broil Potatoes | 191 |
| Potato Rissoles | 192 |
| Potato Puffs | 193 |
| Potatoes a la Maitre d'Hotel | 194 |
| Stuffed Potatoes | 195 |
| To Brown Potatoes and Meat | 196 |
| Mashed Potatoes | 197 |
| Potato Souffles | 198 |
| Potatoes a la Parisienne | 199 |

### BEANS AND PEAS.

| | |
|---|---|
| How to improve Beans | 200 |
| New England Baked Beans | 201 |
| New York Baked Beans | 202 |
| Dry Beans Boiled Pudding | 203 |
| Dry Beans Baked Pudding | 204 |
| Dry Beans Whole, French Style | 205 |
| Beans Stewed | 206 |
| Beans and Bacon, English Style | 207 |
| Beans and Meat | 208 |
| Beans a la Cream | 209 |
| Bean Soup | 210 |
| Succotash in Winter | 211 |
| Succotash in Summer | 212 |
| Green Peas in Winter | 213 |
| Boiled Peas | 214 |
| Green Peas in Summer | 215 |
| Boiled Pea Pudding | 216 |
| Baked Peas | 217 |
| Pea Pudding | 218 |
| Pea Soup | 219 |
| Winter Pea Soup | 220 |

### SAUCES FOR MEATS.

| | |
|---|---|
| Mint Sauce | 221 |
| Onion Sauce | 222 |
| Butter Sauce | 223 |
| Tomato Sauce | 224 |
| Potatoe Sauce | 225 |
| New England Egg Sauce | 226 |
| Celery Sauce | 227 |
| Egg Sauce | 228 |
| Oyster Sauce | 229 |
| Caper Sauce | 230 |
| Maitre d'Hotel Sauce | 231 |
| Salad Sauce | 232 |

### SAUCES FOR PUDDINGS, PIES, AND CAKES.

| | |
|---|---|
| Custard Sauce for Tarts or Puddings | 233 |
| Egg Sauce for Pudding | 234 |
| Fruit Sauce | 235 |
| Wine Sauce | 236 |
| Dried Apple Sauce (French Style) | 237 |
| Cold Brandy Sauce for Puddings | 238 |
| Cold Butter Sauce | 239 |
| Orange Hard Sauce | 240 |
| Banana Sauce | 241 |
| Condensed Milk Hard Sauce | 242 |
| Transparent Sauce | 243 |
| Hot Milk Sauce | 244 |
| Water Sauce | 245 |
| Dried Fruit Sauce of any Kind | 246 |

### MEATS—HEARTS.

| | NO. |
|---|---|
| Roast Heart | 247 |
| Baked Stuffed Heart | 248 |
| Boiled Stuffed Heart | 249 |
| Stewed Heart Whole | 250 |
| Sliced Stewed Heart | 251 |
| Broiled Heart | 252 |
| Fried Heart | 253 |
| Heart Soup | 254 |
| Corned Beef's Heart | 255 |
| Beef's Heart Hash | 256 |
| Beef's Heart Pie Meat | 257 |

### BEEF TRIPE.

| | |
|---|---|
| Tripe Fried Plain | 258 |
| Tripe Fried in Batter | 259 |
| Tripe Broiled | 260 |
| Tripe Baked | 261 |
| Tripe Soused | 262 |
| Tripe Stewed Plain | 263 |
| Tripe Stewed with Onions | 264 |
| Tripe Fricasseed | 265 |

### BEEF'S PALATES.

| | |
|---|---|
| To Prepare Beef Palates | 266 |
| To Stew Beef Palates | 267 |
| To Broil Beef Palates | 268 |
| Fry of Beef Palates | 269 |
| Palates au Friture | 270 |
| Boiled Sheep's Trotters | 271 |
| Sheep's Trotters | 272 |
| Sheep's Head (French) | 273 |

### HOGS' HEADS AND FEET.

| | |
|---|---|
| Hogs' Head Cheese | 274 |
| Improved Hogs' Head Cheese | 275 |
| Hogs' Head Soused | 276 |
| Hogs' Head Stuffed | 277 |
| Hogs' Head Baked | 278 |
| Stew, Hogs' Head, Haslet, and Kidneys | 279 |
| Pigs' Cheek | 280 |
| Boiled Corned Hogs' Head | 281 |

### OX HEADS.

| | |
|---|---|
| Ox Cheek Cheese (American Style) | 282 |
| Ox Cheek Stewed (German Style) | 283 |
| Stew of Ox Cheek (French Style) | 284 |
| Ox Cheek Corned | 285 |
| Ox Cheek Hash | 286 |
| Ox Cheek Pies | 287 |

### ANIMALS' BRAINS.

| | |
|---|---|
| To prepare Ox Brains | 288 |
| To prepare Calves', Hogs', and Sheep's Brains, etc. | 289 |
| Brains Boiled (French Style) | 290 |
| Brains and Tongue | 291 |
| Mock Oysters (Made of Brains) | 292 |
| Brains Fried (French Style) | 293 |
| Brains Baked | 294 |
| Au Beurre Noir | 295 |
| Brains Boiled | 296 |
| Brains Stewed in Wine | 297 |
| Brains en Matelote | 298 |
| Croquettes of Brains | 299 |
| Brains a la Worcestershire | 300 |

### LIGHTS OR LUNGS.

| | |
|---|---|
| To Prepare Lights | 301 |
| To Fry Lights | 302 |
| To Stew Lights | 303 |

### KIDNEYS.

| | |
|---|---|
| To Prepare | 304 |
| Kidney Stews | 305 |
| Stewed Beef Kidneys | 306 |
| Rissoles of Kidneys | 307 |
| Kidneys Fried | 308 |
| Broiled Kidneys | 309 |
| Baked Kidneys | 310 |

# CONTENTS.

| | NO. |
|---|---|
| KIDNEYS SAUTIES OR VIN | 311 |
| KIDNEY GRAVY | 312 |
| ROAST KIDNEYS | 313 |

### HASLETS.

| | |
|---|---|
| TO FRY HASLETS | 314 |
| TO BROIL HASLETS | 315 |
| TO STEW HASLETS | 316 |
| HASLETS AND MILK | 317 |

### OX HEELS.

| | |
|---|---|
| TO CLEAN AND PREPARE OX HEELS | 318 |
| OX HEELS BOILED | 319 |
| OX HEELS STEWED | 320 |
| OX HEELS FRIED | 321 |
| OX HEELS SOUP | 322 |

### PIGS' FEET.

| | |
|---|---|
| PIGS' FEET STEWED | 323 |
| PIGS' FEET FRIED | 324 |
| PICKLED PIGS' FEET | 325 |
| PIGS' FEET BROILED | 326 |
| PIGS' FEET FRIED IN BUTTER | 327 |
| PIG'S FEET FRICASSEED | 328 |
| PICKLED PIGS' FEET | 329 |
| TO COOK PIGS' FEET THIRTY OTHER WAYS | 330 |
| MOCK BRAWN | 331 |
| PIGS' PETTITOES | 332 |
| PIGS' FEET WITH ONIONS | 333 |

### CALVES' HEADS AND FEET.

| | |
|---|---|
| MOCK TURTLE OF CALVES' HEAD | 334 |
| CALVES' HEAD CHEESE | 335 |
| BOILED CALVES' HEAD | 336 |
| CALVES' HEAD STEWED | 337 |
| CALVES' HEAD A LA MAITRE D'HOTEL | 338 |
| COLLARD CALVES' HEAD | 339 |
| FRICASSEE OF CALVES' HEAD | 340 |
| HASHED CALVES' HEAD | 341 |
| LAMBS' HEAD AND PLUCK | 342 |

### LIVER.

| | |
|---|---|
| TO PREPARE LIVER | 343 |
| TO BROIL LIVER | 344 |
| TO FRY LIVER | 345 |
| LIVER AND BACON | 346 |
| TO BAKE LIVER | 347 |
| TO SAUTE LIVER | 348 |
| TO STEW LIVER | 349 |
| LIVER A LA MODE (FRENCH) | 350 |

### HAMS, SHOULDERS, AND BACON.

| | |
|---|---|
| TO PREPARE SMOKED AND SALT HAMS, SHOULDERS, AND BACON FOR COOKING | 351 |
| TO STEAM HAMS, SHOULDERS AND BACON | 352 |
| TO BOIL HAMS, ETC | 353 |
| TO BAKE A HAM, ETC | 354 |
| TO BAKE, BOIL, ETC., A HAM | 355 |

### RARE RECIPES.

| | |
|---|---|
| OX TAIL SOUP | 356 |
| TONGUES | 357 |
| ROLLED BEEF TO EAT LIKE HARE | 358 |
| POTTED OX TONGUE | 359 |
| POTTED BEEF LIKE VENISON | 360 |
| PRESSED BEEF | 361 |
| BOILED MARROW BONES—SERVED ON TOAST | 362 |
| LOIN OF MUTTON TO EAT LIKE VENISON | 363 |
| SHOULDER OF MUTTON SPICED | 364 |

### GENERAL RECIPES FOR COOKING MEATS.

| | NO. |
|---|---|
| SOUPS | 365 |
| STEWS | 366 |
| ROASTING MEATS | 367 |
| BAKING MEATS | 368 |
| BOILING MEATS | 369 |
| TO BROIL MEATS | 370 |
| TO FRY MEATS | 371 |
| SEMI-FRYING MEATS | 372 |
| FRYING COVERED MEATS | 373 |
| TO COOK MEATS WITH TOMATOES | 374 |
| ENTRÉES OF COLD MEATS | 375 |
| TO MAKE GOOD HASHES | 376 |
| COLD MEATS | 377 |
| MEATS | 378 |
| FORCE-MEATS | 379 |

### VEGETABLES—TURNIPS.

| | |
|---|---|
| PLAIN BOILED TURNIPS | 380 |
| MASHED TURNIPS WITH ONIONS | 381 |
| FRIED TURNIPS | 382 |
| PUREE OF TURNIPS | 383 |

### CARROTS.

| | |
|---|---|
| TO FRY CARROTS | 384 |
| CARROTS (FLEMISH WAY) | 385 |
| TO STEW CARROTS | 386 |
| MASHED CARROTS | 387 |

### ONIONS.

| | |
|---|---|
| TO STEW ONIONS BROWN | 388 |
| BAKED ONIONS | 389 |
| ONIONS A LA CREME | 390 |
| TO STUFF ONIONS | 391 |

### CELERY.

| | |
|---|---|
| CELERY WITH MILK | 392 |
| CELERY WITH CREAM | 393 |
| CELERY FRIED | 394 |

### CUCUMBERS.

| | |
|---|---|
| TO STEW CUCUMBERS | 395 |
| TO STUFF AND BOIL CUCUMBERS | 396 |
| TO ROAST CUCUMBERS | 397 |
| TO DRESS CUCUMBERS | 398 |
| CUCUMBERS A LA PAULETTE | 399 |

### BAKED AND BOILED PUDDINGS.

| | |
|---|---|
| BOILED ARROWROOT PUDDING | 400 |
| BAKED ARROWROOT PUDDING | 401 |
| BOILED SAGO PUDDING | 402 |
| BAKED SAGO PUDDING | 403 |
| BOILED MACCARONI PUDDING | 404 |
| BOILED VERMICELLA PUDDING | 405 |
| BAKED MACCARONI PUDDING | 406 |
| BAKED VERMICELLI PUDDING | 407 |
| BOILED TAPIOCA PUDDING | 408 |
| BAKED TAPIOCA PUDDING | 409 |
| BOILED CONDENSED MILK PUDDING | 410 |
| BAKED CONDENSED MILK PUDDING | 411 |
| SEMOLINA PUDDING | 412 |
| SPANISH PUDDING | 413 |
| PORK PUDDING | 414 |

### MAKING AND BAKING CAKES.

| | |
|---|---|
| ROCK CAKES | 415 |
| STRAWBERRY SHORTCAKE | 416 |
| SNOW CAKE (CORN STARCH) | 417 |
| CHOCOLATE CAKES | 418 |
| GINGER SNAPS | 419 |
| HUNTING NUTS | 420 |
| SPONGE CAKE | 421 |
| A RICH POUND CAKE | 422 |
| LEMON CAKE | 423 |
| A RICH PLUM CAKE | 424 |
| A DELICATE CAKE | 425 |
| COMMON GINGER BREAD | 426 |
| JELLY CAKE | 427 |
| SILVER OR BRIDE'S CAKE | 428 |
| WHITE CUP CAKE | 429 |

### PASTRY AND PIES.

| | NO. |
|---|---|
| TO CLARIFY HOUSE FAT | 430 |
| TO MAKE HYGIENIC PIE CRUST | 431 |
| PLAIN PIE CRUST OR PASTE | 432 |
| A FRENCH PUFF PASTE | 433 |
| TO MAKE OTHER PASTES | 434 |
| SWEET APPLE PIE | 435 |
| SOUR APPLE PIE | 436 |
| MOCK GREEN APPLE PIE | 437 |
| MOCK APPLE PIE | 438 |
| APPLE AND PIE PLANT PIE | 439 |
| PIE PLANT PIE | 440 |
| PUMPKIN PIE | 441 |
| SQUASH PIE | 442 |
| SWEET POTATO PIE | 443 |
| CUSTARD PIE | 444 |
| CHERRY PIE | 445 |
| RASPBERRY PIE | 446 |
| BLACKBERRY PIE | 447 |
| WHORTLEBERRY PIE | 448 |
| CRANBERRY PIE | 449 |
| PEACH PIE | 450 |
| PLUM PIE | 451 |
| CURRANT PIE | 452 |
| GOOSEBERRY PIE | 453 |
| MINCE MEAT FOR PIES | 454 |
| IMITATION OF MINCE PIE | 455 |

### INDIAN MEAL, MUSH, BREAD, BISCUIT, CAKES, PUDDINGS, ETC.

| | |
|---|---|
| INDIAN MEAL AND HOGS' HEAD CHEESE | 456 |
| MEAL AND BROTH MUSH | 457 |
| CORN MEAL MUSH | 458 |
| FRIED MUSH | 459 |
| MRS. WINSLOW'S CORN BREAD | 460 |
| MRS. WINSLOW'S BROWN BREAD | 461 |
| NEW ENGLAND BROWN BREAD | 462 |
| SODA BROWN BREAD | 463 |
| WASHINGTON'S BREAD | 464 |
| MRS. SMITH'S YEAST CORN BREAD | 465 |
| TOGUS CORN MEAL BREAD | 466 |
| MRS. WINSLOW'S SUET AND MEAL BREAD | 467 |
| MUSH BREAD | 468 |
| INDIAN MEAL AND WHEAT FLOUR BREAD | 469 |
| WHEAT AND INDIAN BREAD | 470 |
| MEAL JOHNNY BREAD | 471 |
| GRANDMOTHER'S MEAL BREAD | 472 |
| CORN MEAL PONE OR BISCUIT | 473 |
| BLOT'S MEAL BATTER BISCUIT | 474 |
| MOTHER'S MEAL AND RYE BISCUIT | 475 |
| EGG MEAL BISCUIT | 476 |
| INDIAN BISCUIT | 477 |
| MRS. WINSLOW'S MEAL MUFFINS | 478 |
| INDIAN MEAL WAFERS | 479 |
| WHEAT AND CORN CRUMPETS | 480 |
| MEAL FADGE | 481 |
| ALL KINDS OF GRIDDLE CAKES | 482 |
| MEAL GRIDDLE CAKES | 483 |
| MEAL DROP NUTS | 484 |
| MEAL OMELETS | 485 |
| MEAL POUND CAKE (RICH) | 486 |
| MOLASSES MEAL POUND CAKE | 487 |
| CORN MEAL PUDDING (WITHOUT EGGS) | 488 |
| MEAL FRUIT AND COFFEE CAKE | 489 |
| INDIAN SUET PUDDING | 490 |
| BAKED PUDDING | 491 |
| ENGLISH BAKED MEAL PUDDING | 492 |
| NEW ENGLAND PUDDING | 493 |
| FRENCH BAKED INDIAN PUDDING | 494 |
| STEAMED PLUM PUDDING | 495 |
| BOILED CORN MEAL AND CHEESE PUDDING | 496 |

Of *Exercise.*—Its importance to health, what kind for sick and well.

Of *Bathing.*—Ancient and modern bathing compared, how, when, and rules on bathing and swimming, the necessity of it, with facts of interest.

Of *Amusements* of all kinds.—Those rational and beneficial to all.

Of *Labor.*—Its necessity and usefulness.

Of *Love,* and all the Ruling Passions, with advices how to subdue them, with many anecdotes to prove the importance of it.

Of *Tobacco.*—Its abuse, its poisons, the folly of its use in any manner, with facts relating to it.

*The Vices of Mankind.*—How to avoid and prevent them, with many facts.

*How to Make and Save Money.*—Franklin's maxims, Barnum's rules, Rothschild's, Astor's, Stewart's, and many other wealthy men's plans of making and saving money, WITH MANY FACTS, RULES, AND TABLES, TO SHOW HOW IT MAY BE DONE.

*The Tricks of Trade,* by one who knows.—Showing how to beware of them. Very instructive and useful.

*The Adulterations of Food* will be explained, with information how to detect them.

*New Inventions,* as fast as they are made, will be given here.

*Practical Recipes* upon all household matters, many of which are invaluable, and many other subjects will be treated in a calm, rational manner, any one worth the price of the Magazine a year.

---

## OUR RECIPES.

Practical experience has shown us that recipes from cook-books are not always reliable, and generally expensive in spices, eggs, etc. From a large number of books we have used, we are satisfied that they are simply copied from one to another. The practice is a foolish one. Our experienced editress of that department does not allow a recipe inserted, unless tried by her at home, and the ones printed here are those used by her for a long time, many of them thirty years. Her experience is worth much more than all the cook-books printed. This year we shall publish TWO THOUSAND COOKING RECIPES, *which, in a book, would cost two dollars.* We shall also publish Fifteen Hundred Practical Recipes and reasons why, worth in books four dollars; with much other useful information. WE WILL GUARANTEE THAT A FAMILY WHO HAS OUR MAGAZINE WILL SAVE, IN EGGS ALONE, TEN TIMES THE PRICE OF IT. In many recipes where five eggs are used, she uses one, giving a cheap substitute for the other four. Again, by practice she has *found it a fact* that one good spice is better than five or more kinds, as ordered by cook-books. *More recipes will appear every quarter, as well as how to purchase and use the cheaper articles of food.* Besides MRS. WINSLOW'S ECONOMICAL RECIPES, we shall publish FRENCH, ENGLISH, GERMAN, and OTHER STYLES OF COOKING. These will be given in the other numbers. Many of them are quite novel, and worthy of a trial. We shall also give new American recipes as fast as they are invented. This is an age of progress, and families must be informed of any thing practical, good, and cheap in that costliest department —the kitchen.

---

## ANTI-BURNING TEA-KETTLE BOILER.

This new invention is one that every person who cooks, or loves good cooking, will at once appreciate. It is well known that many articles of food are very easily burnt in cooking, especially those of the more delicate nature. To obviate this difficulty, double boilers are sometimes used, but they are twice as expensive, and the food is almost as apt to be spoiled as it would be in a stewpan. The inventor lost so many of them by their being burnt out (as the water is soon boiled away), that necessity caused the TEA-KETTLE BOILER to be invented. Of course every family use a tea-kettle for boiling water. This we use as our water-bath, or first kettle. The Berney boiler is so made as to fit into any tea-kettle perfectly tight. As it is made of tin, it can be kept clean easily. It has a handle, cover, and oval spout; holds from two to five quarts. For BOILING MILK, COOKING CORN STARCH, MAIZENA, FARINA, HOMINY, GRITS, SAMP, RICE, OYSTERS, JELLIES, COCOANUT, and, in fact, any such food, it is superior to all other cooking utensils now in use. They will measure liquids, flour, etc. *Try one.* Price, 75 cents to $1.50, according to the size. Read the recipes for cooking with it. For sale in all the hardware, tinware, and house-furnishing stores.

---

## PRESERVE THE MYSTERY FOR BINDING.

It will make a large and useful volume at the end of the year. A daily newspaper costs four cents a day, over twelve dollars a year, and at the end of the year you have not one. THE MYSTERY costs you one dollar, and fifty cents for binding, and is worth ten dollars at the end of a year. WHY? Because it is useful, and every day will save you money.

## Mrs. Prudence Winslow's
# RULES FOR TRADING ECONOMICALLY.

Having been left a widow, with eight children to support, in 1837, I had to study economy. My husband had been a *wholesale grocer and dealer in provisions*, but the failures of 1837 took both his fortune and his life.

His creditors sold every thing, houses, store, furniture, all, and left me in the streets in February 1838, with the snow three feet deep (there was no exemption law then). With the help of a few relatives my family was cared for, though scattered here and there; after a time I again gathered them together, resolved that they should not leave me, except of their own desire; each one that was able now put all their earnings in the household purse. With nine to feed and clothe, and rent to pay, with the numerous calls for money, it became a duty and a study how to buy the cheapest, yet good articles.

I BOUGHT FOR CASH, AND EVERY THING WHOLESALE except a few unimportant and perishable things. In order to have the means to do that, we were very prudent until enough money had been saved to buy two articles—a bushel of meal and a barrel of flour. After that it was comparatively easy to buy; for the thirty, and sometimes sixty and one hundred per cent. was saved to us. *The advantages of buying wholesale are,*—you have the goods in the original package; you are sure of full weight; you get them pure and uniform. The fine cuts of meat are generally very expensive, now from twenty-five to thirty-five cents per pound; *but the head, feet, heart, liver, tripe, and coarser parts are equally as good* if cooked properly, and give a greater variety. Vegetables are good, but not so important, except potatoes. Many of those now dependent upon the corner grocer and butcher, who give a very limited credit at exhorbitant profits, and the customers are forced to buy just what they have, if they would begin and save enough to buy one article wholesale, they would soon buy all. Why should the poor man labor hard all the week, that when Saturday night comes he must give one-third of his earnings as profit to the retailer, who lives an easy life, and gets rich off of this trade? I give you many recipes for each article, and if you have nothing in the house but meal, you can make a comfortable repast, at least not hunger.

Many would buy largely, they say, but what can we do with it; it would spoil. I will show you, wives and mothers; recollect that the husband who has toiled all day for you and the children, expects you to save, and also to provide him with well-cooked food. How gratified he will be on his return home to find some new, healthy, palatable dish, made out of that bushel of meal that he bought at only three cents a pound; or a nice hash made from yesterday's cold mutton or heart. And when he knows that the food costs him one-third less, sometimes one half, it is an incentive to him to work longer, to get a roof over your heads that can be all your own.

IN BUYING WHOLESALE so as to have the benefit of the market, I will give a list of pounds and gallons you *must buy*, for if you go where they sell less, they will charge retail prices.

There has been much said about co-operative societies and companies. I know of no better company than a large family, or even a small one; or if one, two, or more club together, make out a list, and send one to buy, and then divide, they will have them by the retail at wholesale prices. *Try it once* and you will continue: I have for over twenty years alone, and the saving and comfort is untold. The loss of time of running to the store, the uncertainty of the quality of the articles, and many times the inferiority, totally disappoint the cook.

A friend of mine traded at a fine grocery store. Among the items of his monthly bill was cream of tartar, at one dollar and twenty cents a pound. *Thinking cream of tartar had risen,* he called upon a wholesale druggist to inquire the price; he was asked whether druggists' or grocers'; he answered, What is the difference? Why, said the druggist, one is pure, the other adulterated; grocers' is thirty cents a pound, druggists' fifty-five cents per pound. He took ten pounds, costing $5.50, saving $6.50; then having it pure, twenty-five cents a pound made $2.50 more; saving altogether *nine dollars upon ten pounds.* He bought ten pounds of soda at ten cents, saved one dollar upon that. He took them home, his cook was cautioned not to use but half so much of the tartar, and did not, but the bread was as good as ever. *This is a fact,* and explains the whole subject.

AS TO SAVING AND PURITY. — There are several articles upon which the saving is very large; tea, molasses, syrup, oil, tartar, soda, and in fact all. Tea is rarely found pure except bought of a responsible house: oil will explode if not made as it ought to be. But my space will not allow me to go on as I wish I could, and I refer you to the table and cards of those who will sell you pure, and as low as can be bought in New York. Of course, in tea and a few things, the quality makes a difference in the price. I give the lowest amount that can be bought at the wholesale prices, most of which are in the original packages. Go to the

### WHOLESALE DRUGGIST FOR

| | | |
|---|---|---|
| Cream of Tartar, | bag | 10 lbs. |
| Carbonate of Soda, | " | 10 " |
| Washing Soda, | " | 10 " |
| Pepper, Allspice, | each | 1 " |
| Ginger, Cinnamon, | " | 1 " |
| Cloves, Nutmegs, | " | 1 " |
| Indigo (for bluing), | " | 1 " |
| Kerosene Oil, | bbl. | 40 galls. |
| Essences | | box. |

### WHOLESALE PROVISION DEALER.

| | | |
|---|---|---|
| Salt Codfish, | 7 quintal | 112 lbs |
| Mackerel, | kid or half bbl | 25 to 100 " |
| Tongues & Sounds, | kid | 25 " |
| Butter, | tub, about | 50 " |
| Lard, | " | 40 " |
| Hams & Shoulders | | one or more. |
| Cheese, | | 15 to 40 " |

### WHOLESALE GROCER.

| | | |
|---|---|---|
| Tea, | half chest | 40 lbs. |
| Coffee, | bag | 50 " |
| Chocolate, | box | 25 " |
| Raisins | " | 25 " |
| Figs, | " | 10 " |
| Currents, | bag | 10 " |
| Soap, | box | 70 " |
| Starch, | " | 25 " |
| Sugar, | bbl. | 200 " |
| Molasses, | " | 30 galls. |
| Syrup, | " | 30 " |
| Rice, | bag | 25 lbs. |
| Peas, | half bush. | 16 qts. |
| Beans, | " | 16 " |

### WHOLESALE FLOUR STORE.

| | | |
|---|---|---|
| Flour, | bbl. | 196 lbs. |
| Rye Flour, | " | 196 " |
| Indian Meal, | bag | 100 " |
| Rye Meal, | " | 100 " |
| Oat Meal, | " | 100 " |
| Corn Starch, | box | 25 " |
| Samp, | bag | 25 " |
| Hominy, | " | 25 " |
| Farina, | box | 25 " |

### WHOLESALE BUTCHER.

| | | |
|---|---|---|
| Beef, | quarter, about | 150 lbs. |
| Mutton, | carcass | 50 " |
| Pork | " | 200 " |
| Veal, | " | 100 " |

### WHOLESALE VEGETABLE DEALER.

| | | |
|---|---|---|
| Apples, | bbl. | 3 bush. |
| Potatoes, | " | 3 " |
| Squashes, | " | 3 " |
| Turnips, | one bushel. | |
| Onions, | " | " |
| Carrots, | " | " |
| Beets, | " | " |

IN BUYING WHOLESALE you will save

HEALTH, because you have pure articles.

PATIENCE, because you have them home and uniform.

TIME, because you can buy six months' supply at once.

MONEY, because you can buy as cheap as the retailer, you can save as a general thing, one-quarter to one-third of your money on an average.

IN THE SELECTION OF GOODS you will have but little trouble, for you will deal with men of honor and principle as a general thing, who do a large business and are above misrepresentation. There are also certain brands that are the best, and you will soon find them out, and will use no other.

PROVISIONS.—Buy sweet salt butter to keep, pure lard, sweet hams, and cheese to taste.

SUGARS.—We use only granulated, for it is the cheapest in the end; no drying up, no waste, and it is impossible to adulterate it. Twenty years' use of it only strengthens us in our belief.

COFFEE.—Buy it green, roast it home. Rio and Java, two-thirds Java, one-third Rio, is best; use only pure coffee.

TEA.—Buy black or Japan; green is not so good. Grocers make large profits on tea.

SOAP.—Always buy it long before you want to use it, and cut it up to dry.

STARCH.—All are generally good.

SYRUPS AND MOLASSES.—Buy a good thick syrup or New Orleans molasses; you will save fifty cents a gallon.

FLOURS AND MEALS.—Go to a wholesale store, tell them what you want, and you will generally get it satisfactory.

California flour I found very good.

St. Louis and southern flour will make more bread than any other. Rye flour makes good cheap bread.

Yellow meal is sweeter than white.

FRUITS AND VEGETABLES.—Always buy them fresh, clean looking, and free from decay. As they vary in quality very much, good judgment is better than advice.

DRUGGIST'S ARTICLES.—Get the best always, at first class wholesale drug stores who will sell pure goods when asked for—you must in these things rely upon *their* honor.

FISH.—Fish should always be perfectly fresh when cooked. To select fresh ones observe the eyes, if they have a bright lifelike appearance, the fish is fresh; if on the contrary, the eyes are sunken and dark colored, and have lost their brilliancy, they are certainly stale. Some judge by the redness of the gills, but they are sometimes colored to deceive customers. Do not buy any more fresh fish than you want to use for the day (except in winter, then they will keep), but the fresher the better.

*Dry Salt Fish* should be kept in the cellar; kept cool they will last a year; age does not hurt them. *Pick sweet ones.*

*Pickled Fish* of all kinds keep good a year in a cool place. Keep them always under the pickle; a brick or two will do that. They are handy to have in the house.

*In the selection of Salt Fish*, go to first-class stores, and they will give you good articles.

MEATS, POULTRY, GAME, ETC.—The finest grained beef is the best. The flesh is of a fine red, and the fat a light cream color, but not yellow; the fat, too, is solid and firm. The lean of mutton should be of a red color, and the fat white. The skin of pork should be of a light color, and if young it is tender; the fat should appear firm. A tender goose is known by taking hold of the wing and raising it; if the skin tears easily, the goose is tender; or if you can readily insert the head of a pin into the flesh, it is young. The same remarks will hold good with regard to ducks. Young chickens may be known by pressing the lower end of the breast bone; if it yields readily to the pressure they are not old, for in all animals the bones are cartilaginous when young. The breast should be broad and plump in all kinds of poultry, the feet pliable, and the toes easily broken when bent back.

Meat will keep in winter a long time; at any time you fear it will not keep, have a barrel or keg of salt pickle to put it in. Meat then can be used up without waste.

In summer we need less fresh meat, and need not buy so much. Salt meats, fish, fruits, and vegetables are best. A good refrigerator will keep meat several days in summer.

---

## FRANKLIN'S MAXIMS.

Benjamin Frankin, one of the greatest philosophers and practical men of any age, thus teaches the people the importance of

### FRUGALITY AND ECONOMY.

A man may, if he knows not how to save as he gets, keep his nose all his life to the grindstone, and die not worth a groat at last. A fat kitchen makes a lean will, and

Many estates are spent in getting,
Since women for tea forsook spinning and knitting,
And men for punch forsook hewing and splitting.

If you would be wealthy, think of saving as well as of getting. The Indies have not made Spain rich, because her outgoes are greater than her incomes.

Away then with your expensive follies, and you will not then have so much cause to complain of hard times, heavy taxes, and chargeable families.

What maintains one vice would bring up two children.

You may think perhaps that a little tea or superfluities now and then, diet a little more costly, clothes a little finer, and a little entertainment now and then, can be no great matter; but remember, many a little makes a mickle.

Beware of little expenses! A small leak will sink a great ship, as Poor Richard says; and again: Who dainties love shall beggars prove; and moreover, Fools make feasts, and wise men eat them.

Here you are all got together to this sale of fineries and nick-nacks. You call them goods; but if you do not take care they will prove evils to some of you. You expect they will be sold cheap, and perhaps they may for less than they cost; but if you have no occasion for them, they must be dear to you.

Remember what Poor Richard says: Buy what thou hast no need of, and ere long thou shalt sell thy necessaries.

And again: At a great pennyworth pause awhile. He means, perhaps, that the cheapness is apparent only, and not real; or the bargain, by straitening thee in thy business, may do thee more harm than good; for in another place he says, Many have been ruined by buying good pennyworths.

Many, for the sake of finery on the back, have gone with a hungry stomach, and half starved their families. Silks and satins, scarlets and velvets, put out the kitchen fire, as Poor Richard says. These are not the necessaries of life: they can scarcely be called the conveniences; and yet, only because they look pretty, how many want to have them!

By these and other extravagances, the genteel are reduced to poverty, and forced to borrow of those whom they formerly despised, but who through industry and frugality have maintained their standing, in which case it appears plainly that, A ploughman on his legs is higher than a gentleman on his knees, as Poor Richard says. Perhaps they had a small estate left them which they knew not the getting of; they think, It is day, and will never be night; that a little to be spent out of so much is not worth minding; but always taking out of the meal-bag, and never putting in, soon comes to the bottom, as Poor Richard says, and then, When the well is dry, they know the worth of water.

But this they might have known before, if they had taken his advice. If you would know the value of money, go and try to borrow some; for he that goes a borrowing, goes a sorrowing, as Poor Richard says; and indeed, so does he that lends to such people, when he goes to get it again.

## Mrs. Prudence Winslow's
## ECONOMICAL COOKING RECIPES.

ALL persons who have used Cook-Book recipes know that they give information to cook only fine rich dishes. The very recipes dishearten a prudent housekeeper. How can it be otherwise when some recipes of a single small dish call for ten eggs (at five cents apiece as they are in winter) and ounces of dear spices and outlandish herbs and costly fruits? Mrs. Winslow having for forty years cooked for a large family of her own, and kept a fashionable boarding-house, now getting old, gives to the world the benefit of NEW ENGLAND cooking, with French, English, German, Scotch, Irish, and other national recipes that have been used by her, improved and cheapened.

Mrs. Winslow's struggle through life to support her children caused her to use many of the cheaper foods, and her great love for her offspring caused the old lady to make them good and palatable, but at the same time healthy. It is well known that many, very many families, have nothing but dry bread the most of the time; others have but little meat, others are tired of beef, pork, mutton, and lamb. They want something new; all parties will find their wants supplied here; many of her cheap dishes are as good as the much more costly ones of the modern cook-books. Many of the recipes can be cooked best in MRS. WINSLOW'S TEA-KETTLE BOILER, which saves time and waste.

Where its use is indicated it will be in large type, we will guarantee that any family will reduce their table expenses ONE-HALF BY THESE RECIPES, AND HAVE HEALTHIER AND BETTER DISHES, BESIDES MANY NEW ONES THAT NEVER HAVE BEEN KNOWN TO THE PUBLIC. The families from Europe will recognize many of her dishes, and gladly welcome them.

The great advantage of these recipes are

### CLASSIFICATION.

1st. *We classify the dishes by the name of the principal food of which it is made, and keep them all together, so that one can see at a glance which one of that kind they prefer,* and if they have only Indian corn meal in the house with the few things required, they can select from fifty dishes to suit their palate; thus, bread, porridge, pudding, cakes, etc.

### TIME.

2d. The time is also seen at once; the time it takes without reading the whole recipes, so that if the cook has not time to prepare it one way she can another, so that with meat of any kind it can be cooked to suit the time.

### ARTICLES AND QUANTITY.

3d. The name of each article and the quantity are given separate, so that the cook, after having read the names and quantity, knows if she has the things, the amount, or can get them. If she can, she has but to read the

### 4th, DIRECTIONS,

to go on, and then, if she desires to, can reduce the amount so as to make less, or increase and make more. Many times the spices, soda, cream of tartar, etc., are adulterated, and it takes much more than the recipes say, for these are based upon pure goods. Our

### 5th, REMARKS

upon dishes are to give information of their excellence, and whom they are best for, sick or well, with about the cost of them. We further add that our desire is to improve American cookery; for, as persons who have traveled know, it can be very much improved. Many diseases are caused by bad cooking, and many more diseases originate by eating rich and unhealthy food.

### 1. Milk

Is a very common article of food, enters into a great many dishes, bread, cake, puddings, pies, drinks; it gives, like eggs, a rich flavor without being unhealthy. In large cities and towns it is apt to be adulterated with water; to avoid which use CONDENSED MILK, which is sold in all large cities, or can be bought in tin cans of the grocers and druggists all over the country. It has many advantages over common milk. *See Condensed milk.*

### 2. Boiled Milk.

TIME.—*Twenty minutes.*

ARTICLE.—Milk, two quarts.

DIRECTIONS.—Pour two quarts of milk into the TEA-KETTLE BOILER, have the water in the tea-kettle boiling, place the boiler in the tea-kettle, let it remain twenty minutes, or longer. It will not burn.

REMARKS.—Boiled, is much richer, better, and healthier, than without boiling; the chemical action of heat upon milk condenses and solidifies it. In too many cases milk sold to families is watered or impure; boiling it will correct this in a measure, as all physicians and chemists know that water boiled is made purer. The component parts of milk are about eighty-seven parts of water; sugar, five; caseine, five; butter, three; all perishable. When boiled, it will keep twice as long. In all recipes for cooking, boiled milk is used where milk is required. If the boiler was used for nothing else it is worth the price of it for one month's use for this purpose alone.

# MILK, COFFEE, TEA, AND COCOA.

### 3. Skim Milk.

TIME.—*Twenty minutes.*

ARTICLES.—Milk, two quarts; corn starch, white sugar, butter, each a table-spoonful.

### 4. Condensed Milk.

This article of food is one that we cannot too highly praise, and we recommend our readers to use it. Two of my children were saved by its free use in the last stage of scarlet fever, when too weak to eat anything else, by the recommendation of a physician. My youngest child, only eight months old, could not drink cow's milk without its souring on its stomach, causing great pain, and keeping it awake, and constantly worrying, but, by using CONDENSED MILK, it at once relieved the babe, and it is now a strong, healthy child. I feel it a duty I owe, not only to the CONDENSED MILK Companies, but to the community, to state these facts. The taking out of about 80 per cent. of water, and the chemical action of condensing, improves and enriches it. We now use it for every recipe where milk or cream is directed in this book, and advise our readers to use it also. IT IS CHEAPER, HEALTHIER, HANDIER, LESS LIABLE TO SOUR, AND RICHER, in making Ice Cream, or for any cooking where rich milk is required. FOR COFFEE *use it without water to suit the taste, it imparts a richness that nothing else can.*

MILK is so important an article for babes, children, the sick and invalid's diet that the mother or nurse cannot use too much care to get it pure, good, wholesome, and the very best that the market affords.

SEE ADVERTISEMENTS OF THE CONDENSED MILK COMPANIES IN THIS BOOK.

### 5. To preserve Milk.

Boil it in the TEA-KETTLE BOILER, add a quarter of a tea-spoonful of soda to two quarts.

### 6. Cocoa Milk.

TIME.—*Fifteen minutes.*

ARTICLES.—Quarter of a pound of cocoa; a quart of milk.

DIRECTIONS.—Pour the milk into a TEA-KETTLE BOILER, let the milk boil; then pour in the cocoa first powdered and made to a paste. Chocolate may be made the same way.

REMARK.—Cocoa or chocolate is very healthy and nutritious, and for children excellent.

### 7. Cocoa or Chocolate.

TIME.—*Fifteen minutes.*

ARTICLES. — Quarter pound of cocoa or chocolate; half a pint of milk; water, a quart.

DIRECTIONS.—Pour the boiling water into a TEA-KETTLE BOILER, add the cocoa or chocolate and milk; boil as above.

### 8. Rice Milk.

TIME.—*Fifteen minutes.*

ARTICLES.—Rice ground, a table-spoonful; milk, a pint.

DIRECTIONS.—Boil the milk in a TEA-KETTLE BOILER, then add the rice, sweeten and flavor to taste.

REMARKS.—Rice, flour, corn starch, arrow-root, made in the same proportions is as good. Half a tea-spoonful of magnesia added will correct acidity of the stomach; there is no better food for the sick, feeble, children, and infants.

### 9. Coffee Milk.

TIME.—*Twelve Minutes.*

ARTICLES.—Two table-spoonfuls of ground pure coffee; a pint of milk; water, half a tea-cup.

DIRECTIONS.—Pour the milk into a TEA-KETTLE BOILER; after it boils add the coffee first soaked in boiling water; let it stand covered two minutes; sweeten to taste.

REMARK.—This coffee is perfectly delicious.

### 10. Improved French Coffee.

TIME.—*One minute to make.*

ARTICLES.—African, Mocha, or Java, two parts Maracaibo or Rio, one part; as preferred, or either one alone; boiling water.

DIRECTIONS.—Keep your coffee in a tight can, grind it to a fine powder Just as it is to be used, place the PATENT COFFEE CONE in a pitcher, or china, stone, or earthen water pot; put in the POWDERED COFFEE, pour in BOILING HOT WATER, as much as needed. The liquid coffee runs through as clear and as strong as brandy. Use boiling milk.

REMARKS.—No other is given, for the wretched way of boiling it is not cooking; it is spoiling the aroma of coffee, which is all there is of it fit to drink. Mocha and Java makes the best, except a few costly scarce kinds. Coffee is very stimulating, and, I believe, good for those it agrees with. I would advise families to use nothing but pure coffee. Buy it in the bean, roast it yourselves.

### 11. Tea Milk.

TIME.—*Fifteen minutes.*

ARTICLES.—Milk, one pint; Tea, a table-spoonful.

DIRECTIONS.—Pour the milk into the TEA-KETTLE BOILER, let it boil; then pour in the tea, let it remain five minutes; then strain and serve.

REMARKS.—This is good for the well and sick, especially those feeble. Tea is stimulant and refreshing.

### 12. Tea.

TIME.—*Ten minutes.*

ARTICLE.—A tea-spoonful for each person.

DIRECTIONS.—Scald the tea-pot, put in the tea, add a little water; then add the rest of the water in five minutes. Another way is to drop the leaves in hot water; when the leaves have all sunk, the tea is ready.

REMARKS.—Black tea is the best and healthiest. Teas are very much adulterated now, by mixing damaged and cheap teas with good ones.

### 13. Suet Milk.

TIME.—*One hour.*

ARTICLES. — Mutton suet, two ounces; milk, one pint; flour, one ounce.

DIRECTIONS.—Boil the above in the TEA-KETTLE BOILER one hour. Good for dysentery and diarrhœa.

### 14. Bread and Milk.

TIME.—*Ten minutes.*

ARTICLES.—Old bread, six slices; milk, a pint.

DIRECTIONS.—Boil the milk in the TEA-KETTLE BOILER; when hot pour it over the bread.

# CREAM, WHEYS, AND CUSTARD.

### 15. Real Cream.
TIME.—*Twenty minutes.*
ARTICLES.—Two quarts of milk.
DIRECTIONS—Heat the milk slowly in the TEA-KETTLE BOILER; as the cream arises take it off, then prepare the milk as in recipe for skim milk.
REMARKS.—Cream is often required, but not easily procured; this recipe will show how to get it at once.

### 16. Cream Toast.
TIME.—*Twenty minutes.*
ARTICLES.—Milk, one quart; flour, three table-spoonfuls; butter, two table-spoonfuls.
DIRECTIONS.—Boil the milk in the TEA-KETTLE BOILER; when hot mix the flour in cold milk, strain through a sieve, and stir in rapidly, add the butter and salt to taste, let it boil five minutes. Toast any bread, pour the cream over it, and serve.
REMARKS.—This is far preferable to plain milk, as is most commonly used. Any old bread toasted will answer. All who have eaten this, like it very much.

### 17. Mock Cream.
TIME.—*Twenty minutes.*
ARTICLES.—Milk, one quart; an egg; a table-spoonful of maizena; and butter, the same quantity.
DIRECTIONS.—Boil the milk in the TEA-KETTLE BOILER, stir up the egg, corn starch, and butter, together; add to the milk when hot.

### 18. Milk Porridge.
TIME.—*Half an hour.*
ARTICLES.—Milk, one pint; water, one pint; oat, Graham, rye, or corn meal, grits, farina, or hominy—either of these a large table-spoonful; a little sugar, salt, and butter to taste.
DIRECTIONS.—Put the hot water into the TEA-KETTLE BOILER, mix the meal in a little cold water, add this, and seasoning (add more meal if it is preferred thicker), then add the milk.
REMARKS.—These porridges are good for the sick and well, very easy of digestion, yet nutritious.

### 19. Wheys.
TIME.—*About half an hour.*
ARTICLES.—Milk, a pint, or either one of the following added to it: rennet, or vinegar, or mustard, or alum, or cream of tartar, a tea-spoonful, or an orange or lemon; tamarinds, two ounces; wine, a tumblerful.
DIRECTIONS.—Pour one pint of milk in the TEA-KETTLE BOILER; when boiling hot add either one of the above articles, stir it in rapidly for a few minutes, separate the curd, drink cold or warm. The curd can be eaten by well persons.
REMARKS.—Wheys are made with any thing that will coagulate the milk, and derive their name from that used; for the sick and feeble they are very nourishing.

### 20. Curds.
TIME.—*Half an hour.*
ARTICLE.—Milk, a pint.
DIRECTIONS.—Make a curd as above directed for wheys,—as whey is the watery part of the dish used for the sick, so the curd is for the well,—turn the curd after it is separated, into a mold or dish, or make into cakes; they can be eaten with sauce or plain.

### 21. Plain Custard.
TIME.—*About half an hour.*
ARTICLES.—Milk, one quart; eggs, four; sugar, a quarter of a pound; flavor to taste.
DIRECTIONS.—Pour a quart of sweet milk into the TEA-KETTLE BOILER, stir in the sugar; beat the eggs well, and stir until thick; pour it into a dish or custard cups.

### 22. English Custard.
TIME.—*One hour and a half.*
ARTICLES.—Milk, two quarts; sugar, quarter of a pound; eggs, six.
DIRECTIONS.—Beat the yolks of the eggs; pour the milk into the TEA-KETTLE BOILER, keep the cover off; boil it down to one-half; pour the milk when reduced on the eggs, stir it until nearly cold, then pour back into the BOILER, and boil for one hour; then pour into a buttered mold; let it cool, then turn out; serve with sauce or jellies.

### 23. French Custard.
TIME.—*Half an hour.*
ARTICLES.—Milk, a quart; eggs, four; lemon peel; quarter of a pound of sugar.
DIRECTIONS.—Pour a quart of milk into the TEA-KETTLE BOILER; add one lemon peel; beat the yolks of the eggs, add to the milk, add the sugar; boil all till it is thick.

### 24. Condensed Milk Custard.
TIME.—*Half an hour.*
ARTICLES.—Condensed milk, one pint; water, one pint; sugar, quarter of a pound.
DIRECTIONS.—Pour the milk and water into the TEA-KETTLE BOILER; beat and add the eggs and sugar; boil until it thickens; pour it into cups; grate some nutmeg over each cup; let them get cold, and serve.

### 25. Fruit Custard.
TIME.—*Half an hour.*
ARTICLES.—Custard and fruit.
DIRECTIONS.—Place any preserved fruits or jellies in a deep dish about one inch thick; pour over them any of the above custards when hot, and serve them very cold.
REMARKS.—More or less eggs, sugar, or milk, can be used in any custard; flavor of any kind to suit the taste. Custards may be thickened with maizena, corn starch, or gelatine.

## RICE

Supports millions of people in the eastern countries, and is a very nutritious food, easy of digestion, never does any harm, good for the sick and well. It can be made into many dishes. At present we give only the plain ones, but will hereafter give some thirty others. In boiling, use the TEA-KETTLE BOILER, or a water boiler, or it will be very liable to burn. Rice, when boiled, may be used in custards, bread batter, cakes, muffins, stuffing, fried, etc.

### 26. Rice Water.

To one quart of water, two table-spoonfuls of rice boiled two hours.

### 27. Rice Gruel.

Ground rice, a heaping table-spoonful; ground cinnamon, a tea-spoonful; water, a quart; boil half an hour.

### 28. Rice Boiled.

Wash it in pure water; boil it in salted water in the TEA-KETTLE BOILER. Keep it from boiling to a jelly.

### 29. Rice for Children.

Boil in water until half done; then add a little butter, some sweet milk, sweeten; add eggs if desired.

### 30. Rice Pudding.

Wash the rice; soak it an hour; mix as many raisins in weight as rice; boil it to a hard jelly. It will come out of the BOILER all in one piece. Eat with sauce, or turn hot into cups; it will come out solid when cold.

### 31. Rice Boiled Whole.

Soak a pound of rice, more or less, six hours, in cold water, to which a little salt has been added; pour boiling hot water in the TEA-KETTLE BOILER; pour in the rice; boil twenty minutes; drain it in a calender. It will be very nice.

### 32. Rice and Apples.

TIME.—*Two hours.*

ARTICLES. — Rice, a pound; butter, an ounce; sugar, a table-spoonful; apples, six, or dried apples the same.

DIRECTIONS.—Boil the rice until soft, add the butter and sugar; stew six green or dried apples, sweeten; pour the apples in a dish and cover with the rice, and serve.

### 33. Rice Fritters.

TIME TO FRY.—*Ten minutes.*

ARTICLES, rice, four ounces; eggs, four; milk, one quart.

DIRECTIONS—Boil rice in the milk; when the rice is soft, remove it; when cold add four eggs well beaten, as much flour as will make a batter; drop a spoonful into hot fat, and fry brown. Eat with sugar and sauce.

## FARINA,

One of the products of wheat. It is delicate, yet nourishing; good for the sick and well, especially so for dyspeptics. This and wheaten grits to eat, when costive, are two indispensable articles for them, and no household should be without them. At another time we shall enter more fully upon the subject.

### 34. Boiled Farina, Plain.

TIME.—*One hour.*

ARTICLES. — Water, a quart; farina, a quarter of a pound.

DIRECTIONS.—Have boiling hot water in the TEA-KETTLE BOILER, sprinkle and stir in the farina slowly; boil it an hour; sweeten, salt and flavor to taste. Eat warm or cold. Fried in slices, it is excellent.

### 35. Ice Farina Pudding.

TIME.—*Two hours.*

ARTICLES.—Milk, three pints, or water, a quart; farina, one quarter of a pound; eggs, two.

DIRECTIONS.—Boil the milk in the TEA-KETTLE BOILER; when hot add the farina, sprinkle and stir it in slowly; sweeten to taste, then boil an hour or so until thick; beat the eggs, add; let it boil a little longer, flavor and remove; pour into molds to cool. Eat with milk or sauce. The eggs can be omitted, if desired.

### 36. Boiled Plum Farina Pudding.

TIME.—*Three hours.*

ARTICLES.—Farina, quarter of a pound; milk, three pints, or water, a quart; currants or raisins, a pound.

DIRECTIONS.—Boil the milk, or pour the hot water into the TEA-KETTLE BOILER, then stir in the farina and fruit; boil all together in the boiler three hours, or tie it in a pudding cloth, and boil until done in a pot.

### 37. Baked Farina Pudding.

TIME.—*Two hours.*

ARTICLES. — Farina, four ounces; milk, three pints, or water, one quart; three eggs; half a pound of sugar.

DIRECTIONS.—Boil the farina in the milk or water, in the TEA-KETTLE BOILER for an hour; beat the eggs well, add the sugar; let the farina cook, then add the above, with lemon or vanilla to taste, and bake in a dish.

### 38. Wheaten Grits

Is broken wheat. Wash it well until all the bran is separated. Boil it in the TEA-KETTLE BOILER, using plenty of water. Salt to taste. After it is done, use syrup. A good dish for any one, especially for those costive.

# COCOANUTS

Are at times very cheap, and very little is required to make a rich flavored pudding. A new desiccated cocoanut answers the same purpose; we have tried many pounds of it. It should be cooked in the TEA-KETTLE BOILER when boiled, to prevent burning.

### 39. Cocoanut Bread Pudding.
TIME.—*Three hours.*
ARTICLES.—Milk, one quart; cocoanut, one tea-cupful; bread, two cups; sugar, half cup; eggs, two.
DIRECTIONS.—Boil the milk in the TEA-KETTLE BOILER; when hot add the cocoanut, boil two hours, then add the bread, the eggs well-beaten, and the sugar, boil an hour. Eat it cold; currants or raisins can be added.

### 40. Plain Cocoanut Pudding and Pies.
TIME.—*Four hours.*
ARTICLES.—Cocoanut, half a pound; milk, three pints; eggs, three; sugar, a cupful.
DIRECTIONS.—Boil the cocoanut in the milk in the TEA-KETTLE BOILER, three hours, then add three eggs well-beaten with the sugar boiled until thick; pour into a mold, or bake for pies.

### 41. Cocoanut and Corn Starch Pudding.
TIME.—*Two hours and a quarter.*
ARTICLES.—Milk, a quart; cocoanut, corn starch, sugar, each a tea-cup; eggs, two.
DIRECTIONS.—Boil the cocoanut in the milk in the TEA-KETTLE BOILER two hours; then wet the corn starch in cold milk, beat two eggs, add both to the milk; also the sugar when desired; the liquids can be used for pies.

### 42. A very rich Pudding.
TIME.—*Three hours.*
ARTICLES.—Cocoanut, one pound; milk, one pint; sugar, half a pound; eggs, four; rosewater, one gill.
DIRECTIONS.—Boil the cocoanut in the milk two hours (with the cover on) in the TEA-KETTLE BOILER, beat the eggs well, add the sugar, stir all together. Bake in a pudding dish lined with paste, and boil until thick, and eat cold.

### 43. Rich Cocoanut Custard.
TIME.—*Three hours.*
ARTICLES.—Milk, a quart; sugar, a quarter of a pound; cocoanut, same; eggs, two; maizena, two table-spoonfuls.
DIRECTIONS.—Boil the milk with the cocoanut in the TEA-KETTLE BOILER two hours; then add the sugar, beat the eggs well, add also the maizena; boil until thick, eat cold poured hot over sliced peaches, oranges, pears, or preserved fruits. Eaten cold it is delicious.

### 44. Cocoanut Pie.
TIME.—*Two hours.*
ARTICLES.—Cocoanut, one cup; milk, two cups; sugar, half a cup; soda crackers; three eggs.
DIRECTIONS.—Soak the cocoanut in the milk half an hour, roll the crackers fine, beat three eggs well, stir all together, bake without upper crust in a slow oven.

### 45. Rich Cocoanut Pie.
TIME.—*Two hours and a half.*
ARTICLES.—Cocoanut, half a pound; sugar, a quarter of a pound; lemon rind, one half; eggs, three; milk, a cup; water, a cup.
DIRECTIONS.—Boil the cocoanut and sugar in the water and milk, in the TEA-KETTLE BOILER, two hours; let it cool, add the eggs well-beaten, then the lemon peel well-grated, and bake as before.

### 46. Cocoanut Gingerbread.
TIME.—*Three quarters of an hour.*
ARTICLES.—Cocoanut, four ounces; flour, four ounces; maizena, four ounces; sugar, four ounces; butter, four ounces; peel of a small lemon; a coffee-cup of molasses or syrup; half an ounce of ground ginger.
DIRECTIONS.—Put the syrup into a saucepan with the butter when hot · pour it into the flour and maizena, previously mixed with the sugar, ginger, and grated lemon peel. Beat the mixture well together, set it to become cold, stir into it the prepared cocoanut, beat it for a few minutes, then drop the mixture from a table-spoon, on a buttered tin, any size you prefer the cakes to be, and bake them in a slow oven.

### 47. Cocoanut Pound Cake.
TIME.—*Half an hour.*
ARTICLES.—Sugar, one pound; butter, a quarter of a pound; milk, a tea-cupful; essence of lemon, a tea-spoonful; soda, a tea-spoonful; eggs, three; cocoanut, half a pound.
DIRECTIONS.—Mix the white sugar with the butter beaten to a cream, add the lemon and the milk, beat the eggs separately, then add the soda; beat all thoroughly together with the flour, as much as will make it as thick as pound cake; then lightly stir in the grated cocoanut. If the prepared cocoanut is used, soak it first in milk. Bake it in a quick oven in one or many tins.

### 48. Cocoanut Cake.
TIME.—*Half an hour.*
ARTICLES.—Sugar, half a pound; cocoanut, half a pound; butter, quarter of a pound; eggs, two.
DIRECTIONS.—Beat the sugar and butter up well together, beat the eggs, mix all well together, roll out, cut into cakes, and bake in a moderate oven.

# JELLIES.

### 49. Gelatine and Isinglass.

*Animal Jellies* are nutritious and very cheap, if made according to our directions, and are very pleasant to the taste. They have been considered very expensive and not hearty. This is a mistake. Jellies are the very strength of meat and the vital juices, so to speak. Fruit and farina jellies are the same; try them by our directions; if you do not wish the trouble, prepared gelatine can be easily purchased at the stores. Animal jelly can be made of calf's head and feet, pig's head and feet, cattle's feet in making jellies. The head and feet are good for the table, and make a good meal (see recipes for cooking for the table), so that the jelly is a clear gain; only a little trouble, a trifling expense, and you have a delicacy for well and sick. Use the TEA-KETTLE BOILER in preparing them.

### 50. Plain Jelly Stock.

TIME.—To clean, *half an hour;* to boil, *six hours;* to clarify, *ten minutes.*

ARTICLES.—Calf's feet, four, or a calf's head, or a hog's head, or four ox heels; pig's feet for either; four quarts of water; sugar, two ounces; one egg.

DIRECTIONS.—Take either of the above (not all), scald and clean them in boiling hot water, knock off the hoofs or horned part of feet, take out the eyes and brains if it is the head. Split the feet or head, put them into the pot, add a gallon of cold water, boil six hours, or until very tender; then remove with a skimmer; use no salt or spice in the water (the meat can be used for food as directed below). When it is cold, skim off every grain of fat; a gallon of water generally makes a quart of jelly, which, after it is cold, must be clarified.

### 51. To Clarify Plain Jelly Stock.

TIME.—*Twenty minutes.*

ARTICLES.—Stock, a quart; one egg; sugar, two ounces; flavor.

DIRECTIONS.—Pour a quart of the stock into a TEA-KETTLE BOILER, add the white of an egg, with the shell well beaten together, two ounces of sugar, and any flavor preferred; let it boil six minutes; then skim, pour all into a jelly bag, or through a piece of cotton cloth, run it into a bowl or mold. More eggs can be added if desired.

REMARKS.—If you wish to make it any flavor, do so while the stock is hot. Jellies take their names from the flavor: Lemon, Orange, Cinnamon, &c. The cost of a quart of jelly is but the labor and ten cents at the most; for the meat is worth all that is paid for it.

### 52. Lemon Jelly.

TIME.—*Altogether; one hour.*

ARTICLES.—Peel of four lemons and juice; three glasses of sherry; three-quarters of a pound of loaf sugar; one ounce and a half of gelatine or stock; one pint of water.

DIRECTIONS.—Steep the thin peel of four lemons in half a pint of boiling water until strongly flavored with the peel. Put the sugar pounded with the stock into the TEA-KETTLE BOILER, and boil it slowly for about a quarter of an hour or twenty minutes; then add the strained lemon juice and the water from the peel. Let it just boil up; skim it well, add the wine, and strain it until quite clear.

### 53. Orange Jelly.

TIME.—*About an hour.*

ARTICLES.—Peel of four oranges and two lemons and juice; a quarter of a pound of loaf sugar; a quarter of a pint of water; two ounces of gelatine.

DIRECTIONS. — Grate the rinds of the oranges and lemons, squeeze the juice of each, strain it, and add the juice to the sugar and the water, and boil it until it almost candies. Have ready a quart of jelly, put to it the syrup, and boil it once up. Strain off the jelly, and let it stand to settle before it is put into the mold.

### 54. French Jelly.

ARTICLES.—One quart of calf's foot or clear gelatine or stock; some ripe fruit, or any preserved or brandy cherries.

DIRECTIONS.—Have ready one quart of very clear jelly, select ripe and nice looking fruit, and pick off the stalks; commence by putting some jelly at the bottom of the mold, and let it remain about two hours to harden; then arrange some fruit according to taste round the edge of the mold; if currants, lay them in as they come from the tree, on their stalks, and pour in more jelly to make the fruit adhere, and let that layer also harden; then add more fruit and jelly, until the mold is full. If peaches, apples, apricots, &c., are used, they are better boiled first in a small quantity of syrup; but strawberries, grapes, cherries, or currants may be put in uncooked. An extremely pretty jelly may be made from preserved fruits, or brandy cherries. It may be garnished with any fruit, or an open jelly may have some strawberries piled in the center, or a whipped cream piled up, with strawberries stuck in it, which has a very good effect.

### 55. To make Twenty Kinds of Jelly.

Take a quart of jelly stock, or make it out of gelatine; then make and add any of the recipes to make ice-cream.

# ICE CREAMS,
## WATER ICES, FROZEN CUSTARDS.

HOW TO MAKE ALL KINDS, AND THE COST OF THEM, AND THE PROPER WAY OF EATING THEM.

Many families think because ice cream and water ices are sold so high in the confectionaries that they must be expensive to make. It is a mistake ; it is not so. As we have repeatedly said, a variety of food is essential to the maintenance of human life. Cheap luxuries are also, in moderation, necessary to pleasure and enjoyment after a hard day's work. We know of nothing more delightful and refreshing than ice cream, for milk, sugar, eggs, and fruits are all healthy and very nutritious; so it is not money wasted that you spend for ice cream or water ices. Ices are cheaper, but of course not so substantial. In eating them DO NOT GOBBLE THEM DOWN IN A HURRY, BUT LET THEM MELT IN YOUR MOUTH. THAT IS THE WAY TO EAT THEM, AND WE WILL GUARANTEE NO ONE WILL EVER BE HURT BY EATING ICE CREAMS OR WATER ICES. The swallowing of masses of ice cream upon a heated stomach is enough to make any one sick, but when it is melted in your mouth it can not.

*Condensed Milk used alone, or in proportion of one part water to one part Condensed milk, will be found an excellent substitute for cream, and much richer. Two or three parts water to one of Condensed Milk, will make good cream. If you live where you cannot get it at the door, use the canned milk, which does not require sugar. Try it and you will prefer it to cream, or common milk.*

LEMON JUICE *makes the flavor taste richer.* Sometimes it is not to be put in. It will be stated when.

### 56. How to make Ice Cream.

TIME.—*From ten to twenty minutes.*

ARTICLES.—Sweet milk, a pint; a tablespoonful of sweet butter ; white sugar, half a pound ; juice of one lemon ; two well-beaten eggs (or not); essence, half a teaspoonful, or fresh fruit a pint, or syrup of fruit, half a tea-cupful ; a table-spoonful of maizena, or flour, or pure corn starch.

DIRECTIONS.—Boil the milk in the TEA-KETTLE BOILER ; add the butter, a spoonful of corn starch, maizena or flour, first stirred up in a little cold milk ; add to the milk then two well-beaten eggs ; let it get cool, then stir in the essence or juice of fruit or syrup as directed below; freeze. Cream is richer than milk, but can not be got readily, and is expensive. Those who use cream need no butter or flour.

### 57. Frozen Custards

Are made as above, except using two table-spoonfuls of maizena, and boiling all until thick. Flavor and freezing are the same as ice creams. If you desire, these custards can be made without freezing.

### 58. Water Ices

Are made in the same manner, using ice-water instead of milk, without eggs, and no boiling.

### 59. Fruit Creams, Ices, and Custards.

Juices direct from fresh fruit are the best and the cheapest, where parties raise it. Jam your berries or fruit ; sprinkle half a pound of white sugar over it; squeeze a lemon over the sugar; let it stand one hour, then sift it through a fine sieve, or better, squeeze it through a piece of cotton cloth; then stir it well into the cold milk, as prepared for creams and custards, or water for ices, and freeze at once.

### 60. Spice Creams, etc.

Steep whole spice in a gill of hot water. Use this instead of fruit. Coffee, tea, and chocolate come under this class. If whole spice is not to be had, tie up ground in a cloth.

### 61. Essence Creams, etc.

Where essences can be bought they are the handiest ; half a teaspoonful to a pint of milk. Custards can be made of any of the recipes. We generally use the essences, as they are no trouble.

## TO COLOR.

ICE CREAMS, WATER ICES, JELLIES, AND CUSTARDS *can be made of different colors.*

### 62. Red.

One ounce of cochineal, one ounce of salts of wormwood, one pint of water boiled five minutes ; take it off the fire, add three ounces of cream of tartar, one ounce of rock alum ; put them in slowly or it will boil over; add, if to heap, sugar syrup, instead of water.

### 63. Purple.

Infuse a pound of mallow flowers in a quart of water six hours ; add a little salt of tartar; strain; it gives a deep purple, or boil an hour and add a little huckleberry juice, or use huckleberries or blackberries.

### 64. Yellow.

Use the yolks of eggs, or, for a bright yellow, soak a half pound of turmeric root in a pint of alcohol until it is yellow enough. Color to suit

### 65. White.

Use milk, white of eggs, white sugar, and white essence.

## ICE CREAMS, WATER ICES, FROZEN CUSTARDS.

### 66. Pink.
Use currants, raspberries, or strawberries, or a little red coloring.

### 67. Brown.
Coffee and chocolate creams are brown.

The different kinds of ICE CREAMS, WATER ICES and CUSTARDS are made as follows:—

### 68. Strawberry
Take a pint of fresh strawberries, jam them with a spoon; sprinkle half a pound of sugar over them; then squeeze a good sized lemon over it; add coloring if desired; let it stand an hour; sift it through a fine sieve, or press the juice through a cloth; if the sugar has not all melted, stir it up in the fruit, add half a tea-cupful of water, then stir this juice into the cold prepared cream and freeze at once. If you have no fresh strawberries, use the canned ones, or essence, or syrup, as above directed.

### 69. Raspberry.
Made same as strawberry. A delicate dish, and pink.

### 70. Blackberry.
Made same as strawberry. As healthy a cream as made.

### 71. Whortleberry.
Made same as strawberry. A novel cream ice or custard made a fine purple.

### 72. Gooseberry.
Same as strawberry—*no lemon*. Makes fine green.

### 73. Red Currant.
Made same as strawberry—*no lemon*. A fine pink.

### 74. Pine Apple.
Made same as strawberry.

### 75. Apple.
Boil in enough of water to make a pint of solid stewed apples. Strain through a fine sieve or cloth. Then make as above.

### 76. Pear.
Made same as apple.

### 77. Quince.
Made same as apple.

### 78. Peach.
Peel a dozen large peaches, mash them through a colander, and make same as apple.

### 79. Cherry.
One pint of cherries, mashed, strained, and made as above.

### 80. Grape.
A pint of grapes, mashed, sugared, strained, and made as above.

### 81. Orange.
Juice of four oranges; if desired, boil the peel in the milk and make as above.

### 82. Lemon.
Juice of two lemons, boil the peel in the milk, then make as above.

### 83. Ginger.
Boil the ginger in the milk or water, or use essence to taste.

### 84. Nutmeg.
Same as ginger.

### 85. Cinnamon.
Same as ginger.

### 86. Vanilla.
Same as ginger.

### 87. Clove and Allspice.
Same as ginger.

### 88. Ice Cream Freezers.
There are now in the market many ice cream freezers that will freeze ice cream inside of five minutes, and sold so low that any family can buy one. They rarely get out of order, and last for many years. By the use of one of these the process of freezing is rendered so much more expeditious and satisfactory as to more than compensate for the trifling expense involved in its purchase. They all have the wooden tubs to hold the salt and ice.

### 89. Directions for Freezing
Always accompany them, but we give the following directions that we will always have them, and if you do not have a freezer, you can do so by using a tin pail and a bucket. A quart of ice cream can be frozen, taking care that there are no holes in the freezer to let in the water and spoil the cream. Set the freezer, containing the cream, in a wooden tub or bucket several inches larger, and pack closely around its sides a mixture of pounded ice and salt (mixed in the proportion of six pounds of ice to one of salt), extending to within two inches of the top of the freezer; cover the freezer and keep it in constant motion, removing the cover frequently (if it does not clean itself as some do) to scrape the congealed cream or ice from the sides with a silver spoon or wooden paddle, taking care to keep the sides clear, and stirring it well to the bottom. Keep the tub well filled with salt and ice outside the freezer, and take care that none of the salt water gets in to spoil the cream. The outside tub or bucket should have a hole in or near the bottom, from which the bung can be removed to allow the water to pass out as the ice melts. After the cream is well frozen, it may be packed in molds, and set in salt and pounded ice. When you wish to serve it, wrap the mold with a hot cloth a minute, so as to loosen it; turn out the cream on a dish and serve immediately.

OTHER RECIPES WILL BE GIVEN HEREAFTER.

# MAIZENA.

It is the farinaceous product of corn. It affords many delicate, nourishing, attractive, and palatable dishes, easily simulated by deranged organs, suitable for the use of invalids and children, as well as for family use. In custards for thickening it is preferable to wheat flour. It is the best pudding any cook can make. With a paper of this in the house, and some milk and sugar, an egg or two, a pudding or cake can be had in a few minutes, easy of digestion, a luxury, and very nutritious. It must always be boiled in the TEA-KETTLE BOILER, or some water boiler, to prevent burning, as it is very liable to scorch, and, as the flavor is delicate, spoiled. In adding the maizena to the milk, it must be first wet in cold milk; this prevents its being lumpy; powdered sugar is best to use with it.

### 90. Maizena Custard.
TIME.—*Half an hour.*
ARTICLES.—Maizena, two table-spoonfuls; milk, one quart; egg, one; sugar, a cupful.
DIRECTIONS.—Heat the milk in the TEA-KETTLE BOILER hot, mix the maizena in a little cold milk, beat the egg with the sugar, add all, let it boil three minutes; salt and flavor to taste.

### 91. Maizena Blanc Mange.
TIME.—*Half an hour.*
ARTICLES.—Maizena, five table-spoonfuls; milk, a quart; eggs, two.
DIRECTIONS.—Cook as for custards, flavor, and salt to taste; let it run into molds, eat with sugar and milk or sauce.

### 92. Maizena Lemon Pudding.
TIME.—*Half an hour.*
ARTICLES.—Maizena, three ounces; sugar, six ounces; lemon, one; milk, three pints; eggs, three.
DIRECTIONS.—Heat the milk in a TEA-KETTLE BOILER, grate the rind of one lemon, add the juice and the rind to the sugar, and the maizena, stir this in a little cold water to make it smooth; when the milk is hot, stir it all in; stir until it thickens, beat the eggs well, and add with a little butter; as soon as thick pour it into cups or molds, first wet in cold water; when cold eat with sugar and milk or sauce.

### 93. Maizena Plain Pudding.
TIME.—*Half an hour.*
ARTICLES.—Maizena, five table-spoonfuls; of sugar, same; milk, a quart.
DIRECTIONS.—Heat the milk and sugar in the TEA-KETTLE BOILER; when hot, add the maizena, let it boil five minutes, flavor to taste, pour into a dish, eat with fruits, preserves or jellies, or plain.

### 94. Maizena Baked Pudding.
TIME.—*One hour.*
ARTICLES.—Maizena, four table-spoonfuls; sugar, same quantity; eggs, two; milk, a quart.
DIRECTIONS.—Heat the milk in the TEA-KETTLE BOILER; when hot add the maizena, and sugar, salt, and flavor to taste; let it cool a little, add the eggs well beaten, pour into a buttered dish, and bake half an hour.

### 95. Floating Island.
TIME.—*Half an hour.*
ARTICLES.—Maizena, two table-spoonfuls; sugar, four; milk, three pints; eggs, four.
DIRECTIONS.—Beat the yolks of the eggs and sugar together, mix the maizena with a little of the cold milk, put the remainder in the TEA-KETTLE BOILER to boil; when it boils add the eggs and maizena, stir well until it thickens, put it in an earthen dish, beat the whites of the eggs with a spoon to a stiff froth, place it on the custard; heat the custard in the oven until it is of a light brown, or eat without baking.

### 96. Cream Cake.
TIME.—*To make the cream, fifteen minutes.*
ARTICLES.—Milk, a cup; sugar, half a cup; maizena, a table-spoonful; butter, a tea-spoonful; flavor to taste.
DIRECTIONS.—Boil half the milk and sugar together in the TEA-KETTLE BOILER, mix the maizena in half of the cold milk, and stir in the maizena; boil five minutes.

### 97. To make the Cake.
TIME.—*Half an hour.*
ARTICLES.—Maizena, half a cup; same of wheat flour; sugar, a cup; eggs, three; half a table-spoonful of butter; half a tea-spoonful of soda; one of cream of tartar; flavor with lemon.
DIRECTIONS.—To be baked in round tin pans, about three-quarters of an inch thick; bake two or four, spread the cream on one, cover over with the other, put them together. Jellies can be used instead of cream if desired.

### 98. Sponge Cake.
TIME.—*Forty minutes.*
ARTICLES.—Sugar, half a pound; eggs, four; maizena, three-quarters of a pound; cream of tartar, a tea-spoonful; soda, half a tea-spoonful.
DIRECTIONS.—Beat the eggs and sugar well together, stir the dry tartar well into the maizena, add the soda dissolved in a little hot water; stir all well together; bake in a quick oven.

We will give more recipes in our next number.

# CORN STARCH,

Like the maizena, is the product of Indian corn, and deservedly ranks high as an article of luxurious yet cheap food. It is all nutriment, and differs from maizena in the manufacture; both are good; try both; same recipes for both.

Corn starch has a peculiar thickening property in itself, and owing to being cheap and hearty, should be extensively used for custards, blanc mange, creams, jellies, gravies, omelets, soups for children and invalids, and the well.

The preparation of maizena and corn starch is very simple, when the TEA-KETTLE BOILER is used, giving no care or trouble about burning or spoiling.

CORN STARCH must be first mixed in a little water or milk before being stirred into the TEA-KETTLE BOILER, as it prevents its being lumpy.

READ ARTICLES UPON INDIAN CORN RECIPES.

### 99. Thin Corn-Starch Custard.

TIME.—*Twenty Minutes.*

ARTICLES.—Starch, a table-spoonful; sugar, four; milk, a quart; eggs, three.

DIRECTIONS.—Boil the milk and sugar in the TEA-KETTLE BOILER, beat the yolks of three eggs, mix the maizena in cold milk; then add all to the hot milk, stir and take off; pour this in a deep dish, beat the whites of the eggs to a froth, put on top of the custard; flavor to taste.

### 100. Muffled Cake.

Pour the above over a sponge cake; serve cold.

### 101. Apple Souffle.

Boil a dozen apples, sweeten, and strain through a sieve, pour the above custard over it; eat cold. Dried apples will do as well.

### 102. Orange Corn Starch.

TIME.—*Half an hour.*

ARTICLES. — Starch, a table-spoonful; oranges, four or six; sugar, quarter of a pound; water, nearly a quart; eggs, two.

### 103. Corn Starch Fruit Blanc Manges.

TIME.—*Half an hour.*

ARTICLES.—Starch, a quarter of a pound; sugar, same; any fruit; water, a quart.

DIRECTIONS. — Have a quart of boiling water in the TEA KETTLE BOILER, add the sugar; then add the starch first wet, let it boil until thick; then take any berries, sliced peeled peaches or oranges, mellow pears, or preserved fruit, and lay in a mold or dish; pour the starch over it. Let it cool.

### 104. Coffee Corn Starch.

TIME.—*Half an hour.*

ARTICLES.—Starch, five table-spoonfuls; same of sugar; two of coffee; milk, a quart.

DIRECTIONS.—Boil a quart of milk and the sugar in the TEA-KETTLE BOILER, make a cup of very strong coffee, and add to the milk hot; then add the starch, let it thicken for a few minutes, pour into cups or molds.

### 105. Corn-Starch and Cocoanut Jelly.

TIME.—*Three hours.*

ARTICLES.—Starch, three table-spoonfuls; cocoanut, the same; sugar, two; milk a quart; one egg.

DIRECTIONS.—Boil the cocoanut in half the milk for nearly three hours in the TEA-KETTLE BOILER, to make it tender; then add the starch and sugar and egg; let it boil five minutes, pour into molds, and eat cold.

### 106. Corn-Starch Omelets.

TIME.— *Ten minutes to cook.*

ARTICLES.—Four heaping table-spoonfuls of corn starch; a tea-cupful of milk and three eggs; pepper, salt, and a tea-spoonful of butter; quarter of a tea-spoonful of soda; half a tea-spoonful of cream of tartar.

DIRECTIONS.—Beat the eggs, cream of tartar, and corn starch together, add the milk with the soda dissolved in it, pepper, salt, and butter. Fry brown, turn them over when done, place upon the table hot.

REMARKS.—Eggs are generally dear in price; nothing has ever taken the place of them; but corn starch in its composition is partly a substitute, and that is one of the reasons why it is so good in making omelets. Herbs, ham, or meat can be used to give a flavor, and add to the quantity.

### 107. Cake of Corn Starch.

TIME.—*Half an hour.*

ARTICLES.—Starch, eight ounces; sugar, same; butter, four ounces; eggs, two; baking powder, a tea-spoonful.

DIRECTIONS.—Beat the butter and sugar well together, beat the eggs, add with the starch and powder, flavor to taste. Bake.

### 108. General Recipe for making Creams of Corn Starch.

ARTICLES.—Corn starch, a table-spoonful, more or less; sugar, four table-spoonfuls, or more if desired; milk, a quart; butter, a tea-spoonful; yolks of eggs, from one to ten, as may be preferred; juice of lemons and juice of fruits, essences, or other flavoring that may be preferred.

DIRECTIONS.—Heat the milk and sugar in a TEA-KETTLE BOILER, mix the corn starch in a little cold milk, add the yolks of the eggs well-beaten, the butter and juice of lemon and fruit juice or essences, etc.

REMARKS.—Creams are eaten cold, and if desired thin use less corn starch; if thick, more. The thin is generally whipped to a froth, and poured into glasses to eat, or poured over fruits, preserves, jams, &c. The combination is delicious. If thick, pour into molds.

## 109. General Recipe for making Corn-Starch Jellies.

TIME.—*To make, about ten minutes.*

ARTICLES.—Three to four table-spoonfuls of corn starch, or maizena, one quart of sweet milk, or a half a pint of condensed milk, and three half pints of water, or a quart of water; sweeten to taste with sugar, less than a tea-cupful will do; half a pint of wine improves the jelly. Fruits, essences, spices, juices of lemons, oranges, etc., can be used to flavor, same as for ice creams and frozen custards.

DIRECTIONS.—Boil the milk or water and sugar in a TEA-KETTLE BOILER, mix the corn starch in a little cold water, pour into the boiler, let it boil five minutes. Stir it up, flavor with any fruit, essence, etc., to suit the taste; color with any color, same as for ice creams; two or more colors can be made by dividing the jelly, and coloring one part; turn it into the mold. *Let it cool;* then pour in another part with a different color.

REMARKS.—These jellies are very cheap, easily made with a TEA-KETTLE BOILER, and nutritious and healthy for invalids, children, and well persons. A little practice will enable the cook to make them perfect. Molds of crockery and metals can be bought cheap.

## 110. General Recipe for making Corn-Starch Custards.

TIME.—*To make, about ten minutes.*

ARTICLES.—Corn starch, two or three table-spoonfuls; milk, one quart, or condensed milk, half a pint, and three half pints of water; half a tea-spoonful of salt; one to three eggs; tea-spoonful of butter; juices of fruits, essences, or spices, or any thing to flavor that suits the taste; sugar, four table-spoonfuls or more, according to taste.

DIRECTIONS.—Heat the milk to nearly boiling in a TEA-KETTLE BOILER, and add the corn starch previous dissolved in a little milk; then add the eggs well beaten with the sugar, let it boil five minutes, stirring it; then add the flavor.

## 111. General Recipe for making Corn-Starch Puddings.

TIME.—*About ten minutes.*

ARTICLES.—Corn starch, five table-spoonfuls; same of sugar (more or less to taste); eggs or not, as desired; fruit of any kind or not; milk, a quart; sweet butter, a table-spoonful; and flavor or fruit juices, same for ice creams.

DIRECTIONS.—Heat the milk in a TEA-KETTLE BOILER until hot, add the butter; then the corn starch first mixed in a little cold milk to prevent any lumps; then add the eggs well beaten, if any are used; the flavoring to taste.

## 112. To Color Corn-Starch Creams, Custards, Jellies, Puddings, and Sauces.

For variety and ornament it is sometimes desirable to color them; if any color is desired, use that used to color ice creams.

## 113. Corn-Starch Sauces.

ARTICLES.—Milk, one cup; sugar, one cup; corn starch, three table-spoonfuls; same of wine or brandy; one of butter; juice of half a lemon.

DIRECTIONS.—Heat the milk and sugar in a TEA-KETTLE BOILER, mix the corn starch with the brandy, butter, and juice of lemon; add to the corn starch, and boil ten minutes with the cover on.

REMARKS.—Corn starch sauces can be made of every variety by using the ice cream recipes for flavors, and following the above. Water can be used if no milk is in the house.

## 114. Corn-Starch and Cocoanut Pies.

TIME.—*Three hours and a half.*

Make the above recipe of jelly, line a deep plate with paste, bake it in a quick oven; when done fill with the jelly, and again bake. This is richer than all cocoanut, and will be preferred.

## 115. Milk or Cream in Corn Starch.

It is almost useless to put cream in recipes, as it can not be had without trouble. To obviate that, *mock cream* can be used; or, if our recipes are followed, the expense and trouble to get cream is avoided, except it is made from

## 116. Condensed Milk.

which is now in use, and can be used in all our recipes instead of ordinary milk; we use it as follows:

DIRECTIONS FOR USING CONDENSED MILK.—FOR CREAM, add one part cold water to one of milk; for rich milk, add three; for ordinary milk, add four; for infants, six to nine parts.

## 117. Corn-Starch Snow.

TIME.—*Ten minutes.*

ARTICLES.—Table-spoonful of corn starch; water, half a pint; four table-spoonfuls of white sugar; one lemon; whites of two eggs.

DIRECTIONS.—Dissolve the corn starch in a little water, add the rest of the water, then the sugar, then the juice of the lemon, then the whites of the eggs well beaten; whisk it all together until it becomes thick and white.

## 118. Corn-Starch Charlotte Russe Cake.

ARTICLES.—Half a pound of corn starch; half a pound of powdered white sugar; quarter of a pound of butter; three eggs; essence of lemon to flavor.

DIRECTIONS.—Beat the eggs well with the butter, add the sugar, beat them in; then the corn starch; then the essence of lemon. Bake in a moderate oven, let it get cold; then cut it up in strips half an inch thick.

*The Inside of the Russe.*—Make a cream or custard of any kind, wipe a mold well, see that it is dry; then line the bottom and sides with the cake cut up so as to cover it all over, fill with the cream or custard, and place it on ice. When cold, turn it upside down on a dish, remove the mold; the cake only is seen.

# EGGS.

We have fifty good recipes to cook eggs. We give some of the plain ones, and shall in the future give the rest. Eggs in summer are very cheap, especially in the country, and we know of no better dish than well cooked eggs. They can be cooked for the invalid to digest in an hour, and the hearty man to digest in five hours; they contain a great deal of nutriment, and strengthen the sick and well. In cooking eggs the best way is to break them separately in a cup, for one bad one will spoil all that have been broken before. Always serve hot. As they are cheap and plenty in summer and scarce and dear in winter, it is best to save them for the time when they are expensive.

### 119. To Preserve Eggs.

There are several ways to preserve eggs, but they must in all cases be prepared fresh or new laid, otherwise they will not keep, no matter how they are fixed. The principle of preserving is to keep them fresh, cool, and in the dark.

### 120. To Preserve with Mucilage.

Dissolve the gum arabic in water to any ordinary thin paste, cool them, or dip them in it twice; when dry, which is in a few minutes, lay them away in charcoal dust or bran, or dry sawdust; put the box in a cool, dry closet or cellar, small end downward.

### 121. To Preserve with Mutton Fat.

Melt the suet, dip them in it twice—do not have the suet too hot—and follow the above directions.

### 122. To Preserve with Lime.

To ten quarts of water, add two pounds of salt and two ounces of saltpeter; boil together for twenty minutes; when nearly cold, add eight ounces of quicklime; let it stand three days, stirring it every day; place the small end downward in layers in a jar; when filled pour in the mixture. They will keep for months; the water should cover them two inches.

Do not take out the eggs in any of the plans for preserving, until you wish to use them, as eggs are of a delicate nature, and easily spoiled after being kept some time.

### 123. Poached Eggs.

TIME.—*Three minutes.*

ARTICLES.—Eggs; butter; water, a pint; vinegar, a table-spoonful; a little salt.

DIRECTIONS.—Put the vinegar and salt in the water in the TEA-KETTLE BOILER; let it boil, break and pour the eggs in, boil three minutes; take out. Butter and eat on toast, or not, or heat some cream, or mock cream, and pour on them.

### 124. To Bake Eggs.

TIME.—*Five minutes.*

Butter a dish, break the eggs, pour in pepper, salt, and butter; bake in a slow oven until well set. Serve hot.

### 125. To Boil Eggs.

TIME.—*To boil hard, ten minutes; soft, six minutes; very soft, four minutes, in hot water.*

Place them in an egg boiler or bowl, and pour hot water (not boiling, as it hardens too quick) over them. Eggs cooked soft are the healthiest; hard are a long time digesting.

### 126. Dropped Eggs.

TIME.—*Three minutes.*

Break the eggs so as not to break the yolk; drop them separately in hot water in a flat dish; let them stay three minutes, or until the white coagulates. Serve on toast. Good for the sick and well.

### 127. To Fry Eggs.

TIME.—*Three minutes.*

Melt any ham fat, lard, or butter, in a frying pan, break the eggs in a cup one at a time and pour in the pan; sprinkle the pepper and salt; turn them over or not, as liked; fry until brown on one or both sides. Serve hot.

### 128. Scrambled Eggs.

TIME.—*Five minutes.*

ARTICLES.—Six eggs; milk, a coffee-cupful; flour, tea-spoonful; butter, a table-spoonful; salt.

DIRECTIONS.—Pour the milk into the TEA-KETTLE BOILER, rub the flour into the butter, add this to the milk; salt to taste; beat six eggs light, stir them into the milk when hot; when the whites are well set, serve hot or pour over toast.

### 129. Fricassee Eggs.

TIME.—*Twenty minutes.*

ARTICLES.—Six eggs; butter; a cupful of mock cream or milk.

DIRECTIONS.—Boil the eggs hard, cut them in quarters, take out the yolks, mix them up with hot mock cream; pour this over the whites of the eggs and serve. Salt to taste.

### 130. Plain Omelet.

TIME.—*Five minutes.*

Beat six eggs very light, have a pan of hot fat or butter ready, pour the eggs in, fry till it is a fine brown on one side, sprinkle a little pepper and salt on the top, then lap it over showing the brown side out. Serve hot.

### 131. Herb, or Ham, or Meat Omelet.

Made same as above, but mincing up any meat, herbs, rice, or other articles, and mix with the eggs before frying.

# TOMATOES.

There is no vegetable that grows that can be raised so easy, and that is sold so cheap. Any yard or garden that has a few feet in it to spare, can raise all a family wants; they are very healthy, and are an agreeable addition to any meal. Gather them ripe, but firm to the touch. For pickling or making preserves, gather young and green.

### 132. Raw Tomatoes.

Select the fairest ripe ones, put them on ice; when cold slice, use vinegar, pepper, and salt to taste.

### 133. To Stew Tomatoes.

TIME.—*An hour.*

ARTICLES.—Tomatoes, a dozen; salt, a tea-spoonful; pepper to taste; butter, a table-spoonful; grated bread crumbs, two table-spoonfuls.

DIRECTIONS.—Scald the tomatoes with boiling water, then peel the skins off, put them in the TEA-KETTLE BOILER, with the butter, salt, and bread crumbs and pepper, cover them over; stew an hour, stir up two or three times; serve hot.

### 134. Baked Whole Tomatoes.

TIME.—*One hour.*

ARTICLES.—Tomatoes, a dozen; salt, pepper, and butter.

DIRECTIONS.—Wash, cut off a small piece from the stem end, put a little pepper, salt, and butter in each one, place them in a dish, and bake them in a moderate oven; serve hot

### 135. Baked Tomatoes.

TIME.—*To bake, two hours.*

ARTICLES.—Tomatoes, a dozen; an ounce of bread crumbs; butter.

DIRECTIONS.—Scald, peel, and slice the tomatoes, put a layer of bread crumbs, then a layer of tomatoes, then bread crumbs, then onions with pepper, salt, butter a little, sugar. and last bread crumbs; bake in a moderate oven two hours.

### 136. Tomato Fritters.

TIME.—*Twenty minutes.*

ARTICLES.—Tomatoes, green corn, each a pint; eggs, two; milk, a cupful; flour.

DIRECTIONS.—Take a pint of peeled and mashed tomatoes strained from their liquor, same of green corn cut from the cob in summer (or boiled samp in winter), season with pepper, salt, and sugar, add two well-beaten eggs, one tumbler of sweet milk, and enough of flour to hold it together. Fry in cakes in boiling lard. Serve hot.

### 137. Boiled Tomatoes.

TIME.—*Two hours.*

DIRECTIONS.—Scald a dozen or more tomatoes, put them in the TEA-KETTLE BOILER, boil two hours; season to taste.

### 138. Tomato Paste.

TIME.—*To stew, three hours.*

ARTICLES.—Two quarts of tomatoes; sugar; pepper; nutmeg; vinegar, half a pint.

DIRECTIONS.—Skin and cut up the tomatoes, let them stand twelve hours, strain out the liquor, put the pulp in the TEA-KETTLE BOILER; then season with sugar and spice, add the vinegar, stew three hours or more, with the cover off, or until it is a thick paste, dry upon dishes, and pack in and cork well in open-mouth bottles; keep dry A small piece will make a gallon of soup.

### 139. Tomato Leather.

TIME.—*An hour.*

ARTICLES.—Scald, mash fine through a sieve, add a little sugar; grease panes of glass or tins, spread over the mixture and dry. This can be used in soup, sauce, or stews.

### 140. Tomato Sauce.

DIRECTIONS.—Peel, mash, and boil until tender, rub through a colandar six tomatoes, a table-spoonful of sweet oil and vinegar; mustard, pepper, and salt to taste. Mix all together; excellent for meats. Serve the paste or leather same way for winter use.

### 141. Preserved Tomatoes.

TIME.—*Four hours.*

ARTICLES.—Tomatoes, six pounds; white sugar, four pounds; six lemons; water, a quart.

DIRECTIONS.—Take the small yellow, or red, or green ones (I prefer the green), prick their skins with a fork, cut the lemon in thin slices. Boil the sugar in a quart of water in the TEA-KETTLE BOILER or preserving kettle; when the syrup is clear, and boiling hot, add the lemons and tomatoes, let it boil until the fruit is clear; then skim out the tomatoes, set them to become cold; then pour over them the syrup. Many use a pound of sugar to a pound of fruit. The above is the general way to preserve all fruits with sugar.

### 142. Tomato Figs.

TIME.—*Four hours.*

ARTICLES.—Tomatoes, four pounds; white sugar, one pound; two lemons.

DIRECTIONS.—Do them as above directed; then take them out to become cold, keep the syrup boiling; when the tomatoes are cold, put them back, repeat this twice; then take them out, flatten them, dry in a warm oven. When dry place them in glass jars; dry the lemon at the same time.

# CHEESE.

Cheese is another cheap food, cheap for the amount of nutriment in it; it is not the quantity as much as the quality that gives nutriment. It is a fact, the poorer a cheese, the more muscle-making power it has; chemical analysis giving it the greatest amount of all food, especially skim milk cheese, as will be seen by the table on another page. Dyspeptics or those confined to the house, or costive persons must not use cheese as it is very binding; to those whose digestive organs are strong, and work hard, it is good, or those who do not feel any bad effects after eating it. Persons should eat nothing that disagrees with them.

### 143. Improved Welsh Rabbit.
TIME.—*Twenty minutes.*
ARTICLES.—Cheese, a cupful; milk, a cupful; an egg, pepper, salt.
DIRECTIONS.—Cut or grate the cheese, put it with the milk in a TEA-KETTLE BOILER; after the cheese has melted, add pepper and salt to taste, and one egg well-beaten; pour over dry toast.

### 144. Stewed Cheese.
TIME.—*Half an hour.*
ARTICLES.—Cheese, a tea-cupful; milk, two; bread crumbs, two; mustard, a teaspoonful; pepper and salt.
DIRECTIONS.—Heat the milk and the cheese in the TEA-KETTLE BOILER; when it melts mix in the mustard, salt, and pepper to taste; when all is well mixed, serve.

### 145. Cheese Sandwich.
Spread the stewed cheese (when cold) thick on to slices of bread.

### 146. French Macaroni.
TIME.—*To boil, half an hour; to brown it, six minutes.*
ARTICLES.—Half a pound of pipe macaroni; seven ounces of cheese; four ounces of butter; one pint of new milk; one quart of water and some bread crumbs; a pinch of salt.
DIRECTIONS.—Flavor the milk and water with a pinch of salt; put into a TEA-KETTLE BOILER; when boiling, drop in the macaroni, peel of three grated lemons, whisk the whole up until quite thick, put it into a lawn sieve just large enough to hold the quantity, and let it stand twenty-four hours, before you turn it into a dish for the table.

### 147. Cheese Custard and Macaroni.
Boil half a pound macaroni, and quarter pound of cheese together; when cooked and cold pour over it any custard; serve cold.

### 148. Cheese Fingers.
TIME.—*Quarter of an hour.*
ARTICLES.—A quarter of a pound of puff paste; a pinch of salt; two ounces of cheese; half a tea-spoonful of Cayenne.
DIRECTIONS.—Take the puff paste, and roll it out thin; then take the grated cheese, Cayenne, and salt; mix these, and strew the cheese over half the paste, turn the other over, and cut it with a sharp knife half an inch wide, and any length you like. Bake in a quick oven, and serve them quite hot, shaking a little grated cheese over them.
The fingers must be piled in a dish crossing each other at right angles.

### 149. Pastry Remakins.
TIME.—*A quarter of an hour.*
ARTICLES.—Some good cheese; puff paste; yolk of one egg.
DIRECTIONS.—Take some puff paste, and roll it out rather thin, strew over it some good grated cheese, and fold it over; repeat this three times, rolling it out each time. Then cut the remakins with a paste cutter in any form you please. Brush them over with the yolk of a well-beaten egg, and bake them in a quick oven for about a quarter of an hour. When done serve them quickly on a hot napkin.

### 150. Macaroni.
TIME.—*Half an hour; to boil, five minutes with cream.*
ARTICLES.—Four ounces of macaroni; two table-spoonfuls of good cream; one ounce and a half of butter rolled in flour; some toasted cheese.
DIRECTIONS.—Boil the macaroni until quite tender, and lay it on a sieve to drain; then put it into a pan with the cream, and the butter rolled in flour; boil it five minutes, pour it on a dish, spread toasted cheese all over it, and serve it up very hot.

### 151. Macaroni and Fish.
TIME.—*To boil macaroni, half an hour; to brown it, five minutes.*
ARTICLES.—Some cold cod; twice its weight in macaroni; six ounces of cheese; a large piece of butter.
DIRECTIONS.—Chop any quantity of cold cod very fine, mix with it the macaroni boiled tender, and the cheese; mix the whole well together, put it on a dish, with a few pieces of butter on the top. Grate cheese thickly over it, and brown it before a fire in an oven.

### 152. Mock Crab—Sailor Fashion.
ARTICLES.—A large slice of cheese; a teaspoonful of mustard; the same of vinegar; pepper and salt to taste.
DIRECTIONS.—Cut a slice of cheese rather thin, mash it up with a fork to a paste, mix it with vinegar, mustard, and pepper. It has a great flavor of crab.

# SALT FISH.

There is much nourishment in fish—almost as much as in meat, pound for pound—also, medicinal properties, such as iodine, in them, which have a beneficial effect upon the health. In no class do we see so large families, handsome women, and robust, active men, or greater exemption from maladies than among fisherman and their families. As salt fish are easily procured in any part of the country, and generally at a low price, we give many good and practical recipes, how to prepare them. Any dry, salt, pickled, or fresh fish will answer to cook. Codfish, however, is the best. Dry or pickled fish can be kept almost any length of time in a cool place.

### 153. The Best way to Soak Salt Fish.

Soak that intended for use in plenty of tepid water, adding to each gallon of water a teacupful of vinegar, if the fish is very dry and hard; use a table-spoonful of saleratus or soda to a gallon of water; taste one of the flakes to ascertain when it is sufficiently fresh; too much soaking will render the fish too insipid. Pickled fish must be soaked over night.

### 154. To Cook Fish.

TIME.—*An hour or two.*

Nothing is better to cook salt fish in than the TEA-KETTLE BOILER, as it must be heated gradually, and simmer very gently; boiling will make the fish hard and tough. It is generally to be picked in flakes free from bones, skin, and everything but fish.

### 155. Fish Sauce.

TIME.—*Twenty minutes.*

Mix a little flour in cold water; add it to hot milk in the TEA-KETTLE BOILER; a little butter and salt; add an egg or two if desired; let it boil five minutes; then serve.

### 156. A Down-east Fish Dinner.

TIME.—*To prepare, one hour and a half.*

ARTICLES.—A fish, potatoes, beets, and pork.

DIRECTIONS.—Take more salt fish than you want to eat for this meal, soak, boil until tender in as large pieces as possible; boil more potatoes and beets than you want; cut some fat salt pork in small square pieces and fry brown; peel the beets and slice them into vinegar, or eat without. Serve all separately. This recipe makes a cheap dinner; the balance can be made into that desirable dish called

### 157. Fish Balls.

Take one-third fish, and two-thirds potatoes chopped fine, and fried into balls, brown, and serve with the beets or pickles.

### 158. Croquettes of Fish.

TIME.—*Ten minutes, to prepare.*

ARTICLES.—Fish, eggs, bread crumbs, table-spoonful of flour, and one of milk.

DIRECTIONS.—Take any fish, separate the skin and bones, mince it with seasoning to taste; an egg well beaten with the flour and milk; roll it into balls; brush the outside with egg; dredge it with bread crumbs; fry brown.

### 159. Fish Fritters.

TIME.—*Ten minutes, to prepare.*

ARTICLES.—Fish, bread crumbs, mashed potatoes, equal parts; an egg; half a teacupful of milk; pepper, and any sauce.

DIRECTIONS.—Take the above articles, mix all together to a proper consistency; then cut into small cakes and fry brown.

### 160. Spiced Soused Fish.

TIME.—*Twelve hours.*

ARTICLES.—Any boiled fish, vinegar, pepper, allspice, cloves and mace.

DIRECTIONS.—Put any cool boiled fish into a dish, boil enough vinegar to cover, put in the spices to taste, then pour on the hot vinegar. Let it stand twelve hours; it is then fit for use.

### 161. Lobster Fish.

TIME.—*An hour.*

ARTICLES.—Salt fish, vinegar, pepper, and sweet oil.

DIRECTIONS.—Pick some salt fish into shreds into the TEA-KETTLE BOILER, pour boiling hot water over it; let it cook half an hour, pour off the water, add vinegar, sweet oil, and pepper to taste. Cold fresh fish can be prepared at once without soaking.

### 162. Oyster Fish.

TIME.—*Twenty minutes.*

ARTICLES.—Fish, oysters, butter, bread crumbs, pepper and milk.

DIRECTIONS.—Take any cold boiled salt, or fresh fish, separate from the bones and skin; take as much in quantity of oysters, a cup of milk; boil them slowly in their own liquor in the TEA-KETTLE BOILER for four minutes, then add a little butter, as many bread crumbs as fish, then the fish with spices to suit the taste. This can now be eaten, or it can be poured into a dish and baked.

### 163. Stewed Fish.

TIME.—*Twenty minutes.*

ARTICLES.—Any cold boiled fish, milk, flour, salt, butter.

DIRECTIONS.—Prepare the milk, flour, butter and salt to taste, as for fish sauce, in the TEA-KETTLE BOILER; pick the fish free from bones and the skin; put it into a dish, pour over it the hot sauce, and serve with boiled or baked potatoes.

## SALT FISH—HOMINY.

**164. Fricasseed Fish.**
TIME.—*One hour and a quarter.*
ARTICLES.—Any cooked fish, parsnips, milk, butter, flour, eggs.
DIRECTIONS.—Break the fish into flakes on a dish; boil enough parsnips, mash them, pour enough milk into the TEA-KETTLE BOILER, a piece of butter, little flour wet first in water, two hard boiled eggs minced fine; add the mashed parsnips; when all is boiling hot add the fish; serve with mashed potatoes.

**165. English Baked Fish.**
TIME.—*Twenty minutes.*
ARTICLES.—Any cooked fish, same quantity of mashed potatoes, parsnips, and a quarter of a pound of butter.
DIRECTIONS.—Pick the fish, butter a pie dish, place in it alternate layers of the parsnips, potatoes, and fish; season; bake for twenty minutes; pour over it melted butter or fish sauce.

**166. French Stew of Fish.**
TIME.—*Half an hour.*
ARTICLES.—Fish, cup of milk, two ounces of butter, sprig of parsley, sweet herbs, pepper and salt.
DIRECTIONS.—Any cooked fish; make a sauce of the milk, butter and flour, pepper and salt, parsley and sweet herbs chopped fine; pour in the fish; stew all half an hour.

**167. Parisian Style.**
TIME.—*Half an hour.*
ARTICLES.—Fish, butter, flour, sugar, onions, and vinegar.
DIRECTIONS.—Any boiled fish picked into flakes; brown some butter, dredge in a little flour and sugar; in this, fry some slices of onion; throw in a little vinegar; boil it up; pour it over the fish, and serve.

**168. East India Style.**
TIME.—*Half an hour.*
ARTICLES.—Fish, butter, peppers, nutmeg, parsley, onions, lemons, sweet oil.
DIRECTIONS.—Any cooked fish in flakes; brown some butter, add to it some whole peppers, grated nutmegs, parsley, onions chopped fine, spoonful salad oil; mince and shake this seasoning well. Serve the fish with the sauce; squeeze the juice of a lemon over it.

**169. Italian Style.**
TIME.—*Twenty minutes.*
ARTICLES.—Fish, flour, milk, pepper, salt, cheese.
DIRECTIONS.—Flakes of any fish; thicken the milk with the flour stirred very smooth; two table-spoonfuls grated cheese; stir in the fish, pepper and salt, pour into a dish; strew bread crumbs over it, and brown in an oven.

# HOMINY

Is a coarse preparation of corn. It is cheaper than maizena or starch, and answers for many purposes. It is, however, liable to burn in boiling, and care must be taken to prevent it. With the TEA-KETTLE BOILER there is no danger or trouble.
Hominy is used very much south and west, for children or persons who wish to grow fat. This, with farina, will fatten them very fast.

**170. Hominy Plain Boiled.**
Soak a quart, boil it in the TEA-KETTLE BOILER until soft; eat with syrup, milk, sugar, or butter. Salt to taste.

**171. Hominy Fried.**
Boil as above, pour into a dish; when cold, slice, and fry it brown.

**172. Hominy Cakes.**
TIME.—*Half an hour.*
ARTICLES.—Cold boiled hominy, a pint; flour, half a pint; one egg; lard, a table-spoonful; milk; yeast powder, a tea-spoonful.
DIRECTIONS.—Beat the eggs, mix all together, make a thin batter; fry in cakes brown.

**173. Hominy Bread.**
TIME.—*An hour.*
ARTICLES.—Hominy, cold boiled, three cups; corn meal, a cup; lard, melted, a table-spoonful; eggs, two; milk.
DIRECTIONS.—Beat the eggs well; stir the hominy and meal together; add the eggs; salt and make a thin batter; bake.

**174. Hominy Muffins.**
TIME.—*Half an hour.*
ARTICLES.—Hominy, corn meal, flour, each two table-spoonfuls; lard, one table-spoonful; egg, one; water.
DIRECTIONS.—Make a thin batter, add the egg and salt; bake in rings or pans.

**175. Samp Boiled**
Is large hominy, cracked corn, or whole with the hulls off; it is very palatable boiled in boiler until soft. Eat with milk; salt to taste.

**176. Hominy Gruel.**
TIME.—*To boil, an hour.*
ARTICLES.—Half a pound of hominy; one pint of milk; salt
DIRECTIONS.—Mix the hominy in the milk; boil in the TEA-KETTLE BOILER, salt to taste. Good for invalids and children.

**177. Hominy Cakes.**
A cup of boiled hominy; two eggs; half a cup of sugar; table-spoonful of butter; spice to taste.

# POTATOES.

Plain and sweet potatoes are roots, and are extensively used among all classes. They are, when mealy, light, nourishing, palatable, and healthy; but two-thirds of the potatoes are watery, and require different methods of cooking them from the ordinary way of boiling. When bought, if over FIFTY CENTS A BUSHEL is paid, they are not profitable as compared with meal and flour; yet for a change it is well to have some once or twice a week; but potatoes at a dollar a bushel are dear food, at two dollars they are extravagant. Many families never save their cold potatoes; it is a mistake, for many of the best recipes require cold cooked potatoes. Potatoes are improved by soaking in cold water over night, or for an hour or two before cooking.

### 178. Steam Potatoes.
TIME.—*Forty minutes.*
DIRECTIONS.—This is a good way: pare or not, wash in cold water, put them in a steamer, steam until a fork goes through them easily; serve hot.

### 179. To Boil Old Potatoes.
TIME.—*Nearly an hour.*
DIRECTIONS.—Pare or not, wash in cold water, and put them in cold water in the pot with a little salt; boil slowly, the slower the better; if the water boils too fast, set it further off from the fire. Try with a fork; when done, pour off the water, put the pot on the stove, the cover off to dry the potatoes; serve hot as soon as dry. Never let the water stop boiling, as it makes them watery.

### 180. To Boil New Potatoes.
Scrape off the skins, and lay them in cold water for an hour or two; boil as above.

### 181. To Bake Potatoes.
TIME.—*One hour.*
DIRECTIONS.—Wash, wipe dry, put in a hot oven, and bake an hour, or until done; many prefer them this way. IN COOKING *the four ways above,* if not peeled cut off a thin slice from each end, it lets the water out from them.

### 182. Mashed Potatoes.
Boil the potatoes, peel and mash, season with milk, pepper, salt, and butter to taste.

### 183. Browned Mashed Potatoes.
Prepare as above, turn them into a pudding dish or pan, and set in an oven to brown; this is an excellent way to cook poor watery potatoes.

### 184. Potato Cakes.
Take seasoned mashed potatoes, make them into cakes nearly an inch thick. Bake or fry them.

### 185. Stewed Potatoes.
Cut cold boiled potatoes into slices, cover with hot mock cream. Stew slowly until hot in a TEA-KETTLE BOILER.

### 186. Baked Chopped Potatoes.
Chop cold boiled potatoes in a chopping tray till very fine, turn them into a pudding dish, cover with mock cream, and bake half an hour.

### 187. Fried Cold Potatoes.
Slice cold boiled potatoes, or chop fine, fry brown with pork fat, or any grease or lard; pepper and salt to taste.

### 188. Fried Raw Potatoes.
TIME.—*Twenty minutes.*
DIRECTIONS.—Peel some good potatoes, throw them in cold water, heat pure lard so as to have the frying pan have an inch or more in it. Slice the potatoes very thin; when the fat is boiling hot, put them in; when of a delicate brown and crispy, remove. This is a quick cheap way, for they do not soak fat, and well done are a delicacy. Sprinkle a little salt on while hot.

### 189. Potato Ribbons.
Prepare and cook in the same manner as fried raw potatoes, except they are pared round and round into ribbons.

### 190. To Fry them Light or Swelled.
When fried, turn into a colander, and have the fat over a brisk fire; leave the potatoes in the colander only about half a minute, then put them back in the very hot fat, stir about one minute and put them again in the colander; salt them and serve hot. If the fat is very hot when dropped into it for the second time, they will certainly swell. There is no other way known to do it. It is as easily done as it is simple.

### 191. To Broil Potatoes.
Cut some cold boiled potatoes up lengthwise, a quarter of an inch thick, dip each piece in flour, lay them on a gridiron over a clear fire; when both sides are browned, put them on a hot dish, butter, pepper, and salt them. Serve hot.

### 192. Potato Rissoles.
TIME.—*To fry, ten or twelve minutes.*
ARTICLES.—Some boiled potatoes; bread crumbs; egg; pepper and salt; a piece of butter.
DIRECTIONS.—Boil some potatoes; when done, drain the water from them, and set them by the side of the fire to dry; then peel and mash them with a fork in a clean stew pan, with a seasoning of pepper and salt, and a piece of fresh butter; stir the mash over the fire for a few minutes, and then turn it out on a dish. When cool roll it into small balls, cover them with a beaten egg and bread, and fry them in hot lard or beef-drippings. When a light brown let them drain before the fire, and serve.

## POTATOES—BEANS AND PEAS.

### 193. Potato Puffs.
ARTICLES.—Three ounces of flour; three ounces of sugar; three well-boiled potatoes; a piece of butter the size of a nutmeg; two eggs; a little grated nutmeg.

DIRECTIONS.—Boil and mash the potatoes, mix them with sugar, flour, nutmeg, butter, and beaten eggs. Make them into cakes, fry a nice brown, and serve them with white sauce.

### 194. Potatoes a la Maitre d'Hotel.
ARTICLES.—Some boiled potatoes; a little melted butter; pepper; salt; and the juice of half a lemon.

DIRECTIONS.—Take some potatoes boiled and peeled; when nearly cold, cut them into rather thick slices, and put them into a stew pan, with a little melted butter, seasoned with pepper, salt, and the lemon. When very hot, put them in a dish, and serve with the sauce over them.

### 195. Stuffed Potatoes.
TIME.—To roast, one hour.

ARTICLES.—Some of the largest potatoes; one table-spoonful of cheese; pepper and salt; a little flour; two ounces of fresh butter.

DIRECTIONS.—Take some potatoes, boil them well, cut off the tops, and scoop out the inside completely. Rub this quite fine through a sieve, and add a table-spoonful of grated cheese, pepper, and salt; melt the butter in a stew pan; put in the potato flour, and make it hot; fill the skins of the potatoes with it, put them into the oven, and serve them up quite hot.

### 196. To Brown Potatoes and Meat.
DIRECTIONS. — Boil some fine, large, mealy potatoes, take off the skins carefully, and about an hour before the meat is cooked, put them into the dripping pan, having well dredged them with flour. Before serving them, drain them from any grease, and serve them up hot.

### 197. Hashed Potatoes.
Any cold boiled, baked, fried, or cooked in any way, left over, and minced with cold meat or fish of any kind, and seasoned well, make a palatable and healthy dish of food.

### 198. Potato Souffles.
Steam a quart of potatoes, then peel and mash them in a TEA-KETTLE BOILER, and mix an ounce of butter with them; set on the fire, pour into it, little by little, stirring the while, about half a pint of milk; stir a little longer after the milk is in, and until they are turning rather thick; dish the potatoes, smooth or scollop them with the back of a knife, and put them in a quick oven till of a proper color, and serve.

### 199. Potatoes a la Parisienne.
Chop an onion fine and partly fry it with butter, then put in it some potatoes cut in dice, add a little water, salt and pepper; boil gently until done; take from the fire, add chopped parsley, and serve.

## BEANS AND PEAS

Are among the best and most nutritious of foods, and for the amount of nourishment and strength they give, to the actual cost of them, are among the cheapest of foods. A quart swells to over two quarts; if old, they require more soaking. Add a little salt to the water in which they are soaked. These recipes answer for dry and fresh beans and peas.

They are too hearty for dyspeptics, and should not be eaten by those of weak stomachs.

The New England people eat them often, and especially every Sunday morning, and for dinner that day or the next. The founders of the six New England States almost lived upon them and corn. We give all the varieties of cooking them known.

### 200. How to Improve Beans.
Soak dry beans for sixty hours before cooking them; it takes out the strong taste and bilious nature in them.

### 201. New England Baked Beans.
TIME.—All day or night.

ARTICLES.—Dry beans, a quart; lean pork, half a pound; two table-spoonfuls of molasses; water.

DIRECTIONS.—Wash and soak the beans in double as much water from two to six hours; put the beans into a boiler with the pork, scored fine on the skin; add double as much water, boil until the skin cracks (not mashed), pour the water away, then skim the beans into an earthen pot; add the pork last; pour in hot water—not that in which they were boiled—so as to cover them; add two table-spoonfuls of molasses; set them in the oven to bake, cover over the pot; make a good coal fire, shut up the stove, let them cook all night. In the morning you have a good hot breakfast. If preferred dry, use less water in baking them.

### 202. New York Baked Beans
TIME.—To bake, two hours.

ARTICLES.—Dry beans, a quart; lean pork, two pounds; water.

DIRECTIONS.—With the pork, first scored, boil the beans until the skins break, pour away the water, then put the pork into a shallow pan, then the beans, then boiling water until it covers them; bake; eat with vinegar and pepper. Not so good as the New England style. The pork should be covered with the beans, except the top of it.

### 203. Dry Beans Boiled Pudding.
TIME.—To boil second time, an hour.

ARTICLES.—Dry beans, one quart; pork, half a pound, seasoning.

DIRECTIONS.—Wash and soak the beans over night; boil the beans, until very soft, with the pork; mash the beans through a colander, cut the pork fine, put all into a pudding cloth, boil an hour, season to taste.

## BEANS AND PEAS.

### 204. Dry Beans Baked Pudding
Is made as above, but baked in a pan instead of boiling.

### 205. Dry Beans Whole, French Style.
TIME.—*To boil, about an hour.*
ARTICLES.—Dry beans, a quart; two table-spoonfuls of butter.
DIRECTIONS.—Wash, soak, and boil the beans until tender, but keep them whole; put them in a TEA-KETTLE BOILER with the butter, a pint of hot milk, pepper and salt; boil them all for five minutes; serve hot.

### 206. Beans Stewed.
TIME.—*Two hours.*
ARTICLES.—Dry beans, a quart; pork, half a pound.
DIRECTIONS.—Wash, soak, boil to a thin mash; boil the pork with them in small pieces; serve hot, with pepper to taste.

### 207. Beans and Bacon, English Style.
TIME.—*To cook, about two hours.*
ARTICLES.—Dry beans, a quart; bacon, half a pound; six small onions, flour, butter, salt and pepper.
DIRECTIONS.—Wash and soak them about an hour; put at the same time into the stew-pan, the bacon; in an hour, add the beans with the onions whole; boil gently until cooked (whole); drain; then put into the TEA-KETTLE BOILER a tablespoonful each of flour and butter, a half pint of milk, a half pint of the water the beans were cooked in; boil ten minutes, then pour it over the beans, etc. Eat hot.

### 208. Beans and Meat.
Boiled beans, prepared in the French style, are a very good addition to a dinner.

### 209. Beans a la Creme.
TIME.—*Two hours.*
ARTICLES.—Dry beans, a pint; two eggs; two table-spoonfuls of cream, same of butter, one of vinegar.
DIRECTIONS.—Wash, soak an hour, boil until tender in salted water; beat up two eggs with the cream and butter; put it into the TEA-KETTLE BOILER; when hot put in the vinegar and then the beans; let them boil ten minutes; serve hot.

### 210. Bean Soup.
TIME.—*Four hours.*
ARTICLES.—Beans, a pint; pork, half a pound.
DIRECTIONS.—Wash the beans, boil in two quarts of water in the TEA-KETTLE BOILER until they are mixed with the water; strain the soup through a sieve, and serve hot.

### 211. Succotash in Winter.
TIME.—*To boil, four hours.*
ARTICLES.—A pint of Lima beans, a pint of sweet corn, half a pound of bacon or pork, a pint of milk, and the same quantity of water.
DIRECTIONS.—Soak the beans and corn all night, cut up the bacon in small pieces; put into the TEA-KETTLE BOILER, pour in the beans and corn, and boiling milk and water; cook about four hours. *Excellent.*

### 212. Succotash in Summer.
Use green corn and beans; cook as above.

### 213. Green Peas in Winter.
Take green marrowfat peas just before they are ripe; shell and dry. They can be bought in all the stores, dry.

### 214. Boiled Peas.
Soak all night, boil them until soft, not mashed; add a little butter and salt when done. As good as canned peas.

### 215. Green Peas in Summer.
Cook same way without soaking.

### 216. Boiled Pea Pudding.
TIME.—*To boil second time, an hour.*
ARTICLES.—Dry peas, one quart; pork, half a pound, with pepper and salt.
DIRECTIONS.—Wash and boil the peas, until very soft, with the pork, mash the peas through the colander; cut the pork fine; put all into a pudding cloth, boil an hour, season to taste.

### 217. Baked Peas.
TIME.—*To bake, an hour.*
ARTICLES.—A quart of peas, half a pound of lean pork.
DIRECTIONS.—Soak the peas an hour, boil in the TEA-KETTLE BOILER with the pork until quite soft; pour all into a deep dish and bake an hour, or until quite stiff; be careful not to burn them while baking.

### 218. Pea Pudding.
TIME.—*To boil, two hours.*
ARTICLES.—One pint of peas, butter, salt, and pepper.
DIRECTIONS.—Soak the peas several hours in plenty of water, pour them into the TEA-KETTLE BOILER; when tender turn them out, mash them, season with pepper, salt, and butter; strain through a sieve, turn them back into the boiler to get hot, then serve.

### 219. Pea Soup.
TIME.—*To boil, three hours.*
ARTICLES.—Peas, a pint; pork, a quarter of a pound.
DIRECTIONS.—Boil the peas and pork in the TEA-KETTLE BOILER with three pints of water until they are dissolved; strain through a sieve, serve hot, season to taste.

### 220. Winter Pea Soup.
TIME.—*To boil, four hours.*
ARTICLES.—Split peas, a pint; three quarts of water; a pound of lean beef; quarter of a pound of pork, seasoning.
DIRECTIONS.—Boil the peas in the TEA-KETTLE BOILER, in the water with the beef and pork cut up, until all is soft; serve hot; season to taste; fried bread, cut small, improves it.

# SAUCES FOR MEATS.

Well-made sauces are the best testimonials of the skill of a good cook, and the very essential part of a dinner. They often give a zest to poor meat, or cheap pudding. It is economical to use good sauces, and we regret to say that many families use but one or two a year in and out again, because they have no practical recipes for others. Most of ours are made in the TEA-KETTLE BOILER; it prevents burning, and waste of material and time.

### 221. Mint Sauce.
TIME.—*To make, three minutes.*

ARTICLES—Green mint, two table-spoonfuls; sugar, same quantity; vinegar, half a tea-cupful. *Good for any meat.*

DIRECTIONS.—Mix the sugar in the vinegar, add the mint, first chopped fine; let it stand ten minutes, and it is fit for use.

### 222. Onion Sauce.
TIME.—*Half an hour.*

ARTICLES.—Onions, four; milk, a pint; butter, a tea-spoonful; pepper and salt.

DIRECTIONS.—Heat a pint of milk in the TEA-KETTLE BOILER, peel and chop fine the onions, put them into the milk, boil until soft, add the butter and seasoning, serve hot or boil the onions in water; then add to the hot milk. *Add flour* to thicken if desired.

### 223. Butter Sauce.
TIME.—*Five minutes to boil.*

ARTICLES. — Flour, two tea-spoonfuls; butter, four tea-spoonfuls; half a pint of milk or water; a little salt.

DIRECTIONS.—Put the flour and salt into the bowl, mix them smooth with the milk; then pour it into a TEA-KETTLE BOILER, add the butter, and boil ten minutes.

### 224. Tomato Sauce.
TIME.—*Five minutes to prepare.*

ARTICLES.—Six large tomatoes, or a pint of canned ones; table-spoonful of sweet oil; same of vinegar; half a tea-spoonful mixed mustard, pepper, and salt to taste.

DIRECTIONS. — Mix the above together, and eat cold, or heat up for warm meats in the TEA-KETTLE BOILER.

### 225. Potato Sauce.
TIME.—*Forty minutes.*

ARTICLES.—Equal quantities of potatoes and onions; piece of butter; pepper, and salt; and a cup of milk.

DIRECTIONS.—Boil, when done, mash together, heat a cup of milk in the TEA-KETTLE BOILER, add the mash and seasoning, boil two minutes, and serve with seasoning.

### 226. New England Egg Sauce
Is made the same way, using eggs instead of capers.

### 227. Celery Sauce.
TIME.—*One hour to boil.*

ARTICLES.—Six stalks of celery; a pint of fresh milk; a table-spoonful of flour; same of butter.

DIRECTIONS.—Boil the milk in the TEA-KETTLE BOILER, add the celery cut up in small pieces, boil until tender, add the flour mixed with the butter, salt to taste. *Extracts or the seeds bruised can be used.*

### 228. Egg Sauce.
TIME.—*Twenty minutes.*

ARTICLES. — Two eggs; a cup of butter; a little salt; a cup of milk.

DIRECTIONS.—Boil the eggs hard, shell them, cut them up into small square pieces; melt the butter with milk into the TEA-KETTLE BOILER, heat it very hot, add the salt, put the chopped eggs into a sauce bowl, and pour the butter over the eggs.

### 229. Oyster Sauce.
TIME.—*Half an hour.*

ARTICLES. — A tumblerful of oysters; tumblerful of milk; table-spoonful of butter; tea-spoonful of flour.

DIRECTIONS. — Heat the milk and the liquor in the TEA-KETTLE BOILER, chop the oysters fine, add to the milk; add the flour and butter first rubbed together. Boil well.

### 230. Caper Sauce.
TIME.—*Boil five minutes.*

ARTICLES. — A cup of butter; flour, a table-spoonful; pint of sweet milk; four table-spoonfuls of capers.

DIRECTIONS.—Heat the milk in the TEA-KETTLE BOILER, add the butter and flour mixed together; add the capers.

### 231. Maitre d'Hotel Sauce.
TIME.—*Ten minutes.*

ARTICLES.—Three ounces of butter; juice of one lemon; a tea-cup of milk; same of gravy; a sprig of parsley.

DIRECTIONS.—Mix the butter smoothly with the juice of the lemon; then mix the boiling milk with any gravy from the meat in the TEA-KETTLE BOILER, heat it hot; then stir in the butter until it is melted, mix the parsley leaves in the sauce.

### 232. Salad Sauce.
TIME.—*Three minutes.*

ARTICLES.—Yolks of two hard-boiled eggs; a tea-spoonful of sweet oil; table-spoonful of finely grated horse-radish; a table-spoonful of strong vinegar; a tea-spoonful of mustard; salt and pepper to taste; a table-spoonful of white sugar.

DIRECTIONS.—Mix all together using more or less of each article, according to taste, it can be made thick or thin by using more or less vinegar.

# SAUCES FOR PUDDINGS, PIES, AND CAKE.

### 233. Custard Sauce for Tarts or Puddings.
TIME.—*Ten minutes.*
ARTICLES.—One pint of milk; two eggs; half a wine-glass of brandy; sugar to your taste.
DIRECTIONS.—Stir two well-beaten eggs into hot milk and pounded sugar, quantity to your taste; add half a glass of brandy, and pour it all into a TEA-KETTLE BOILER, and stir it the same way till it is of the consistency of thick cream; serve it over pudding, or in a tureen.

### 234. Egg Sauce for Pudding.
TIME.—*Ten minutes to boil.*
ARTICLES.—Yolks of four eggs; a glass of wine; a lemon; sugar to your taste.
DIRECTIONS.—Put the yolks of the eggs into a TEA-KETTLE BOILER, and whisk them for two minutes; then add the wine and lemon juice strained, and the rind grated; boil. Then pour it over the pudding.

### 235. Fruit Sauce.
TIME.—*Fifteen minutes.*
ARTICLES.—A quart of any berries; six ounces of sugar, and five table-spoonfuls of water.
DIRECTIONS.—Put the berries, sugar, and water into a TEA-KETTLE BOILER, and then strain it through a sieve, and serve it with any pudding that you think the flavor will improve. Berry or jams boiled and strained will be quite as good in the winter when fresh fruit can not be obtained.

### 236. Wine Sauce.
TIME.—*Ten minutes.*
ARTICLES.—Half a pint of melted butter; four table-spoonfuls of wine; the peel of half a lemon; sugar to your taste.
DIRECTIONS.—Add to the butter wine, and grated rind of half a lemon, and the sugar pounded and sifted; let it boil in the TEA-KETTLE BOILER, and serve with any pudding, etc.

### 237. Dried-Apple Sauce (French Style).
TIME.—*Fifty hours, to stew.*
ARTICLES.—Dried apples, lemon, sugar.
DIRECTIONS.—Wash as many apples as you wish to stew, soak them in water all night, the next morning put them on to stew in the same water in a porcelain kettle. Stew all the next day after, add the sugar to taste, then strain through a sieve.
REMARKS.—This is a fine sauce: by cooking so long it loses the dried-apple taste. If you prefer the old style, cook four hours as above directed.

### 238. Cold Brandy Sauce for Puddings.
ARTICLES.—A quarter of a pound of loaf-sugar; a quarter of a pound of fresh butter; one wine-glass of brandy.
DIRECTIONS.—Beat the butter with the sugar to a froth; then beat in gradually the brandy.

### 239. Cold Butter Sauce.
TIME.—*Three minutes to make.*
ARTICLES.—Butter, half a cupful; sugar, two cupfuls; two eggs; flavoring.
DIRECTIONS.—Beat all together, flavor with any essence, lemon, orange, or spice, to taste.

### 240. Orange Hard Sauce.
The juice of three oranges, powdered sugar enough to make the hard sauce.

### 241. Banana Sauce.
Peel and mash three ripe mellow bananas; the juice of half a lemon; enough sugar to make a hard sauce.

### 242. Condensed Milk Hard Sauce.
TIME.—*Two minutes.*
ARTICLES.—A tea-cupful of condensed milk; a grated nutmeg; powdered sugar; a wine-glassful of sherry wine.
DIRECTIONS.—Mix all together, using sugar enough to make a hard sauce.

### 243. Transparent Sauce.
TIME.—*Half an hour.*
ARTICLES.—A coffee-cupful of water; a table-spoonful of butter; a coffee-cupful of white sugar; the whites of two eggs; essence of lemon or vanilla.
DIRECTIONS.—Put the sugar, water, and butter into a TEA-KETTLE BOILER, let it heat ten minutes, stirring it well; let it cool; then beat the whites of the eggs into the cool sauce.

### 244. Hot Milk Sauce.
TIME.—*To boil, five minutes.*
ARTICLES.—Milk, a pint: two eggs; a cup of sugar.
DIRECTIONS.—Heat a pint of milk hot in a TEA-KETTLE BOILER, beat up the eggs and sugar, flavor to taste, add to the milk, boil.

### 245. Water Sauce.
Made as above, using water instead of milk, and adding juice of a lemon.

### 246. Dried Fruit Sauce of any kind.
Wash the fruit, soak, stew, and sweeten to taste. Can be made thick or thin, by adding more or less water.

# MEATS.

As all know, meats of all kinds are expensive. This has not always been the case; but now it is, and many parts of animals are as good when cooked properly, or even better than the costly and fashionable parts. In Europe, all parts of the animals are used, nothing is wasted, and it will be so here as soon as people understand how to cook them. This is most important, and when the wife or cook can make a wholesome, palatable dish at a saving of from one-half to three-quarters in price, it is her duty to do it, and save money.

## BEEF'S HEARTS

Are sold very low, and when cooked by any of these recipes, are very nourishing and good. They require to be well cooked. These recipes answer for hogs, sheep, or calves' hearts. Soak all kinds two hours in salt or warm water, and trim them of every waste, which is quite small.

### 247. Roast Heart.

TIME.—*Two hours to roast.*
ARTICLE.—One heart.
DIRECTIONS.—Wash and soak, then bake or roast it well, and taste same as for beef.

### 248. Baked Stuffed Heart.

TIME.—*Two hours and a half.*
ARTICLES.—One heart; loaf of bread; sage, salt, and pepper.
DIRECTIONS.—Wash and soak, cut out the lobes or strings, trim it; then fill it with bread stuffing, season with sage, etc., cover over the large end with strong paper. Bake two hours and a half.

### 249. Boiled Stuffed Heart.

TIME.—*Three hours to boil.*
DIRECTIONS.—Prepare as above, tying the heart up in cloth; then boil.

### 250. Stewed Heart Whole.

TIME.—*Two to three hours.*
ARTICLES.—Heart; bread; seasoning; one egg; a carrot; three onions; cloves; allspice; half a lemon.
DIRECTIONS.—Prepare as for boiling, make stuffing, fill it; then place it in a stew pan with water, let it stew two hours; then add a sliced carrot, three onions, twenty cloves, and same of allspice, let it stew an hour longer. Take out the heart, add a tablespoonful of flour, juice of half a lemon, let it boil up once, pour over the heart, and serve.

### 251. Sliced Stewed Heart.

TIME.—*Two to three hours.*
Cook as above, slicing the heart in pieces.

### 252. Broiled Heart.

ARTICLES.—Heart, pepper, salt, and butter.
DIRECTIONS.—Prepare the heart; then cut it lengthwise in slices half an inch thick, broil over a clear fire. Pepper, salt, and butter to taste.

### 253. Fried Heart.

Prepare as for broiling; fry with hot fat, pepper, and salt.

### 254. Heart Soup.

TIME.—*Three hours.*
ARTICLES.—Half a heart; six turnips; six onions; two carrots; eighteen potatoes; salt and pepper.
DIRECTIONS.—Prepare as for stewing; then boil nearly two hours, add the vegetables and seasoning.

### 255. Corned Beef's Heart.

Put a heart in a bucket of strong salt water for two days; then boil with vegetables. It is equal to any corn beef.

### 256. Beef's-Heart Hash.

When any heart is left from the above dishes, cut the fat off, as it is not good in hash; then cut it up fine with as much cold potatoes (and onions to taste), cook it in a frying-pan; salt and pepper to taste; an onion chopped fine, and added will give it a good flavor.

### 257. Beef's-Heart Pie Meat.

To make mince pies nothing is better or so cheap as beef's hearts. Wash, but do not soak them; boil until tender.

## BEEF'S TRIPE,

One of the healthiest and cheapest of animal foods, and will give as much nutriment as the meat. Plain boiled and tender it is good for weak stomachs and dyspeptics. As it is always cheaper in price than beef, veal, mutton, or pork, it is very economical. It should be boiled tender; the thick parts are the best. In the recipes the tripe is first boiled tender.

### 258. Tripe Fried Plain.

TIME.—*Ten minutes.*
DIRECTIONS.—Cut up the tripe in convenient pieces, and fry brown in any fat; season to taste.

### 259. Tripe Fried in Batter.

TIME.—*Half an hour.*
ARTICLES.—Tripe, two pounds; flour, eight ounces; table-spoonful of butter; one egg; water, half a pint.
DIRECTIONS.—Make a batter of the last four (as for recipe for batter), dip the pieces of tripe in, and fry brown.

### 260. Tripe Broiled.

TIME.—*Ten minutes.*
DIRECTIONS.—Broil the tripe plain over a bright coal fire. Butter, pepper, and salt; eat hot.

### 261. Tripe Baked.

TIME.—*One hour.*
ARTICLES. — Tripe, butter, and bread crumbs.
DIRECTIONS.—Spread butter and a thick layer of bread crumbs on one side of a piece of tripe, roll it up, the bread, etc., inside. Tie it around tight with a cord. Bake one hour. Serve with onion sauce. Cut across the roll to serve.

### 262. Tripe Soused.

After it is boiled tender, put it in weak vinegar, add whole cloves, allspice, mace, pepper, to the vinegar. It is good eaten cold. (Can be cooked in any of these recipes same as if fresh.)

### 263. Tripe Stewed Plain.

TIME.—*Half an hour.*
ARTICLES.—Tripe, a pound; water, a pint; flour, two table-spoonfuls.
DIRECTIONS.—Pour a pint of boiling water into a TEA-KETTLE BOILER, mix the flour in a little cold water, strain into the water, stir; then cut the tripe in small pieces, add pepper and salt to taste. Boil all nearly half an hour.

### 264. Tripe Stewed with Onions.

TIME.—*One hour.*
ARTICLES.—Tripe, two pounds; onions, three; milk, a quart; flour, two table-spoonfuls.
DIRECTIONS.—Cut three onions up, cook them in a frying-pan with little water until soft; while doing this have a quart of milk on heating in the TEA-KETTLE BOILER; when the milk is hot add the onions, and the tripe cut up in small pieces; then add the flour, as before, salt and pepper to taste ; boil half an hour, serve hot.

### 265. Tripe Fricasseed.

TIME.—*Half an hour.*
ARTICLES. — Tripe, a pound; mace, a blade; egg, one; water, a pint; one lemon; spice to taste; butter.
DIRECTIONS.—Cut the tripe up to pieces, two inches square, put it into a stewing pan with the water hot, slice in a lemon, a great spoonful of butter, the mace, let it stew; pepper, salt, and spice to taste. Boil an egg hard; when done, pour out the tripe, ornament the dish with slices of the egg.

### BEEF PALATES

Is another part of the ox, scarcely if ever eaten in this country, but they are in Europe, and make a fine addition to the bill of fare. Butchers will gladly furnish them, upon being called for, at a low price.

### 266. To Prepare Beef Palates.

TIME.—*To boil, four hours.*
Soak them for five hours in lukewarm water, then put them into a pot, scald them whole—they are hard—scrape off the skin if it does not come off easily; scald again until they look white and clean; boil them until they are tender.

### 267. To Stew Beef Palates.

TIME.—*Half an hour.*
ARTICLES.—Three palates, three onions, a quart of milk, a dozen cloves and some allspice.
DIRECTIONS.—Prepare and boil as above, then cut them in small pieces with the onion and cloves; stew in a TEA-KETTLE BOILER until all is done, then serve.

### 268. To Broil Beef Palates.

TIME.—*To broil, five minutes.*
ARTICLES. — Three palates, pepper and salt, bread crumbs and egg sauce.
DIRECTIONS. — Prepare, boil as directed above until tender, press them flat; dip them in egg, then bread crumbs or meal and broil brown; serve with Worcestershire sauce.

### 269. Fry of Beef Palates.

TIME.—*To fry, ten minutes.*
ARTICLES.—Three palates, some bacon or pork, flour, butter, pepper, salt, horse-radish.
DIRECTIONS.—Prepare and boil the palates, cut them in square pieces and fry brown with pork or bacon; make some rich gravy, thickened with flour and butter, seasoned with the pepper, salt, and horse-radish; serve hot.

### 270. Palates au Friture.

TIME.—*To fry, ten minutes.*
ARTICLES.—Three palates, two eggs, flour, butter, salt, and pepper.
DIRECTIONS.—Prepare and boil; cut them in two; make a thick batter, dip the palates into the batter; fry brown, and serve hot.

REMARKS.—Any person desiring more spices can add them to these dishes.

### 271. Boiled Sheep's Trotters.

TIME.—*Three hours.*
ARTICLES.—Four trotters; a table-spoonful of flour; a salt-spoonful of salt.
DIRECTIONS.—Perfectly clean and blanch the trotters, taking care to remove the little tuft of hair which is found in the fourche of the foot; beat up a spoonful of flour and a little salt in the water you use for cooking them in, and let them stew till the bones come out easily.

## 272. Sheep's Trotters.

TIME.—*Three hours and a half.*

ARTICLES.—Sheep's trotters, some force meat, pepper and salt, a spoonful of sauce.

DIRECTIONS.—Stew the sheep's trotters for about three hours; then take out the bones without injury to the skin, and fill the part from which the bones have been removed with force-meat; put them into the TEA-KETTLE BOILER, with a sufficient quantity of the liquor in which they were boiled to cover them, adding a tea-spoonful of sauce and a little pepper and salt; let them stew for about half an hour; take them out, strain the gravy and boil it down to a glaze, with which glaze the trotters; serve.

## 273. Sheep's Head (French).

TIME.—*Two hours to boil.*

ARTICLES.—One head, two onions, two carrots, two turnips, a piece of celery, five cloves, a sprig or two of thyme, two tablespoonfuls of salt, a quarter of an ounce of pepper, two quarts of water.

DIRECTIONS.—Put the head into a gallon of water, and let it soak for two hours or more; wash it thoroughly; saw it in two from the top; take out the brains; cut away part of the uncovered part of the skull and the ends of the jaws; wash it well; put in a TEA-KETTLE BOILER the onions, carrots, celery, cloves, thyme, a bay leaf, salt, pepper, and water; let it simmer very gently, take out the vegetables and herbs; skim off the fat, lay the head on a dish; have the brains ready boiled—it will take ten minutes to do —chop it up fine, warm it in parsley and butter; put it in under the head and serve; any of the spices may be left out.

## HOGS' HEADS AND FEET

Are the cheapest parts of the hogs, and full as good as any; in fact, many delicacies may be made of them. Always bear in mind that *economy is wealth.*

## 274. Hog's-Head Cheese.

TIME.—*Five hours.*

ARTICLES.—One hog's head, ears, feet, and tongue; salt, pepper, and sage.

DIRECTIONS.—Let the butcher split the head open, and remove the eyes, and cut off the nostrils; cut off the ears, clean them and the head well; also, the feet and tongue (do not boil the brains); boil altogether until tender; while warm remove all the bones, cut it up coarsely, then season with salt, pepper, and sage; pour it into a pan or dish; eat cold, or fry.

## 275. Improved Hog's-Head Cheese.

TIME.—*Five hours.*

ARTICLES.—Three quarts of liquor, salt, Indian meal.

DIRECTIONS.—Cook as above for cheese, strain the liquor, wipe out the pot; first strain off the fat; have about three quarts of liquor to use (if you have not as much, add water enough to make three quarts), strain it, return into the pot, stir in Indian meal until it becomes almost thick, let it cook, stirring constantly, to prevent burning, about ten minutes; salt, then stir in the meat; it must be well seasoned so as to season the meal; pour into pans; when cool, cut in slices, roll in meal, and fry brown. This will make a good dish.

## 276. Hogs's Head Soused.

Prepare as for cheese, without meal, adding a little vinegar to the mass to suit the taste; pack in jars; keep a cloth wet with vinegar over it; eat cold, or fry.

## 277. Hog's Head Stuffed.

TIME.—*To cook, four hours.*

ARTICLES.—One hog's head, heart, liver; bread; pepper and salt.

DIRECTIONS.—Split open the head at the top, leaving the under part whole; remove the eyes, brains, and all the bones; strew the inside with salt, let it drain; make a stuffing of the haslet by chopping up the heart and liver, adding bread; season with pepper and salt; sew up the head where it is split open; now stuff it with the stuffing, sew over the back part a piece of white cloth; if to bake, it is ready; if to boil, wrap it in a towel; either way will take four hours (if a large one) to cook; serve hot or cold.

## 278. Hog's Head Baked.

TIME.—*Three hours.*

ARTICLES.—A head; one egg; sage, pepper, salt, butter.

DIRECTIONS.—Divide the head, take out the eyes, save the brains in a dish. Thoroughly clean the head, bake it two hours. Scald the brains, beat them up with an egg, sage, pepper, and salt, and a little butter; fry them brown. Serve with the head.

## 279. Stew, Hog's Head, Haslet, and Kidneys.

TIME.—*Four hours.*

ARTICLES.—One head, haslet, kidneys; onions, potatoes, and flour.

DIRECTIONS.—Clean the head, and boil as before described, taking the upper part only, adding the kidneys and haslet, boil until tender; remove, cut up with a knife coarsely. Mix and add to the meat sliced onions and potatoes. When the meat is removed stir flour in the broth to thicken it. Serve hot.

## 280. Pig's Cheek.

TIME.—*Three hours.*

ARTICLES.—Pig's cheek; one ounce of bread crumbs.

DIRECTIONS.—Boil and trim in the shape of ham.

## 281. Boiled Corned Hog's Head.

Boil hog's head with vegetables: it makes a cheap good dish. *Boil the head four hours.*

## OX-HEADS

Are used only by our foreign-born citizens, who understand the value and use of them; they contain a great deal of nutriment, and can be bought very cheap.

## 282. Ox-Cheek Cheese (American Style).

TIME.—*Four hours.*

ARTICLES.—Half an ox-head, one teaspoonful of fine salt, half a tea-spoonful of pepper, one table-spoonful of powdered thyme, enough water to cover the head.

DIRECTIONS.—Split an ox-head in two, take out the eyes, crack the side-bones, and lay it in water one hour; then put it in a saucepan, with sufficient water to cover it, let it boil very gently, skimming it carefully; when the meat loosens from the bones, take it from the water with a skimmer, and put it into a bowl; take out every particle of bone, chop the meat very fine and season it with thyme and pepper; tie it in a cloth and press it with a weight; when cold, it may be cut in slices for dinner or supper; the gravy remaining will make a rich broth if a few vegetables be stewed in it.

## 283. Ox-Cheek Stewed (German Style).

TIME.—*Seven minutes, altogether.*

ARTICLES.—Half an ox-head, one head of celery, some pepper and salt, four small onions, six cloves, two quarts and a half of water.

DIRECTIONS.—Well wash part of an ox-head, and let it soak in cold water several hours; then put it into a stew-pan with a little pepper and salt, onions, celery cut into slices, cloves; pour in the water and set it over a gentle fire to simmer slowly; when tender, take out the head, and cut the meat from it in rather small pieces, strain the gravy and put about a third part of it in a stew-pan, with some force-meat balls and pieces of head; make all very hot and serve.

## 284. Stew of Ox-Cheek (French Style).

TIME.—*Four hours.*

ARTICLES.—An ox-cheek, a little salt, and a few cloves, three onions, six carrots, four or five turnips, a head of celery.

DIRECTIONS.—Clean and well wash an ox-cheek, cut off the fleshiest parts and break the bones into an available size, then put it into a pot with enough water to cover it, and season with pepper and salt, then with a few cloves, the onions and carrots, celery cut into pieces, and turnips of tolerable size; stew it slowly; before serving, the meat may be removed and the gravy thickened and browned; serve it very hot with the meat in the gravy. A shin of beef is excellent, dressed in this fashion.

## 285. Ox-Cheek Corned.

Cut them off and salt; boil with vegetables; serve as for corned beef.

## 286. Ox-Cheek Hash.

Boil, corned or fresh, and use for hash. See hash recipes.

## 287. Ox-Cheek Pies

Boiled, it is first rate for mince pies, in place of costly meat.

## ANIMALS' BRAINS

Are cheap, palatable, eatable, and a good many persons are fond of them. Believing nothing in this world should ever be wasted, we give these recipes, hoping our people will try them. Although they are generally thrown away, butchers will save them if purchasers can be obtained.

## 288. To Prepare Ox-Brains.

Soak the brains in lukewarm water and clean them well from blood, fibers, and skin them; soak them ten hours in cold water in winter, and five hours in summer.

## 289. To Prepare Calves', Hogs', and Sheep's Brains, etc.

Put the brains in cold water, with a table-spoonful of vinegar for each brain; soak them from one to five hours; remove the skin, fibers, etc.

An ox-brain is as large as three or four of the smaller animals, but all are good to eat—there is no perceptible difference.

## 290. Brains Boiled (French Style).

TIME.—*To boil, one hour.*

ARTICLES.—An ox-brain, or three other brains; two ounces of bacon, one carrot, four small onions, salt and pepper, a lemon, water.

DIRECTIONS.—Slice all the articles (not the brains); put all into the TEA-KETTLE BOILER, boil until the vegetables are done, then strain the sauce, boil all again fifteen minutes; serve with potatoes.

## 291. Brains and Tongue.

TIME.—*To boil, ten or fifteen minutes.*

ARTICLES.—A little parsley, thyme, pepper and salt, two table-spoonfuls of melted butter or cream; juice of a quarter of lemon, a pinch of cayenne.

DIRECTIONS.—Clean the brains, boil them in a little water fifteen minutes in the TEA-KETTLE BOILER; take them up, drain and chop them, and put them to warm in the boiler, with the herbs chopped, the melted butter or cream, and the seasoning; squeeze a little lemon juice over them; stir them well together; boil the tongue; skin it, take off the roots, lay it in the middle of the dish, and serve the brains round it.

## 292. Mock Oysters (Made of Brains).

TIME.—*To boil, twenty minutes.*

ARTICLES.—Brains, milk, vinegar, whole cloves, allspice, cinnamon, pepper, salt.

DIRECTIONS.—Take brains from the heads as whole as possible, remove the skin and throw them into salt and water; let them remain in this two hours, then boil them until done in sweet milk in the TEA-KETTLE BOILER; take them up in an earthen bowl or dish, and pour over weak vinegar to cover them; prepare sufficient vinegar to cover them by adding to it whole cloves, allspice and cinnamon to taste; season well with pepper, using part red pepper; scald the vinegar; pour off the weak vinegar, cover with the spiced vinegar. Eat cold, or stewed with crackers, as oysters.

## 293. Brains Fried (French Style).

ARTICLES.—Brains, pepper, salt, sage, flour, and bread crumbs.

DIRECTIONS.—Wash the brains, parboil them, remove all the skin, season them with pepper, salt, and sage; dust flour, meal, or bread crumbs over them, and fry a delicate brown.

## 294. Brains Baked.

TIME.—*One hour to bake.*

ARTICLES.—One ox or three hogs', calves', or sheeps' brains; two eggs; four table-spoonfuls of milk or cream; two of corn starch; one-third as much bread crumbs as brains; pepper, salt, and sage to taste.

DIRECTIONS.—Soak and clean as directed the brains, parboil ten minutes, beat the eggs up with the corn starch; then beat all the articles together, season to taste. If too moist, add more bread crumbs; grease a dish well with butter, pour in the mixture, cover it over with bread crumbs.

## 295. Au Beurre Noir.

When prepared and boiled as above directed, put two ounces of butter in a frying pan, and when melted, turn into it two table-spoonfuls of vinegar, boil two or three minutes; then throw into it half a dozen stalks of parsley, take them off immediately with a skimmer, turn the butter and vinegar over the brains, spread the parsley around, and serve.

## 296. Brains Boiled.

ARTICLES.—Brains of one ox, or more of the others; four table-spoonfuls of vinegar; two onions; ten cloves; same of allspice; salt and pepper to taste.

DIRECTIONS.—When prepared put the brain in a TEA-KETTLE BOILER, cover it with cold water, add the vinegar, onions sliced, parsley, cloves, allspice, salt and pepper; boil about five minutes, and take off the fire; cut each half of the brain in two from side to side; place the four pieces on a dish, the cut part upward.

## 297. Brains Stewed in Wine.

When prepared as directed put in a TEA-KETTLE BOILER, and cover it with claret wine, add half an onion, sliced, one clove of garlic, one clove, two sprigs of parsley, one of thyme, salt, six pepper corns, and boil. Cut and dish it as directed above, turn the broth over it through a strainer, and serve.

## 298. Brains en Matelote.

TIME.—*Twenty minutes.*

ARTICLES.—The brains; a spoonful of vinegar; one of salt; three small onions; half a glass of white wine; half a pint of milk, and two ounces of butter; pepper, sage.

DIRECTIONS.—Clean and soak the brains; then put them into a TEA-KETTLE BOILER of boiling water, with the vinegar and salt, and let them scald for ten minutes; take them out and pass them through more cold water. Fry the onions in butter and flour; then pour them in the milk, the white wine, stir all well together. Put in the brains, mix them with the sauce, and stew them until done, season to taste. Throw away the vinegar when used.

## 299. Croquettes of Brains.

TIME.—*Ten minutes.*

ARTICLES.—Brains; one spoonful of sage leaves; one egg; some bread crumbs; pepper and salt; a little milk.

DIRECTIONS.—Blanch the calf's brains, and beat them well together with a spoonful of sage leaves chopped very fine, seasoned with pepper and salt; mix them with bread crumbs soaked in a little milk and a well-beaten egg. Make them into balls, and fry them in butter. Serve them piled upon a dish.

## 300. Brains a la Worcestershire.

TIME.—*A quarter of an hour.*

ARTICLES.—The brains; a spoonful of salt; one table-spoonful of vinegar; three ounces of butter; some Worcestershire sauce.

DIRECTIONS.—Prepare the brains; then boil them in salt water and vinegar. Cut some thin slices of bread in the shape of scallop shells, and fry them in butter, lay these on a dish, divide the brain in two, and place on the fried bread, pour the sauce over them, and serve.

## LIGHTS OR LUNGS

Of sheep, calves, and hogs, if sound, are good and healthy eating. Like all the vitals and extremities, in this country, they have not been eaten and perfected, as they have in Europe; yet they are better eaten than wasted. If any part of an animal is diseased, none of it is fit to be eaten; if any part is, the whole is, and if any heart, liver, or lungs, are diseased, it is easily seen.

### 301. To Prepare Lights.

Trim and cut them up in slices, soak in cool water three hours, wash them in lukewarm water well twice, squeeze the blood out of them.

### 302. To Fry Lights.

Prepare as above, slice and fry brown with pork fat.

### 303. To Stew Lights.

ARTICLES.—Lights, butter, flour, onions, yolks of three eggs; salt and pepper, any other spice to taste.

DIRECTIONS.—Prepare as above, parboil them three minutes, throw the slices of lights into cold water, drain them, cut into dice, fry them five minutes with butter, sprinkle them with flour, add six sliced onions, a pint of hot milk, salt, pepper, spice to taste; cook all in the TEA-KETTLE BOILER until all is tender. Beat the yolks of the eggs with a table-spoonful of vinegar, mix with the whole, and turn on a dish and serve hot.

LIGHTS COOKED otherwise by any of the haslet recipes.

## KIDNEYS.

Beefs', calves', lamb's, hogs', are all good, cheap, and hearty for the strong and well, but not fit for the weak and feeble. They make many excellent dishes. All butchers keep them; but never buy only fresh ones.

### 304. To Prepare.

Wash, soak them in warm water half an hour, trim. Beef kidneys three hours.

### 305. Kidney Stews.

TIME.—*Two hours.*

ARTICLES.—Kidneys, onions, salt pork, flour, milk, and pepper.

DIRECTIONS.—Wash, trim, and cut up in thin slices any kidneys, put them into the TEA-KETTLE BOILER, with onions sliced to taste, and two slices of salt pork. Cover with boiling hot water, stew two hours. Make a cup of gravy of flour in cold milk, pour into the BOILER; then add salt and pepper to taste, let it boil five minutes, serve hot.

### 306. Stewed Beef Kidneys.

TIME.—*Half an hour.*

ARTICLES.—A beef kidney, pepper, and salt.

DIRECTIONS.—Cut the kidney into slices, and season it highly with pepper and salt, and fry it a light brown; then pour a little warm water into the pan, dredge in some flour, put in the slices of kidney, and let it stew very gently.' Serve hot.

### 307. Rissoles of Kidneys.

TIME.—*Half an hour.*

ARTICLES.—Some slices of cold kidneys; the same quantity of ham or bacon; yolks of two eggs; one ounce of butter; pepper and salt, and some bread crumbs.

DIRECTIONS.—Cut some neat slices from a cold beef kidney, with about the like quantity of ham or bacon cut into the same-sized slices, and two hard-boiled eggs; lay the bacon over the kidney, then the slices of eggs, season with pepper and salt, and bind them together with a little melted butter and the yolk of a beaten egg. Dip them into beaten bread crumbs, fry them lightly and serve, with a little gravy in the dish.

### 308. Kidneys Fried.

TIME.—*Ten minutes.*

ARTICLES.—Kidneys, flour, salt, pepper, butter, vinegar.

DIRECTIONS.—Trim, parboil, cut in thin slices, dredge them well with flour, fry on both sides, season with salt and pepper, make a gravy of butter and flour, add a little vinegar, serve hot.

### 309. Broiled Kidneys.

TIME.—*Eight minutes.*

ARTICLES.—Kidneys, pepper, salt, bread crumbs, and butter.

DIRECTIONS.—Cut each kidney through without dividing it, take off the skin, and season highly with pepper and salt, dip each kidney into melted butter, and strew bread crumbs over them, pass a small skewer through the white part of them to keep them flat, and broil them over a clear fire, serve them with hollow part uppermost, filling each hollow with the sauce. Use small kidneys.

### 310. Baked Kidneys.

TIME.—*One hour to bake.*

ARTICLES.—Kidneys, salt-pork, pepper.

DIRECTIONS.—Prepare and slice the kidneys, place alternate layers of slices of salt pork and kidney on a skewer, put these in a pan, a little cold water under the pan grate, and bake until done.

## KIDNEYS—HASLETS—OX HEELS.

### 311. Kidneys Sauties or Vin.
TIME.—*Ten minutes.*
ARTICLES.—Kidneys, a table-spoonful of butter; same of chopped onions and parsley; one salt-spoonful of salt, and one of pepper; brown sauce; a tea-cup of any wine.
DIRECTIONS.—Cut the kidneys into rather thin slices, put them into a pan with a little butter. When they are nearly done, add the chopped onion and parsley, with pepper and salt to taste. Pour in a little good sauce, and any wine. Boil it up and serve. This is a nice dish.

### 312. Kidney Gravy.
TIME.—*One hour and three-quarters.*
ARTICLES.—Four kidneys; two ounces and a half of butter; a few sweet herbs; a little salt and cayenne; one tea-spoonful of ketchup; half an onion; one pint of water.
DIRECTIONS.—Slice four kidneys, cut them into pieces, and dredge them with flour; put them into a TEA-KETTLE BOILER, with the butter, a few sweet herbs, and half an onion. Shake these over the fire for eight minutes, and then add the water. Let it simmer for two hours skimming it carefully, strain the gravy, and set it by for use.
This gravy can be made from one beef kidney, instead of four sheep's kidneys which is about equal.

### 313. Roast Kidneys.
Prepare as above, and roast.

### HASLETS.
Sheep's, lambs', calves', and hogs' haslets.

### 314. To Fry Haslets.
Cut the heart and liver in slices, and fry with salt-pork fat, pepper to taste. Haslets should be well-cooked.

### 315. To Broil Haslets.
Cut them up in slices and broil until well-done; butter, salt, and pepper to taste.

### 316. To Stew Haslets.
Cut up in small pieces a haslet and two onions, put all into a TEA-KETTLE BOILER, add boiling water, and stew until tender; season with pepper, salt, and butter to taste, serve hot. It can be thickened with flour if desired.

### 317. Haslet and Milk.
TIME.—*Half an hour.*
ARTICLES.—Milk, liver, pepper, salt, butter, flour, vinegar.
DIRECTIONS.—To a quart of boiling hot milk add the liver only from a haslet; boil half an hour in the TEA-KETTLE BOILER. Pepper, salt, and butter to taste; add a little flour to thicken, wet first in cold milk, then boil a few minutes, add three table-spoonfuls of vinegar, stir it in briskly, and serve at once.

### OX HEELS
Are not used much in the Northern States, except by a few who know how good they are.
They make nutritive, agreeable, economical, and healthy dishes. Any butcher will furnish them cheap. A set of four will make a meal for twenty persons. Try these recipes.

### 318. To Clean and Prepare Ox Heels.
Dip them in boiling water, let them remain sufficient time to loosen the horny parts and hair, scrape, put the knife under the horn, and pry it off; wash until white and clean.

### 319. Ox Heels Boiled.
TIME.—*About four hours to boil*
ARTICLES.—Two or more heels; potatoes and other vegetables; pepper and salt.
DIRECTIONS.—Put two or more in a pot with plenty of water, boil until the bones can be taken out easily, season with pepper, salt, etc., eat with potatoes and other vegetables.

### 320. Ox Heels Stewed.
TIME.—*Four hours.*
Prepare and cook the heels as above, with less water, add onions, potatoes, and seasoning to taste, a little flour to this.

### 321. Ox Heels Fried.
TIME.—*Ten minutes to fry.*
ARTICLES.—Cow heel; yolk of an egg; bread crumbs; a sprig of parsley; cayenne pepper and salt; a piece of butter.
DIRECTIONS.—Having boiled, cut the heels into pieces about two inches long, and one inch wide, dip them into the yolk of a beaten egg, cover them with fine bread crumbs mixed with chopped parsley, cayenne, and a little pepper and salt; fry them in boiling fat, and arrange them neatly on a hot dish.
Ox heels can be cooked the same as pigs' feet in any of the pigs' feet recipes.

### 322. Ox Heel Soup.
TIME.—*Six hours.*
ARTICLES.—Two feet; six carrots; six turnips; three small onions; ten potatoes, and a spoonful of black pepper; two heads of celery.
DIRECTIONS.—Cut up the feet; then put them into a TEA-KETTLE BOILER; cut the carrots and turnips in slices; three small onions; add the black whole pepper, and about five quarts of water. Let it boil, and then simmer slowly till reduced to a pulp, and serve with vegetables.

## PIGS' FEET.

Buy them before they are boiled, as they are much cheaper, and you can clean and and boil them better than they usually are at the store. Besides they can be procured fresh and good.

### 323. Pigs' Feet Stewed.

TIME.—*Forty minutes.*

ARTICLES.—Pigs' feet, onions, pepper, allspice, salt, flour, vinegar.

DIRECTIONS.—After they are boiled tender cut them up, put them into the TEA-KETTLE BOILER, with enough hot water to cover them, add an onion or two sliced at the bottom. Pepper, allspice, and salt to taste. Stew half an hour, turn off the gravy, thicken with flour and butter, add vinegar to taste, pour it back on the feet. Boil ten minutes, serve hot.

### 324. Pigs' Feet Fried.

Take split boiled pigs' feet, rub them in meal, bread crumbs, or batter; fry until brown.

### 325. Picked Pigs' Feet.

ARTICLES.—Feet, meal, pepper, salt, vinegar, egg, flour.

DIRECTIONS.—Boil the feet until tender; while hot pick off the meat, season with pepper, salt, and vinegar to taste, put the meat in pans, press it down. When cold cut in slices, dip it in meal, fry until slightly brown; to prevent it falling to pieces dip the slices in egg, or fry in flour batter.

### 326. Pigs' Feet Broiled.

Take split boiled pigs' feet, broil until brown. Spread sweet butter on them, eat with mustard.

### 327. Pigs' Feet Fried in Butter.

TIME.—*Twenty minutes.*

ARTICLES.—Pigs' feet; one egg; one table-spoonful of flour; one and a half gill of milk; a pinch of salt; a little lard for the pan.

DIRECTIONS.—Make a nice batter of an egg, a table-spoonful of flour, a gill and a half of milk, and a pinch of salt. Split the feet in halves, and dip them into the batter. Fry them a nice brown, and serve.

### 328. Pigs' Feet Fricasseed.

TIME.—*One hour.*

ARTICLES.—One pint of milk; one small onion; half a lemon peel; a small piece (size of a nut) of butter rolled in flour; one salt-spoonful of salt; pigs' feet.

DIRECTIONS.—Cut the feet in neat little pieces, and boil them in a little milk in the TEA-KETTLE BOILER with a small onion, a little lemon peel. Before you serve them, add a little butter, flour, and salt.

### 329. Pickled Pigs' Feet.

TIME.—*One day.*

ARTICLES.—Vinegar, whole clove, mace, allspice, pepper.

DIRECTIONS.—After they are boiled tender, put them in plain weak vinegar (add with whole clove, mace, allspice, and pepper if desired in the vinegar); scald the vinegar every week or two to keep it.

### 330 To Cook Pigs' Feet thirty other Ways.

They can be cooked in every style that heads, tripe, and calves' heads are. See those recipes.

### 331. Mock Brawn.

TIME.—*Four hours.*

ARTICLES.—Two hocks, feet, and ears.

DIRECTIONS.—Take two hocks, feet, and ears, boil them so tender that you may run a quill through them. Then pick the meat off the bones, have an oval pan, and lay the skin at the bottom and round the sides of it, put the meat in the middle, fill it as full as you can, and lay a heavy weight on it for a couple of days. Then take it out of the pan quite whole, bind it round with a broad piece of coarse tape, and put it into a pan with salt and water, changing the water every two or three days. It will keep for a fortnight or three weeks.

### 332. Pigs' Pettitoes.

TIME.—*Forty minutes.*

ARTICLES.—Feet, heart, and liver of a pig; a small piece of butter (size of a walnut); half a tea-spoonful of pepper; a little salt; one pound of toasted bread.

DIRECTIONS.—Put them in just sufficient water to cover them, add the heart and liver, boil them ten minutes; then take out the liver and heart, and mince them small, return them to the feet, and stew until quite tender; thicken with flour and butter, season with pepper and salt, and serve up with sippets of plain or toasted bread, make a pyramid of the minced heart and liver, and lay the feet around them. When pettitoes are fried they should be first boiled, then dipped in butter, and fried a light brown.

### 333. Pigs' Feet with Onions.

TIME.—*To boil, one hour and a half; to broil, ten minutes.*

ARTICLES.—Four boiled pigs' feet; two onions; one tea-spoonful of made mustard; two ounces of butter; one tea-spoonful of flour.

DIRECTIONS.—Split the feet in halves; egg and bread; crumb them and broil them; cut the ears into fillets; put them into a TEA-KETTLE BOILER, with two sliced onions, the butter, and the flour. When they are browned, take them up, add the mustard, and lay them on a hot dish. Put the feet on the top of them, and serve.

## CALVES' HEADS AND FEET

Are generally sold cheap. They are healthy, nutritious, and palatable when cooked properly. If you buy them uncleaned, dip the head and feet into scalding water, with a little rosin added to it; remove the hair and scrape well. After it is cleaned, cut it open, take out the brain and eyes, let it soak all night in cold water, and cook as per recipes.

### 334. Mock Turtle of Calf's Head.

TIME.—*One hour.*

ARTICLES.—Calf's head and feet, mace, cloves, nutmeg, red pepper, sweet herbs, a large onion, salt, butter, flour.

DIRECTIONS.—Take a calf's head, split it open, and lay it for two or three hours in cold water, then put it on to boil in as much water as will cover it; when it is done enough to take off the bones, cut the meat into square pieces, and put them into the TEA-KETTLE BOILER with some mace, cloves, nutmeg, red pepper, some sweet herbs and a large onion; salt to taste; put in as much of the liquor as will cover it, and let it stew gently one hour; then take one quarter of a pound of butter, rolled in flour, and some browned butter, mix it with the stew, and let it boil half an hour; when done, fry the liver and lay it round the dish. Use as much spice as desired.

### 335. Calf's-Head Cheese.

Made precisely like hog's-head cheese; very good.

### 336. Boiled Calf's Head.

TIME.—*About three hours.*

DIRECTIONS.—Clean, keep the skin on, remove the eyes, jaws, and nose, remove the brains; put the head and tongue, with enough warm water to cover them, in a pot, tie the brains in a cloth, boil all together until tender; any vegetables can be added. Serve plain, or with brain sauce.

### 337. Calf's Head Stewed.

Cook same as for boiling, using less water, stirring in flour to thicken; when done, season to taste.

### 338. Calf's Head a la Maitre d'Hotel.

TIME.—*One hour and three-quarters.*

ARTICLES.—Remains of a cold calf's head, three-quarters of a pint of maitre d'hotel sauce.

DIRECTIONS.—Remove the bones from the head and cut it into thin slices. When the sauce is sufficiently thick to cover the meat nicely, lay the slices in it, warm in gradually, and as soon as it boils up place it on one side to simmer for a few minutes.

### 339. Collard Calf's Head.

TIME.—*Six hours, altogether.*

ARTICLES.—A calf's head, a few thick slices of ham, three table-spoonfuls of minced parsley, three blades of pounded mace, half a tea-spoonful of white pepper, six eggs.

DIRECTIONS.—Scald the head and scrape off the hair, clean it nicely, divide it and take out the brains, boil it for two hours, or until the meat leaves the bones, which must be taken out; then flatten the head on the table, cover it with a thick layer of parsley, a layer of slices of ham, the yolks of the eggs boiled hard, and cut into thin rings, between each layer put a seasoning of the pepper and spices; roll the head in a cloth very tightly, boil it for four hours, at least, then take it up and put it under a heavy weight; let it remain until cold; remove the cloth, etc., and serve.

### 340. Fricassee of Calf's Head.

TIME.—*One hour and a half.*

ARTICLES.—The remains of a boiled calf's head, a bunch of savory herbs, two dessert-spoonfuls of lemon juice, one onion, one blade of mace, pepper and salt, two eggs, a piece of butter, flour, and a quart of the liquor in which the head was boiled.

DIRECTIONS.—Cut the meat from the head into nice thin pieces, and put the bones into a TEA-KETTLE BOILER, with nearly a quart of the water in which the head was boiled, a bunch of savory herbs, a blade of mace, the onion browned, and a little pepper and salt; let it simmer for nearly an hour, then strain it into a TEA-KETTLE BOILER, put in the slices of head, thicken the gravy with a little butter and flour, and bring it nearly to a boil; when done, take out the meat, and stir gradually in two dessert-spoonfuls of lemon-juice, and the yolks of two well-beaten eggs, but do not let it boil or it will curdle; pour it over the meat, and serve it up very hot.

### 341. Hashed Calf's Head.

TIME.—*One hour and a half.*

ARTICLES.—Half a calf's head, a bunch of savory herbs, a little cayenne pepper, salt, one lemon one onion, one carrot, one quart of broth, or the liquor in which it was boiled.

DIRECTIONS. — Cut the meat from the remains of a boiled calf's head into small pieces of about two inches across; put a quart of broth, or the liquor in which the head was boiled, into a TEA-KETTLE BOILER with a carrot, and one small onion; boil it until reduced to nearly half the quantity, then strain it through a hair sieve and add the wine, the juice of a lemon, two dessert-spoonfuls of mushroom ketchup, and a piece of butter rolled in flour; lay in the slices of head, and when gradually well heated, let it just boil up; then serve it on a hot dish, with rolled bacon, and force-meat balls as a garnish.

### 342. Lamb's Head and Pluck.

TIME.—*One hour and a quarter to boil.*

ARTICLES.—A lamb's head, egg, bread crumbs, a cup of milk, a piece of lemon-peel pepper, salt, and nutmeg.

DIRECTIONS.—Soak the head in water for two hours, then boil it until nearly done, take it out and brush it over with the yolk of a well beaten egg, cover it thick with bread crumbs; again add the eggs and repeat the bread crumbs; season it with pepper and put it into a moderate oven until sufficiently brown; in the meantime, after scalding the pluck and setting it too cool, mince it up fine, mix in the brains and season them with pepper, salt, and grated nutmeg; put them in a TEA-KETTLE BOILER, with a piece of lemon-peel cut thin; put the mince into a dish, and serve the lamb's head on it.

## LIVER.

The livers of all domestic animals that are eaten, are cheap, good, and healthy, and are generally sold for about one-third to one-quarter the prices of a carcass.

### 343. To Prepare Liver.

When to be roasted whole soak them three hours in cold water; when to be boiled, wash only; when to be cooked in slices, have water with a little salt, on the fire; as soon as it boils throw the liver in for about five minutes, then take it out and drain it.

### 344. To Broil Liver.

Cut the liver in slices about a quarter of an inch thick, sprinkle on them salt and pepper, place them on a gridiron over a sharp fire, turn over only once, and serve with butter spread on the slices; a few drops of lemon juice may be added.

### 345. To Fry Liver.

Cut in slices as above; slice fat salt pork, fry the pork brown, take out the pork when done, leaving the fat in, then put in the liver, cook until done, with salt, pepper, vinegar.

### 346. Liver and Bacon.

TIME.—*Quarter of an hour.*

ARTICLES.—Two pounds and a half of liver one pound of bacon, juice of one lemon; two ounces of butter, a little flour, pepper and salt.

DIRECTIONS.—Soak the liver in cold water for half an hour, then dry it in a cloth and cut it into thin, narrow slices; take about a pound of bacon, or as much as you may require, and cut an equal number of thin slices as you have of liver, fry the bacon lightly, take it out and keep it hot; then fry the liver in the same pan, seasoning it with pepper and salt, dredging over it a little flour. When it is a nice brown, arrange it round the dish with a roll of bacon between each slice; pour off the pan, put in about two ounces of butter well rubbed in flour to thicken the gravy, squeeze in the juice of a lemon, and add a cupful of hot water; boil it and pour it into the center of the dish.

### 347. To Bake Liver.

TIME.—*From thirty to ninety minutes, according to size.*

DIRECTIONS.—Envelop the liver with buttered paper, place it in an oven and baste often; a few minutes before it is done, take the paper off, and baste continually; serve with the gravy or sauce.

### 348. To Saute Liver.

TIME.—*About ten minutes.*

ARTICLES.—Two ounces of butter, an onion, liver, flour, a wine-glass of warm milk, same of claret wine, salt, pepper, allspice.

DIRECTIONS.—Put two ounces of butter in a frying-pan, and set it on a sharp fire; when melted, add an onion, then the liver cut in slices (after having been prepared as above); sprinkle on a salt-spoonful of flour, then half a wine-glass of warm milk, same of claret wine, salt, pepper, and a pinch of allspice; serve when done.

### 349. To Stew Liver.

Prepare the liver as directed above, and when drained and cold, lard it well; have butter in a frying-pan on a brisk fire; when hot, put the liver in for about five minutes, turning it over on every side; have in a TEA-KETTLE BOILER four ounces of bacon, cut in dice, set it on a good fire, and when hot, lay the liver in, then add pepper and salt, a sprig of thyme, two cloves, and a small carrot cut in two, cover the TEA-KETTLE BOILER, subdue the fire, and let it simmer three hours, stirring now and then; place the liver on a dish, strain the sauce on it, and serve.

### 350. Liver a la Mode (French).

TIME.—*Two hours and a quarter.*

ARTICLES.—A liver, or part of one; seven ounces of bacon, two ounces and a half of butter, a bunch of sweet herbs, two onions, six cloves, one clove of garlic, three carrots, two turnips, one wine-glass of brandy, one of wine, one table-spoonful of sauce.

DIRECTIONS.—After well washing the liver, soak it a short time in cold water, then wipe it dry and insert lardoons of bacon at equal distances in the interior part of the liver; put it into a stew-pan with about two ounces and a half of butter, a small bunch of herbs tied together, half a blade of mace, and a small onion stuck with six cloves, and fry it a nice brown; then add three carrots, two turnips, an onion cut, and a wine-glass of brandy, with sufficient water to just cover the whole; baste it frequently with its own gravy, and let it simmer slowly for two hours; when done take out the liver and put in on a dish, garnished with the cut vegetables; strain and skim the gravy, and the sauce, and glass of wine; boil it to the quantity required, pour it over the liver, and serve it up hot.

## HAMS, SHOULDERS, AND BACON.

HOW POOR ONES ARE MADE GOOD BY COOKING.

Hams, shoulders, bacon, and pickled pork are very economical and handy dishes, as they are so hearty that a person can not eat much; properly cooked, they are a luxury. By our mode of cooking, a common ham or shoulder is made as good as the best sugar-cured ones. Never buy them unless warranted sweet.

### 351. To Prepare Smoked and Salt Hams, Shoulders, and Bacon for Cooking.

Soak any of them from twenty to fifty hours, according to the size, in three pails of water; trim it neatly, removing any rusty parts—this soaking opens and fills the pores of the meat, which salting, smoking, and drying has hardened, and which cooking, without long soaking, does not fill. By this process much waste is prevented. Try it, and this one recipe will pay for the book.

### 352. To Steam Ham, Shoulders, and Bacon.

TIME.—*About six hours.*

DIRECTIONS.—After preparing as above, pour over some boiling in a pot, with an ounce of whole cloves, an ounce of allspice, an ounce of pepper; then put the meat in a steamer, cover tight and steam until tender; eat hot or cold.

### 353. To Boil Hams, etc.

TIME.—*Five or six hours.*

DIRECTIONS.—Prepare the ham as above, pour in enough water in a pot to cover the ham, add half an ounce each of whole cloves, allspice, mace, and nutmeg, half a pound of sugar; boil until the skin peels and it is tender; as the scum rises skim it off carefully; take off the pot and let it cool in the liquid until cold; remove the skin whole. If to eat hot, of course take it out before cooling.

### 354. To Bake a Ham, etc.

TIME.—*Five hours.*

DIRECTIONS.—Prepare it as above; cover it over with a quite thick paste, then put it in a pan, bake it in a moderate oven until done; baste it; the flour prevents its drying up; when done, remove the crust and skin; serve hot or cold.

### 355. To Bake, Boil, etc., a Ham.

Prepare and boil a ham as above directed for boiling three hours, no longer; then put it in a moderate hot oven from the pot, and bake it two hours more. This gives a fine flavor to the ham.

REMARKS.—Any family once using the above recipes to cook hams, shoulders, bacon, and pickled pork, will use no other. We have repeatedly tried the most inferior hams this way, and then tried the old way with the best cured hams, costing much more, and found the common hams the best.

### 356. Ox-Tail Soup.

TIME.—*Two hours.*

ARTICLES.—One ox-tail, white or Russia turnips, onions, potatoes, carrots, salt, pepper, and flour.

DIRECTIONS.—Ox-tail makes a rich soup, rich in strength and nutriment. Cut up an ox tail in three-inch pieces, wash it, put it in the soup pot, cover with cold water, heat it slowly, as the scum rises to the top skim it off until all is removed; when boiled two hours to a gallon of soup, peel and slice six white or two Russia turnips, six large onions or more small ones, also a dozen Irish potatoes, and two carrots; add salt and pepper to taste; when almost done add flour, beaten up in water, strain boil up, then remove and serve.

REMARKS.—Rice and barley can be added to soups, if preferred to flour. Any meat can be used—beef, mutton, pork, or veal.

### 357. Tongues

Are good corned, or smoked, boiled tender.

### 358. Rolled Beef to eat like Hare.

TIME.—*A quarter of an hour to each pound.*

ARTICLES.—The inside of a sirloin of beef; half a pound of bacon; some rich gravy; two glasses of port wine; two of vinegar; twenty pounded allspice; currant jelly, and melted butter.

DIRECTIONS.—Soak the beef for a day and night in a glass of port wine, and the same of vinegar; lay some good force meat over it, lard it with shreds of bacon, and bake it. Baste it frequently with port wine and vinegar, in the same proportion that you used for soaking it, and season it with some pounded allspice. Serve it up with a rich gravy poured round it, with currant jelly in a tureen.

### 359. Potted Ox Tongue.

ARTICLES.—One pound and a half of boiled tongue; six ounces of butter; a little Cayenne; a small spoonful of pounded mace; nutmeg and cloves.

DIRECTIONS.—Remove the rind of the tongue, cut and pound it in a mortar as fine as possible with the butter, and the spices beaten fine. When perfectly pounded, and the spice well blended with the meat, press it into small potted pans, and pour clarified butter over the top. A little roast veal added to the potted tongue is an improvement.

### 360. Potted Beef like Venison.

TIME.—*To bake, two hours to two hours and a half.*

ARTICLES.—Four pounds of buttock of beef; two ounces of saltpeter; two ounces of bay salt; a quarter of a pound of common salt; half an ounce of salprunella; half an ounce of cloves and mace, a quarter of an ounce of pepper; half a nutmeg.

DIRECTIONS.—Take four pounds of buttock of beef, and cut the lean into four pieces; beat the saltpeter, bay salt, common salt, and salprunella very fine, mix them well together, and rub them into the beef. Let it remain in the pan four days, turning it night and morning; after that put it into a pan, cover it with water and a little of the brine.' Send it to the oven, and bake it until very tender; then drain it from the gravy, and take out all the skin and sinews; pound the beef in a mortar, put it on a broad dish, and strew over it the mace, cloves, and pepper, all beaten very fine, and grate in half a nutmeg, mix the whole well with the pounded meat, and add a little fresh butter clarified to moisten it. Then press it down into pots, set them at the mouth of the oven just to settle, and then cover them two inches deep with clarified butter. When quite cold, cover them with white paper tied over, and set them in a dry place.

The beef will keep good a considerable time.

### 361. Pressed Beef.

TIME.—*Five hours.*

ARTICLES.—Ten or eleven pounds of the flank; two pounds of salt; half a pound of moist sugar; a quarter of an ounce of saltpeter.

DIRECTIONS.—Take about ten or eleven pounds of the thin flank, and rub well into every part two pounds of salt, and half a pound of moist sugar, mixed with the saltpeter dissolved; repeat the rubbing with the pickle every day for a week; then roll it round, and bind it with a wide piece of tape. Have ready a stew pan of scalding water, put in the beef, and when it simmers allow five hours for ten pounds of meat. When sufficiently done drain off the water in which it was boiled, and pour cold water over it for six or eight minutes, drain it on a sieve reversed, and then place it on a board with a weight on it to press the meat well. Then remove the tapes, trim it neatly, and serve it when required.

### 362. Boiled Marrow Bones. — Served on Toast.

TIME.—*Two hours.*

ARTICLES. — Flour, **bread**, pepper, and salt.

DIRECTIONS.—Saw the bones any size you may prefer, cover the ends with a common paste of flour and water, tie a cloth over them, and place them in a small stew pan, with sufficient boiling water to cover them. When sufficiently boiled, serve them upright; or when boiled, take out the marrow, and spread it on toasted bread cut into small square slices; season it with pepper and salt, and send it to the table quickly.

### 363. Loin of Mutton to eat like Venison.

TIME.—*Three hours.*

ARTICLES.—A large fat loin of mutton; one onion; a sprig of thyme and parsley; a little whole pepper and salt; one pint of port wine.

DIRECTIONS.—Bone a large and fat loin of mutton, take the skin off the fat, and put the bones and mutton into a stew pan with an onion, a sprig of thyme and parsley, and a little whole pepper and salt; add a pint of port wine, cover the pan close, and set it over a very slow fire to stew. Then skim off the fat from the gravy, and serve it very hot with sweet sauce in a tureen.

### 364. Shoulder of Mutton Spiced.

TIME.—*To stew, four hours.*

ARTICLES.—Two ounces of coarse sugar to one pound of meat; one salt-spoonful of cloves to the same; mace and pepper mixed, one tea-spoonful; ginger, a pinch; half an ounce of salt; beef gravy to a whole joint, one pint and a half.

DIRECTIONS. — A shoulder of mutton, boned, may be rubbed with the seasoning above given, increased in proportion to its weight. The salt to be added the day after the sugar, cloves, mace, ginger, and pepper have been rubbed into the meat. Turn and rub the meat with this pickle every day for a week or a little longer.

Roll it up tightly, bind it with a string, and stew it gently in beef broth. Serve it in its own gravy with good piquante sauce.

## GENERAL RECIPES

FOR COOKING MEATS, ETC.

We give some general rules for soups, stews, roasting, baking, broiling, and frying meats

### 365. Soups

Are a compound of meats and vegetables, or meats and vegetables separately. Soups are called by the name of the principal meat or vegetables of which it is made. Meats should always be put in cold water for soups, heat gradually, and boiled gently. This takes nearly all the goodness from the meat into the soup. *Soups are cheap, healthy, and nutritious,* can be made out of the liquors that meats are boiled in, or shins and coarse pieces of meat, and are just as good. All kinds of vegetables, also rice and barley, are used to suit the taste. The Germans, French, and Russians are fond of soup.

# GENERAL RECIPES.

### 366. Stews

Are similar to soup, but much thicker and richer; less water makes a stew.

### 367. Roasting

Is simply turning the meats before a fire until cooked. As it is very seldom done, we will only say it is a good way to, but we do not think worth going to much trouble to do if you have a good oven, and use one of BERNEY's PATENT ROASTING PANS, which will roast as well, and be more convenient.

### 368. Baking is more Economical.

All cooking in range, stove, or any oven, is baking; therefore meats cooked in an oven is baking. Meats should be put on a grate in a pan to raise it an inch from the bottom of the pan, pour in a pint of salted water to keep the oven moist, *bake slowly* and steadily, baste frequently with the gravy; the gravy is good plain or mixed with flour; season to taste.

### 369. Boiling

Either salt or fresh meats, is a good way to cook meats; *boil them tender*, if fresh; to be cooked whole, drop it in hot water; if corned, drop it in warm water. The first closes the pores of the meat, the second draws out the salt. Corned beef is a healthy dish.

### 370. To Broil Beef Steak, Veal Cutlets, Pork and Mutton Chops, Liver, Fowl, Game.

Grease the bars of your gridiron (use the kind that turns over instead of turning the meat), place the meats on it, and broil over a hot coal fire; cut the meats one-half an inch thick; do not stick a fork in them while cooking, as it allows the juice to run to waste. The meats should not have too much fat on them. After they are done lay in a hot dish (if not done return to the gridiron at once). Salt and pepper to taste. Spread on good sweet butter; *recollect, serve and eat hot*. This is the plain way of broiling any kind of meat, fowl, and game. Before broiling or frying livers or hearts, soak in salt and water a few minutes if preferred.

### 371. To Fry Steaks, Chops, Cutlets, Fowl, Game, etc.

A large deep wrought-iron frying-pan is best. *Always let the fat be hot before putting in the meat (I prefer salt-pork fat fried out of clear salt pork to any other)*; lard, oil, or butter can be used. Have enough to cover the meat. All meats except beef should be well cooked.

Watch the meat carefully, and turn often; don't let it then burn. Salt and pepper to taste; *but do not salt until the meats are done; salt hardens meats.* Spread sweet butter over the meats hot. Put on a hot dish. Persons who like onions can cut up one or more, fry and cook in the gravy.

### 372. Semi-Frying, or Broiling in the Frying-Pan.

Heat it very hot, grease it, lay it in the meat, turn it constantly until done; finish as above.

### 373. Frying Covered Meats.

Roll the meats in flour, meal, or bread crumbs, shake off what will not adhere, and cook as above. Tomatoes, mustard, vinegar, wine, or any seasoning.

### 374. Cutlets, Steaks, Chops, Beef's Heart, Liver, Tripe, etc., with Tomatoes.

A pint of canned or whole tomatoes, an onion, a table-spoonful of sugar, salt and pepper to taste, a table-spoonful of butter, and three of fine bread crumbs, a tumbler of hot water. Let these simmer gently together, while the meat is being fried or broiled; take them out when done; pour the tomatoes over them.

### 375. Hashes, Entrees of Cold Meats.

All meats (which are often) left over, also potatoes, will make good entrees, hashes, etc.

### 376. To make Good Hashes,

Take out all the bones, and leave only one-quarter of fat to three-quarters of lean meat. Onions, parsley, pepper and salt to taste; chop all fine, heat up well, serve hot.

### 377. Cold Meats

Are often as good as hot eaten with the salad, or maitre d'hotel sauce.

### 378. Entrees of Cold Meats, etc.,

Are made in most any style to suit the taste, by slicing and warming them in sauces, gravies, spiced and seasoned highly.

### 379. Forcemeats,

Or stuffings for poultry, and game, meats or vegetables, can be made of ham or bacon suet, veal, oysters, bread crumbs, soaked bread, or eggs: any spice or sweet herbs to taste.

A selection can be made from any of the above list and flavor as desired. Sometimes milk, butter, wine, and brandy, are used. Onions are used with bread to stuff geese, ducks, or strong game.

Any meat or vegetables can be stuffed, and, by using good taste, can be improved. Hereafter we will give many recipes for forcemeats and stuffings.

# VEGETABLES

Are healthy, but not very nutritious. The various ways of preparing them given below will repay a trial of them.

## TURNIPS.

Cheap, hardy, and plenty. Keep all winter.

### 380. Plain Boiled Turnips.

Peel, and boil them until soft, with any corned meats.

### 381. Mashed Turnips with Onions.

Mash the boiled turnips with a few boiled onions, salt, pepper, and butter to taste.

### 382. Fried Turnips.

Cut cold boiled turnips lengthwise in slices half an inch thick; fry brown; eat hot.

### 383. Puree of Turnips.

TIME.—*To prepare, ten minutes.*

ARTICLES.—Six turnips, three table-spoonfuls of butter, same of milk, pepper and salt to taste.

DIRECTIONS.—Wash, peel, slice six turnips when tender, press them through a sieve, mix in the butter, milk, and seasoning; put the mass in the TEA-KETTLE BOILER, and cook half an hour.

## CARROTS.

### 384. To Fry Carrots.

Boil, slice, and fry brown.

### 385. Carrots (Flemish Way).

TIME.—*Forty minutes to boil.*

ARTICLES.—Six or eight good-sized carrots, five small onions, a sprig of parsley, salt and pepper, a pint of milk, a quarter of a pound of butter.

DIRECTIONS.—Boil the carrots forty minutes, or until they are tender; cut them into dice, then stew them in a TEA-KETTLE BOILER with the small onions, chopped parsley, a little pepper and salt, a pint of milk, melted butter; serve very hot.

### 386. To Stew Carrots.

TIME.—*To parboil them, fifty minutes; nearly twenty minutes to simmer.*

ARTICLES.—Some carrots, a piece of butter rolled in flour, cream.

DIRECTIONS.—Cut into large slices five carrots scraped and washed, parboil them, and then simmer until tender in about a quarter of a pint of milk, and five large spoonfuls of cream, in a TEA-KETTLE BOILER. Add a seasoning of pepper and salt, and a piece of butter rolled in flour; when done serve on a hot dish.

### 387. Mashed Carrots.

TIME.—*To boil the carrots, one hour and a half to one hour and three-quarters.*

ARTICLES.—Some carrots, butter, pepper and salt.

DIRECTIONS.—Scrape off all the skin, wash them well and boil them tender in a stew-pan of boiling water. Then take them up with a skimmer, mash them smooth, add a piece of butter and salt; place them in the center of a dish piled up and marked over with a knife; serve with boiled or roast meat.

## ONIONS.

### 388. To Stew Onions Brown.

TIME.—*Two hours.*

ARTICLES.—Some onions, good beef gravy.

DIRECTIONS.—Strip off the skin and trim the ends neatly, taking care not to cut the onions; place them in a TEA-KETTLE BOILER cover them with some very good beef gravy, and let them stew very slowly for two hours, or until they are perfectly tender without breaking. The onions may be dredged lightly with flour and fried a light color, before they are stewed, if preferred.

### 389. Baked Onions.

Wash and bake them with the skins on same as potatoes; peel when done; eat with sauce.

### 390. Onions a la Creme.

TIME.—*Two hours.*

ARTICLES.—Four or five onions, three ounces of butter, a little flour, pepper, salt, and a cupful of milk.

DIRECTIONS.—Boil the onions in two or three waters to take off the strong taste, then put them into a TEA-KETTLE BOILER, with the butter, a little flour rubbed smooth, pepper, salt, and milk; stir them frequently until sufficiently done; serve them with the sauce poured over them.

### 391. To Stuff Onions.

TIME.—*To fry, ten minutes; to stew, two hours.*

ARTICLES.—Some large onions, a little fat bacon, a little lean beef, bread crumbs, a sprig of parsley, lemon peel, pepper, salt, and mace, one or two eggs, a piece of butter, some brown gravy.

DIRECTIONS.—Peel some onions, parboil and drain them, then take out the inside, but be careful to keep the onions whole, chop up the inside of the onion, a little beef and a little fat bacon; add some bread crumbs, a sprig of parsley, a lemon peel minced up, and a seasoning of pepper, salt, and mace; beat it all up with a well-beaten egg or two, into a paste, and stuff the onions with it; dredge them all over with flour, and fry them a nice brown; then put them into a TEA-KETTLE BOILER with sufficient brown gravy to cover them, and stew them gently for two hours. If stewed in water, a little flour and butter must be added.

# CELERY—CUCUMBERS.

## CELERY.

### 392. Celery with Milk.

TIME.—*To boil the celery, three-quarters of an hour.*

ARTICLES.—Six heads of celery, a pint of milk, a piece of butter rolled in flour, nutmeg, and salt.

DIRECTIONS.—Take celery, cut them about three or four inches long, wash them very clean, and boil them in water until they are tender, put in the milk, mix the butter and flour, and a little salt and grated nutmeg, boil it up till it is thick and smooth, put in the celery, warm it up, and serve with the sauce poured over it.

### 393. Celery with Cream.

TIME.—*To boil the celery, three-quarters of hour; to thicken the sauce, six or eight minutes.*

ARTICLES.—Three or four heads of celery, yolks of four eggs, half a pint of cream, a little salt, and grated nutmeg.

DIRECTIONS.—Cut the white part of three or four heads of celery into lengths of three or four inches long, boil it until tender and strain it from the water; beat the yolks of four eggs and strain them into the cream, season with a little salt and grated nutmeg, put it into a TEA-KETTLE BOILER with the celery until it boils and is of a proper thickness, and then send it to the table on toasted bread.

### 394. Celery Fried.

TIME.—*Twenty minutes.*

ARTICLES.—Three stalks of celery, two eggs, salt, nutmeg, two ounces of butter, four spoonfuls of white wine, two ounces of flour, two ounces of lard.

DIRECTIONS.—Make a batter with the yolks of two eggs well beaten, the white wine, salt and nutmeg, and stir the flour in thoroughly; dip each head of the celery into the batter and fry in lard; serve quite hot, with melted butter poured over them.

## CUCUMBERS.

### 395. To Stew Cucumbers.

TIME.—*To fry, five or six minutes; to stew, six or seven minutes.*

ARTICLES.—An equal quantity of cucumbers and onions, two ounces of butter, six table-spoonfuls of wine, and a half a blade of mace, a little salt, and cayenne, a piece of butter rolled in flour.

DIRECTIONS.—Cut into slices an equal quantity of cucumbers and onions, and fry them in the butter, strain them from the butter and put them into a TEA-KETTLE BOILER with the milk, wine, and mace, stew for about six or seven minutes in the boiler, stir in a bit of butter rolled in flour, a seasoning of salt and a very little cayenne; boil the sauce, thicken, and then serve it up hot.

### 396. To Stuff and Boil Cucumbers.

TIME.—*One hour and five minutes.*

ARTICLES.—Two large cucumbers, a little forcemeat, a pint of milk, two ounces of butter, seasoning to taste.

DIRECTIONS.—Peel two large cucumbers, cut a piece off the large end, and scoop out the seeds, fill it with forcemeat, replace the pieces from the end, and secure it with a very small skewer, put the milk into a TEA-KETTLE BOILER, with two ounces of good butter and seasoning, put in the cucumbers and let them boil very slowly for one hour, then take them out and boil down the sauce for a few minutes; pour it over the cucumbers and serve hot.

### 397. To Roast Cucumbers.

TIME.—*Twenty minutes, or half an hour.*

ARTICLES.—Two large cucumbers, some forcemeat, a little butter, half a pint of gravy.

DIRECTIONS.—Boil the cucumbers ten minutes, then cut them down and take out all the inside; fill them with forcemeat and tie them together, dredge over them a little flour, and place them in an oven to become brown, basting them frequently with fresh butter; when done put them on a hot dish.

### 398. To Dress Cucumbers.

ARTICLES.—Five table-spoonfuls of vinegar, three of sweet oil, pepper, and salt.

DIRECTIONS.—Pare the cucumbers and commence cutting them at the thick end with a sharp knife, shred them as thin as possible on a dish, sprinkle them with pepper and salt, pour over them the above proportion of oil and vinegar.

### 399. Cucumbers, a la Poulette.

TIME.—*Twenty-five minutes.*

ARTICLES.—Three large cucumbers, a little salt, two table-spoonfuls of vinegar, yolks of two eggs, a piece of butter, a little flour, two spoonfuls of cream, and half a pint of broth.

DIRECTIONS.—Take the cucumbers, pare off the rind and cut them into slices of an equal thickness, pick out the seeds and boil them tender in boiling water, with salt and vinegar; when done take them carefully out with a slice, and when drained, put them into a TEA-KETTLE BOILER with half a pint of milk, butter, flour, cream; skim off any fat which may rise, and boil it gently for a quarter of an hour, taking care that the slices of cucumbers are not broken; when ready to serve, stir in the eggs, beaten with a spoonful of vinegar.

# BAKED AND BOILED PUDDINGS.

Puddings are generally cheap, and a healthy way of cooking food, nutritious and agreeable to the taste.

For boiled puddings you will require either a mold, a TEA-KETTLE BOILER, or a pudding-cloth: the former should have a close-fitting cover, and be rubbed over the inside with butter before putting the pudding in it, that it may not stick to the sides. A pudding-cloth must be kept very clean, and in a dry place. Bread, flour, and meal puddings should be tied very loosely as they swell very much in boiling.

The water must be boiling when the pudding is put in, and continue to boil until it is done. If a pudding is boiled in a cloth, there must always be water enough to cover the pudding; but if boiled in a tin mold or a TEA-KETTLE BOILER, it is best not to let the water quite reach the top. When the pudding is done, take it out from the water, plunge whatever it is boiling in, whether cloth or mold, suddenly into cold water; then turn it out immediately; this will prevent its sticking. If there is any delay in serving the pudding, cover it with a napkin, or the cloth in which it was boiled; but it is better to serve it as soon as removed from the cloth, basin, mold, or TEA-KETTLE BOILER.

Bread or rice puddings require a moderate heat for baking; batter or custard requires a quick oven. The time needed for cooking each particular pudding is given with the recipe.

Eggs for puddings are beaten enough when a spoonful can be taken up clear from strings.

Soufflés require a quick oven. These should be made so as to be done the moment for serving, otherwise they will fall in and flatten.

### 400. Boiled Arrow-Root Pudding.

TIME.—*One hour to boil.*

ARTICLES.—Three table-spoonfuls of arrow-root; one pint of milk; two eggs; sugar and flavoring to your taste.

DIRECTIONS.—First mix the arrow-root smooth in a few spoonfuls of cold milk, stir into it the remainder, add two well-beaten eggs, and sugar and flavoring to your taste, put it into a TEA-KETTLE BOILER, and boil it for one hour with the lid close on.

### 401. Baked Arrow-Root Pudding.

TIME.—*Half an hour to bake.*

ARTICLES.—Three dessert-spoonfuls of arrow-root; a pint and a half of new milk; peel of half a lemon; a piece of butter, the size of a walnut; moist or loaf sugar; three eggs, and a little nutmeg; puff paste.

DIRECTIONS.—Mix into a rather thick smooth batter the arrow-root, with a little cold milk. Put the remainder of the milk into a TEA-KETTLE BOILER, with the lemon peel and sugar to taste. When it boils strain it gradually into the batter stirring it all the time, adding the butter. When nearly cold stir in three well-beaten eggs, and pour the whole into a pie dish, round which has been placed a border of puff paste. Grate a little nutmeg over the top, and bake it in a moderate oven.

### 402. Boiled Sago Pudding.

TIME.—*Three-quarters of an hour.*

ARTICLES.—Two ounces of sago; one pint of milk; two eggs; two biscuits; one glass of brandy; sugar to your taste.

DIRECTIONS.—Boil the sago in a TEA-KETTLE BOILER in the milk until it is quite tender. When cold add the eggs, biscuits, brandy, and sugar, beat all together, and put it into a buttered basin. Boil it three quarters of an hour, and serve it with wine sauce poured over it.

### 403. Baked Sago Pudding.

TIME.—*One hour to bake.*

ARTICLES.—One quart of milk; four table-spoonfuls of sago; rind of one lemon; three eggs; two ounces of butter; two ounces and a half of sugar; puff paste.

DIRECTIONS.—Boil the milk in a TEA-KETTLE BOILER with the lemon peel; then strain it through muslin, and stir in the sugar and sago, set it over a slow fire, and let it simmer for twenty minutes. Then put it into a bowl to cool. Add the butter and the eggs well-beaten, put it into a pudding dish with some puff paste round the edge, and bake it for an hour in a moderate oven.

### 404. Boiled Macaroni Pudding.

TIME.—*One hour and a quarter.*

ARTICLES.—Two ounces and a half of macaroni; one quart of milk; three eggs; a wine-glass of brandy or wine; a peel of one small lemon.

DIRECTIONS.—Simmer the macaroni in the milk and the peel of a lemon for about an hour, or until it is tender, take out the lemon peel. Well-beat the eggs, add the sugar pounded, the brandy or wine, and stir all into the milk; when cool then boil again ten minutes.

### 405. Boiled Vermicelli Pudding.

TIME.—*To boil the vermicelli, one hour.*

ARTICLES.—Three ounces of vermicelli; three tea-cupfuls of milk; two ounces of butter; three eggs; three table-spoonfuls of sugar.

DIRECTIONS.—Wash the vermicelli, and put it into a TEA-KETTLE BOILER with the milk; boil it for an hour; then add the butter. Well-beat three eggs with the sugar, and when the vermicelli is cool, stir in the eggs and sugar. Boil it one hour, and serve with sauce.

## BAKED AND BOILED PUDDINGS.

### 406. Baked Macaroni Pudding with Almonds.
TIME.—*One hour; three-quarters of an hour to simmer the macaroni.*
ARTICLES.—A quarter of a pound of pipe macaroni; three pints of new milk; a piece of butter the size of an egg; a quarter of a pound of loaf sugar; four eggs; a little nutmeg.
DIRECTIONS.—Break a quarter of a pound of pipe macaroni into small pieces; then soak, simmer until tender in a TEA-KETTLE BOILER. Then mix with the eggs, butter, sugar, add it to the macaroni and milk, beat all well together, and pour it into a buttered dish, grate a little nutmeg and lemon peel over the top, and bake it for one hour in a moderate oven.

### 407. Baked Vermicelli Pudding.
TIME.—*To bake, an hour.*
ARTICLES.—Three ounces of vermicelli; three tea-cupfuls of milk; two ounces of butter; three eggs; three table-spoonfuls of powdered sugar.
DIRECTIONS.—Wash the vermicelli, and put it into a saucepan with milk, bake it for a quarter of an hour; then add the butter. Well-beat the eggs with the sugar, and when the vermicelli is quite cold, stir in the eggs and sugar; bake it one hour, and serve with sauce to taste.

### 408. Boiled Tapioca Pudding.
TIME.—*One hour to boil.*
ARTICLES.—One quart of new milk; three ounces of tapioca; an ounce and a half of butter; four eggs; grated lemon peel or any other flavoring; three ounces of sugar.
DIRECTIONS.—Put the tapioca into a TEA-KETTLE BOILER with the milk, and let it boil; turn it out to cool, and then stir into it the sugar, the flavoring, and the eggs well-beaten; return it to the boiler, and boil ten minutes. Serve hot with sauce.

### 409. Baked Tapioca Pudding.
TIME.—*One hour to bake.*
ARTICLES.—One ounce and a half of tapioca; a pint of milk; two eggs; sugar to taste; grated lemon peel.
DIRECTIONS.—Soak tapioca in cold water until soft, stirring it now and then; well-beat the eggs with sugar to taste, and mix them with the milk, stir the tapioca into it, and pour the whole into a buttered dish. Grate the peel of a lemon on the top, and bake it in a moderate oven.

### 410. Boiled Condensed Milk.
TIME.—*Three-quarters of an hour.*
ARTICLES. — Half a pint of condensed milk; half a pint of water; two eggs; three ounces of sugar; a little cinnamon.
DIRECTIONS.—Boil a little cinnamon with the sugar, milk, and water in a TEA-KETTLE BOILER. When cold add the eggs well-beaten, and stir it over the fire until it thickens; then set it to get quite cold. Butter and flour a cloth, and tie the custard in it, put it into the boiler, and boil it three-quarters of an hour.

### 411. Baked Condensed Milk.
TIME.—*Three quarters of an hour.*
ARTICLES.—Four eggs; one pint of condensed milk; half a nutmeg; sugar to your taste; a tea-spoonful of vanilla; one pint of water.
DIRECTIONS.—Beat the eggs very light, stir them into the cream, sweeten it to your taste, and add the nutmeg and the vanilla. Bake it one hour in a quick oven, in a dish with or without a bottom crust.

### 412. Semolina Pudding.
TIME.—*Ten minutes.*
ARTICLES.—A quart of new milk; half a tea-cupful of semolina orange marmalade.
DIRECTIONS.—Put the milk into a TEA-KETTLE BOILER, and when boiling, stir in the semolina, and continue to stir it over the fire for ten minutes; then put it into a mold to cool, turn it out, and serve with jam or marmalade round it. It is delicious iced.

### 413. Spanish Pudding.
TIME.—*Ten or twelve minutes to fry.*
ARTICLES. — Half a pint of milk; one ounce of butter; some flour; yolks of three eggs.
DIRECTIONS.—Put the milk and butter into a TEA-KETTLE BOILER, and just before it boils dredge in sufficient flour to make it a thick dough, stirring it all the time with one hand as you add the flour; then take it off the fire, and stir in, one at a time, the yolks of three well-beaten eggs, mixing each well in before adding the other; then put it on a dish. Fry it in small round pieces in boiling butter until a light brown. When done drain them from the fat, and serve on a folded napkin, with sifted sugar over them.

### 414. Pork Pudding.
TIME.—*Boil from three to six hours.*
ARTICLES.—A cup of chopped pork; two cups of chopped raisins; a tea-spoonful of soda; five cups of flour; three cups of milk; one coffee-cup of molasses; one cup of dried apples.
DIRECTIONS.—Chop up the pork, raisins, and dried apples together, mix the flour with the milk and the molasses, dissolve the soda in a little of water, and add; then mix all together, put into a cloth, and boil, the longer the better, up to six hours. Serve with rich sauce.

# MAKING AND BAKING CAKES.

Cakes are luxuries not necessary, and, where fat butter and spices are used are generally expensive, indigestible, and unhealthy; yet civilized life seems to demand them and pay the penalty for eating them by sickness, loss of health, time, and money. We give the best known general directions for cooking that can be followed with confidence.

An oven to bake well should have a regular heat throughout, but particularly at the bottom, without which bread or cakes will not rise or bake well.

An earthen basin is best for beating eggs or cake mixture.

Cakes should be beaten with a wooden spoon or patent cake beaters. Butter may be beaten with the same.

Eggs should be beaten with a broad fork; or use the patent egg beaters: they cost but little, and are the best. Eggs should be clean and fresh for a cake. It is well, as a general rule in cake making, to beat the butter and sugar (which must be made fine) to a light cream; indeed, in the making of pound cake, the lightness of the cake depends as much upon this as upon the eggs being well-beaten; then beat the eggs and put them to the butter, and gradually add the flour and other ingredients, beating it all the time.

In common cakes, where only a few eggs are used, beat them until you can take a spoonful up clear from strings.

In recipes in which milk is used as one ingredient, either sweet or sour may be used, but not a mixture of both.

Sour milk makes a spongy, light cake; sweet milk makes a cake which cuts like pound cake.

In making cakes, if you wish them to be pleasing to the palate, use double-refined sugar, although light brown sugar makes a very good cake.

To ascertain whether a cake is baked enough, if a small one, take a very fine splint of wood and run it through the thickest part; if not done enough, some of the dough, or unbaked dough, will be found sticking to it; if done, it will come out clear. If the cake is large, pass a small knife blade through it, instead of the splint. Cakes to be kept fresh, should be placed in a tin box tightly covered, in a cool dark place.

Other recipes for cake will be found in the Corn Starch, Meizenia, and Cocoanut recipes.

### 415. Rock Cakes.

TIME.—*Half an hour to bake.*

ARTICLES.—Half a pound of butter; one pound of flour; half a pound of moist sugar; forty drops of essence of lemon; two eggs; and half a glass of brandy or wine.

DIRECTIONS.—Rub the butter into the flour and sugar, mix the whole with the eggs and half a glass of brandy or wine. Drop them on a baking-sheet and bake.

### 416. Strawberry Shortcake.

ARTICLES.—One large table-spoonful of butter; two of loaf sugar; one well-beaten egg; two even tea-spoonfuls of cream of tartar; three cupfuls of flour; one small tea-spoonful of soda; one cupful of milk; strawberries and sugar.

DIRECTIONS.—Beat butter with sugar to a cream and egg, rub the tartar in the flour, dissolve the soda in the milk, add it last; bake in a flat pan in a quick oven; when done let it get cold, cut it in three layers, or in half, cover one layer with strawberries and sugar, lay on the top layer, and dust sugar over it.

### 417. Snow Cake (Corn Starch).

TIME.—*One hour and a quarter to one hour and a half.*

ARTICLES.—One pound of corn starch; eight ounces of loaf sugar; eight ounces of fresh butter; whites of seven eggs; flavoring of essence of lemon.

DIRECTIONS.—Beat the butter to a cream before the fire, and add the sugar pounded, and the starch, beating the mixture all the time. When well mixed stir in the whites of the eggs, whisked to a stiff froth, and the essence of lemon to your taste. Again whisk the mixture for nearly half an hour, pour it into a buttered tin, and bake in a moderate-heated oven.

### 418. Chocolate Cakes.

ARTICLES.—One pound of flour; one pound of sugar; one pound of butter; eight eggs; two table-spoonfuls of brandy; a pinch of salt; chocolate glazing.

DIRECTIONS.—Mix the above ingredients well together with a wooden spoon, putting the butter (melted before the fire) in last. Spread a baking-sheet with butter, put over it the mixture half an inch thick and bake it. Cut the cake into oblong pieces and glaze them thickly with chocolate.

### 419. Ginger Snaps.

TIME.—*Twenty minutes to bake.*

ARTICLES.—Half a pint of syrup; quarter of a pound of brown sugar; one pound of flour; one table-spoonful of ground ginger; one of caraway seed.

DIRECTIONS.—Work the butter into the flour, then mix it with the syrup, brown sugar, ginger, and caraway seed. Work it all well together, and form it into cakes; place them on a baking-tin in a moderate oven, when they will be dry and crisp.

## GENERAL RECIPES.

### 420. Hunting-Nuts.
TIME.—*Fifteen to thirty-six minutes.*
ARTICLES.—One pound of flour, half a pound of molasses; half a pound of brown sugar; six ounces of butter and ginger.
DIRECTIONS.—Mix the above ingredients well together, make them into small nuts, and bake them on a baking-sheet.

### 421. Sponge Cake.
TIME.—*Three-quarters of an hour to one hour.*
ARTICLES.—Four eggs; half a pound of sifted loaf sugar; the weight of two eggs and a half full (in their shells) of flour; one lemon.
DIRECTIONS.—Take the sugar, break the eggs over it, and beat all together for full half an hour. After you have beaten the eggs and sugar together for the time specified, grate into them the peel of a lemon, and add the juice if approved. Stir the flour into the mixture and pour it into a tin. Put it instantly into a cool oven.

### 422. A Rich Pound Cake.
TIME.—*One hour.*
ARTICLES.—One pound and a half of flour; one pound of butter; one pound of white sugar; six eggs; a wine-glassful of brandy; half a nutmeg; a tea-spoonful of vanilla or essence of lemon.
DIRECTIONS.—Beat the butter and pounded sugar to a cream; whisk the eggs to a high froth; then put all the ingredients together and beat until light and creamy. Put it into a tin lined with buttered paper, and bake it in a moderate oven for one hour. When done, turn it gently out, reverse the tin, and set the cake on the bottom until cold. Let the paper remain on until the cake is to be cut; use more eggs if desired.

### 423. Lemon Cake.
TIME.—*One hour.*
ARTICLES.—Four eggs; half a pound of pounded sugar; seven ounces of flour; peel of one lemon or two small lemons.
DIRECTIONS. — Beat the pounded sugar with the yolks of the eggs until it is smooth; whisk the whites to a froth stiff enough to bear the weight of an egg, and add to the beaten yolks; then stir in gradually the flour and the grated peel of the lemon; line a tin with buttered paper, pour in the cake mixture and bake it.

### 424. A Rich Plum Cake.
TIME.—*Two hours or more.*
ARTICLES.—One pound of fresh butter; twelve eggs; one quart of flour; one pound of moist sugar; half a pound of mixed spice; three pounds of currants; one pound of raisins; half a pound of almonds; half a pound of candied peel; half a pound of citron.
DIRECTIONS.—Beat the butter to a cream, and stir into it the yolks of the eggs well beaten with the sugar, then add the spice and the almonds chopped fine. Stir in the flour, add the currants washed and dried; the raisins and citron peel chopped. As each ingredient is added, the mixture must be beaten by the hand; then butter a piece of paper, place it round a tin, put in the cake; and bake it for two hours, or more if required. Slice the citron.

### 425. A Delicate Cake.
TIME.—*About one hour.*
ARTICLES. — One pound of sugar; one pound of flour; seven ounces of butter; whites of six eggs; half a nutmeg grated; a little lemon extract.
DIRECTIONS.—Beat the butter to a cream and stir into it the sugar and flour; then add the whites of the eggs beaten to a froth; the nutmeg grated and the lemon extract. Beat all well together, and put it into a tin lined with buttered paper. Five or six ounces of pounded almonds may be added to this cake, according to your taste.

### 426. Common Gingerbread.
ARTICLES.—Half a pound of butter; half a tea-cupful of ginger; one pint of molasses; two pounds of flour, one table-spoonful of saleratus.
DIRECTIONS.—Rub the flour and butter together, and add the other ingredients. Knead the dough well, roll it out, cut it in cakes, wash them over with molasses and water, and bake them in a moderate oven.

### 427. Jelly Cake.
ARTICLES.—Half a pound of white sugar; one-fourth of a pound of butter; six eggs; one pound of flour, juice and grated rind of one lemon; half a tea-spoonful of yeast powder; jelly or marmalade.
DIRECTIONS.— Beat and mix well for pound cake, and bake very thin on tins. While hot spread each layer with nice jelly or marmalade, placing one layer upon another. Ice the top or sift loaf sugar very thickly upon it.

### 428. Silver or Bride's Cake.
ARTICLES.—The whites of ten eggs; one pound of pulverized loaf sugar; three quarters of a pound of butter, and one pound of sifted flour; lemon, vanilla, rose, or almond.
DIRECTIONS.—Beat the eggs to a froth; stir in the sugar; cream together the butter and the flour; add all together; flavor with lemon, vanilla, or rose. Almonds blanched and pounded are an improvement. Use rose water with the almonds to prevent them from oiling. *Use no spices.*

### 429. White Cup Cake.
Four tea-cups of sifted flour, two of loaf-sugar, one of butter, one of sour cream or rich milk, a small tea-spoonful of soda, the whites of four eggs well beaten. Flavor with lemon or other flavor.

# PASTRY AND PIES.

We could all exist without pastry or pies, and no doubt live longer, healthier, and wealthier, and we do not advise their indiscriminate use, yet plain pastry (for the mischief is caused by rich paste) in pies would do no particular harm.

First, the cook should have smooth, cold hands, very clean, for making paste or crust. She should wash them well, and plunge them in cold water for a minute or two, in hot weather, before beginning her paste, drying them well first.

The pastry slab, if possible, should be made of marble; or a wooden paste-board. They should be kept scrupulously clean.

The crust used for common pies may be made of clarified beef dripping, or lard, instead of butter.

Be careful about the proper heat of the oven for baking pies, as, if it be too cold, the paste will be heavy and have a dull look; if too hot, the crust will burn before the pie is done.

Try if the oven is hot enough by holding your hand inside of it for a few seconds; if you can do so without snatching it out again quickly, it is too cold. It is best, however, to try it by baking a little piece of the crust in it first.

Always make a hole with a knife at the top of the pie to allow the gases, generated in it by cooking, to escape. This aperture is also useful for pouring gravy into the meat pie when done, if more is required. The hand of a pastry cook should be light, and the paste should not be worked more than is absolutely required for mixing it.

We give first a plain recipe for pie crust, such as people of small means can use and will find good. A puff paste, and one which will be found good enough for all ordinary purposes, of butter, flour, and eggs made stiff, will also suit raised pies. Use spices to suit the taste.

We begin by giving instructions for clarifying house fat so as to render it fit for use.

### 430. To clarify House Fat.

Put the fat in a pan, fry it out, then peel some raw potatoes, slice them in it, fry them brown, pour boiling hot water in the fat, let it all boil half an hour, then strain fat and water, and all the small impurities drop down into the water.

This fat is good for any thing, except cake. Mix all kinds, mutton, beef, pork, or ham fat, all together; only it must be sweet.

### 431. To make Hygienic Pie Crust.

TIME.—*Fifteen minutes.*

Equal quantities of flour, Graham flour, and corn meal; rub evenly together, and wet with sweet cream or milk; use same as other paste. This is excellent for the dyspeptic and feeble, as a change, good for all.

### 432. Plain Pie Crust or Paste.

TIME.—*Ten minutes.*

ARTICLES. — Flour, a pound; fat, four ounces; water.

DIRECTIONS.—Put the flour into a bowl and work it into a smooth paste with water; divide the fat into four parts; roll out the paste; put over it in rows one portion of the fat in pieces the size of a bean; flour it; fold over the edges, and again roll it; repeat the whole again three times, dredging a very little flour over the paste, and rolling thin each time; do not touch with your hands any more than you can help; use a large knife or spoon; use ice water; do this in as cool a place as possible.

### 433. A French Puff-Paste.

TIME.—*Ten minutes.*

ARTICLES.—Flour, a pint; butter, a pound; two eggs; one lemon; a pinch of salt.

DIRECTIONS.—Pour the flour into a bowl; make a hole in the center of it, in which put the yolks of two eggs, the juice of the lemon, salt, and ice-water, and a quarter of the butter into a paste; dredge the board and rolling-pin with flour; roll out the paste very thin; put little pieces of butter on the paste; fold over three times, still buttering (as the butter separates the paste and forms the flakes); do so three time: this forms nine flakes; keep it cool, and at each turning let it cool, if convenient in a refrigerator, a few minutes.

### 434. To make other Pastes.

The above is the way to make paste. Any amount of butter or fat, not to exceed pound for pound, may be used; lemon juice and eggs may be omitted.

### 435. Sweet Apple Pie.

Pare mellow sweet apples, and grate them upon a grater (a very large grater is necessary for this purpose). Then proceed as for pumpkin pie.

### 436. Sour Apple Pie.

Take nice tart apples, slice them; add cinnamon. Fill the under crust an inch thick; sprinkle sugar over them; add a spoonful or two of water. Cover with a thin crust, and bake three-quarters of an hour, in a moderate oven.

### 437. Mock Green Apple Pie.

To five soda-crackers add five cups of boiling water; cover in a dish, let them soak; add three full cups of sugar, two lemons—grate the rind, and add both rind and juice. Bake with two crusts.

### 438. Mock Apple Pie.

One large grated lemon, three large soda crackers, two even table spoonfuls of butter, two teacups of sugar, one egg, a wineglass of water, poured over the crackers. These will make two pies. Bake with two crusts.

## PASTRY AND PIES.

### 439. Apple and Pie-Plant Pie.

Equal quantities of apple and pie plant made in the same manner as all pie plant, make excellent pie.

### 440. Pie-Plant Pie.

Remove the skin from the stalks; cut them in small pieces; fill the pie dish evenly full; put in plenty of sugar, a tea-spoonful of water; dredge a trifle of flour evenly over the top, cover with a thin crust, and bake the same as apple pie.

### 441. Pumpkin Pie.

Select a pumpkin which has a deep rich color, and firm, close texture. Stew and sift it. Boil some milk in the TEA-KETTLE BOILER, add to make it thin. Sweeten with equal quantities of sugar and molasses, and bake about one hour in a hot oven; add ginger or nutmeg to taste.

### 442. Squash Pie.

This is superior to pumpkin, as it has a richer, sweeter flavor, and is better. It is made in precisely the same manner as pumpkin pie. Eggs and nutmeg can be added.

### 443. Sweet-Potato Pie.

Boil and sift through a colander any sweet potatoes, add milk, boiled in the TEA-KETTLE BOILER, and make the same as pumpkin pie; or bake, or boil and slice, same as for sour-apple pie.

### 444. Custard Pie.

ARTICLES.—Corn starch, one table-spoonful; sugar, two; one egg; milk, a quart.

DIRECTIONS.—Boil the milk in the TEA-KETTLE BOILER, add the starch and sugar; when it is all boiled five minutes let it cool, then add the egg well beaten, nutmeg, and a little butter, line some plates with pie-crust, pour in the custard and bake.

### 445. Cherry Pie.

Choose fair ripe cherries, the large black English being the best for this purpose; wash and look them over carefully; fill the pie plate evenly full; strew sugar over the top; dredge in plenty of flour; cover with a moderate thick upper crust, and bake one hour.

### 446. Raspberry Pie.

Take nice ripe berries, either red or black are about equally good; wash and pick them carefully; place them an inch or more thick on the under crust; strew a small quantity of sugar, and a trifle of flour over them; put on the upper crust and bake half an hour.

### 447. Blackberry Pie.

This is made in the same manner as the preceding. All berries for pies should be ripe or nearly so, and as fresh as possible.

### 448. Whortleberry Pie.

Whortleberries make excellent pies, and are in market usually longer than any of the summer fruits. It is made in the same manner as raspberry.

### 449. Cranberry Pie.

Wash the berries in a pan of water, rejecting all the bad ones; simmer them until they become soft and burst open; strain through a fine wire sieve, removing all the hulls; add sugar to the taste; bake on a thick under crust in a moderate oven.

### 450. Peach Pie.

Select rich juicy peaches, of a rather small and nearly uniform size. They should be very ripe; peel and slice them, fill the pie dish with them, sprinkle sugar and a little flour over them; add a table-spoonful of water, cover and bake one hour

### 451. Plum Pie

Is made in the same manner as the peach pie. It requires much more sugar to make it at all palatable.

### 452. Currant Pie.

Currants are made into pies by stewing them and sweetening according to the degree of acidity, and baking between two crusts in the ordinary manner. Or better still, merely fill the pie with them without any previous cooking, sprinkle sugar over, dredge in a little flour, and bake the same as apple pie.

### 453. Gooseberry Pie.

This is made in precisely the same manner as currant pie; it is very palatable.

### 454. Minced Meats for Pies.

One pound of currants, four pounds of peeled and chopped apples, one pound of suet chopped fine, one beef's heart boiled tender and chopped fine; pull the strings from the suet and add one pound of raisins stoned and cut in two; the juice of four oranges and two lemons, with the chopped peel of one; add of ground mace and all-spice each a spoonful, and a tumblerful of brandy. Mix all well together, and boil the liquor down, and when done cover the mince meat over with the liquor and keep it closely covered in a cool place, until wanted for use. When you want to use the mince meat add cider to your taste.

### 455. Imitation of Mince Pie.

An excellent imitation of mince pie may be made by placing between the layers of raisins, currants and chopped apples; season precisely as for a mince pie.

# INDIAN MEAL,

## MUSH, BREAD, BISCUIT, CAKES, PUDDINGS, &c.

It consists of Indian corn ground coarse. In many parts of our country it is eaten in every variety of form, not only on account of its cheapness, but of its health and strength-giving qualities; it agrees with most every one. Perhaps less of this is used in New York city and vicinity than in any other part of the country; yet it is not because the New Yorkers do not like it. No, it is because their wives and cooks do not know how to cook meal. At a celebrated eating house in New York they sell five times as much corn biscuit as wheat.

Dr. IRA WARREN, the eminent Boston, Mass., physician, says, "Corn needs no praise from me. It is comparatively cheap, nutritive, and wholesome, and is perhaps worked up into more savory dishes than any other, very nourishing as well as cheap."

Dr. JOHN KING, of Cincinnati, Ohio, the head of the Eclectic Medical Fraternity, says of corn, "It furnishes a very healthy, nutritious, and palatable diet, and is especially adapted for the support of the energetic and hard-working classes. It is certainly preferable to the wheat bread."

Dr. W. BEACH, of New York city, the distinguished head of the Reform Practice, says, "Indian corn is probably the most healthy, nutritive food in the world. In fact, every physician recommends its use, where it agrees with the stomach for the weak and dyspeptics."

The estimate of the cost to support a man on Indian meal at present prices (wholesale) is $2.50 a hundred pounds. Now, a pound when cooked makes two pounds and a half; this would be about ten dollars a year. Of course, no one would live on corn meal alone; but where is the food that will compare with it? Not one, not one. Comparison of Indian meal with other products will be found in another column. If families would or have to economize, they should bear in mind that a pound of meal swells to more than double in cooking; that it is nearly all nutriment; that it takes four pounds of meat or potatoes to equal one pound of meal; in reality, one pound of flour does not go as far as a pound of meal.

WE GIVE MORE RECIPES FOR COOKING INDIAN MEAL, AND IN GREATER VARIETY THAN EVER WERE GIVEN BEFORE BY ANY AND ALL THE COOK-BOOKS COMBINED; TRY THEM.

And recollect that every pound of meal used where flour would have been, saves you at least five cents, and any of the very palatable dishes are cheaper than any others.

Many families now use fried mush in place of potatoes; children ninety-nine in a hundred prefer it.

In all cases buy yellow meal; it is sweeter and stronger than the white. It comes to the market sifted; but in our recipes always sift it again. Buy meal made from old corn; it costs more, but keeps longer. Keep meal in a cool, dry place, uncovered.

### 456. Indian Meal and Hog's-Head Cheese.

TIME.—*Five hours.*

ARTICLES.—Meal and hog's head; seasoning.

DIRECTIONS.— Clean and boil a hog's head; when tender remove the bones, chop the meat fine, put the meat back into the broth (first skim and strain off the fat), season and salt well, stir into the broth as much meal as will make a thick mush; let this simmer half an hour, taking care not to let it burn; pour into pans, let it cool; then cut into slices, and fry.

For a hearty strong meal, none can excel it.

### 457. Meal and Broth Mush.

TIME.—*Three hours.*

ARTICLES.—Meal; bones; broth; salt.

DIRECTIONS.—Take the broth of any boiled meat or poultry, or get some beef bones, boil them in water without salt, two hours and a half; then skim out the bones, salt to taste, sift in the meal until thick, boil twenty minutes, eat hot, or pour in pans, and fry in slices when boiled.

### 458. Corn-Meal Mush.

ARTICLES.—Indian meal, a quart; salt to taste.

DIRECTIONS. — Take a quart of Indian meal, sift it, wet it up in water; then pour into the BOILER, pour in boiling hot water until thin, cook an hour, salt to taste. (We say an hour, but it can be eaten before that, if in a hurry.) Eat with milk, butter, syrup, or sugar. This can be cooked in any boiler with care, in any amount.

### 459. Fried Mush.

Any of the above mushes left over can be poured into a pan; when cold cut in thin slices; fry brown. YOU WILL LIKE IT.

### 460. Mrs. Winslow's Corn Bread.

TIME.—*Forty minutes.*

ARTICLES.—Sour milk, a quart; two eggs; soda, two tea-spoonfuls; molasses, four table-spoonfuls; salt meal.

DIRECTIONS.—Into the milk mix the meal and molasses to a thin batter, beat the eggs, dissolve the soda in water, add a little salt, stir all into thin batter, bake it in pans, in a hot oven, forty minutes.

## INDIAN-MEAL BREAD.

### 461. Mrs. Winslow's Brown Bread.

TIME.—*To bake, two hours; to steam, two hours.*

ARTICLES. — Sour milk, two quarts; Indian and rye meal; soda, three tea-spoonfuls; molasses, six table-spoonfuls; salt.

DIRECTIONS.—To the milk add one-third rye and two-thirds corn meal. Dissolve the soda in warm water, add with the salt and molasses, bake in a deep pot, tin, or stone, two hours; then steam from two to ten hours, the longer the better, or place the pot in a boiler, but prevent the water from boiling over.

### 462. New England Brown Bread.

TIME.—*Five hours or longer to bake.*

ARTICLES. — Corn meal, six cups; rye meal, three cups; yeast, one cup; molasses, one cup; salt.

DIRECTIONS.—Scald the corn meal; when lukewarm add the rye meal and the yeast, molasses and salt. Bake in a stone or iron pot.

REMARKS.—This is the justly celebrated New England Brown Bread, made and used by every New England family, cheap, wholesome, and good. Put it in an earthen or iron pot, cover it over, and bake it all night; it is then hot for breakfast. Thousands and hundreds of thousands of these loaves are eaten every morning, and especially Sunday morning, with baked beans.

### 463. Soda Brown Bread.

TIME.—*Three hours to bake.*

ARTICLES.—Corn meal, two large cups; rye flour, one large cup; molasses, half a small cup; vinegar, two table-spoonfuls; same of fat; soda, half a tea-spoonful; salt; water.

DIRECTIONS.—Scald the meal, add a little cold water and the rye flour and salt; add the vinegar and molasses; stir all together, dissolve the soda in a little warm water, add, and make it a thick batter, pour into a deep dish or pan, and bake three hours. Eat hot.

### 464. Washington's Bread.

DIRECTIONS. — Mix Indian meal with a little salt, wet with cold water, and make a thick batter; put into tin pans, and bake well; to be eaten with butter. This is preferred to wheat bread at the South and West, and was the only bread used by General Washington.

### 465. Mrs. Smith's Yeast Corn-Bread.

TIME.—*To bake, fifty minutes.*

ARTICLES. — Meal, a quart; two table-spoonfuls of lard; yeast, a tea-cupful.

DIRECTIONS.—Put a quart of meal in a pan, pour boiling water on it, add the butter and yeast, make it into a batter, beat well, set it to rise. When light, grease your pans, pour in the batter, about half an inch thick, and bake in a moderate oven.

### 466. Togus Corn-Meal Bread.

TIME.—*To steam, four hours or longer.*

ARTICLES.—Corn meal, three cups; flour, one cup; milk, three cups; molasses, half a cup; soda, a tea-spoonful; salt.

DIRECTIONS.—Mix all together, first dissolving the soda in warm water, mixing it with the milk; pour in a TEA-KETTLE BOILER, or other cone-shaped pot; steam it in an iron pot, four hours or longer,—the longer the better; very fine.

### 467. Mrs. Winslow's Suet and Meal Bread.

TIME.—*To steam, five hours.*

ARTICLES.—Milk, one quart; suet, a tea-cupful; molasses, same; soda, a tea-spoonful; cream of tartar, two.

DIRECTIONS.—Boil a quart of milk, stir in some meal to a batter, and the suet chopped fine, add the soda and tartar, bake an hour, or steam five hours.

### 468. Mush Bread.

TIME.—*To bake, one to two hours.*

ARTICLES. — Corn meal mush, three quarts; flour; yeast, half a pint.

DIRECTIONS.—Boil meal enough to make three quarts, add a little salt and the yeast, and enough wheat flour, to form a soft dough, let it rise; when light, add only enough flour to prevent it adhering to the board or pan; make it into loaves, put them in pans, let them rise again, and bake. It makes fine cheap bread.

### 469. Indian Meal and Wheat-Flour Bread.

TIME.—*To bake, two hours.*

ARTICLES.—Indian meal, two quarts; wheat flour, one quart; yeast, half a pint; molasses, half a tea-cupful; salt, a tea-spoonful.

DIRECTIONS.—Scald the meal with boiling water; when cooled add the salt, molasses, and yeast; stir in some flour, set it to rise, knead well with flour, make it into loaves, put it in pans, let it rise a second time, and bake.

### 470. Wheat and Indian Bread.

Make as for the above recipe, except use only one quart of meal, and no molasses, using two quarts of flour.

### 471. Meal Johnny Bread.

TIME.—*To bake, half an hour.*

ARTICLES. — Indian meal, three cups; flour, a cup; molasses, third of a cup; salt; sour or butter milk; soda, a tea-spoonful.

DIRECTIONS.—Mix the meal, flour, molasses, and salt, dissolve the soda in the milk, make a batter; bake in a quick oven.

### 472. Grandmother's Meal Bread.

TIME.—*Half an hour*
ARTICLES.—Meal, a pint; lard, a teaspoonful; salt.
DIRECTIONS.—Mix the meal, lard, and salt in boiling water, stir it up to a dough, spread it on a tin pan, and bake before a fire, or in an oven.

### 473. Corn-Meal Pone or Biscuit.

TIME.—*Bake forty minutes.*
ARTICLES.—Indian meal, a quart; wheat flour, a pint; milk; cream of tartar, two tea-spoonfuls; soda, one; eggs, two; sugar, three table-spoonfuls; lard, the same.
DIRECTIONS.—Beat the eggs with the sugar, rub the tartar into the meal and flour, add the eggs and sugar, and the soda first dissolved, thin down to a batter, with milk or water. Eat all biscuits hot, with sweet butter.

### 474. Blot's Meal-Batter Biscuit.

TIME.—*To bake, forty minutes.*
ARTICLES.—Corn meal, a pint; eggs, two; butter, two ounces; salt and sugar to taste.
DIRECTIONS.—Beat the eggs, melt the butter, mix with the meal, sugar, and salt; then pour in hot milk till it makes a thick dough; put in a pan and bake.

### 475. Mother's Meal and Rye Biscuit.

TIME.—*Forty minutes to bake.*
ARTICLES.—Meal, three cups; rye meal, one; lard, a table-spoonful; molasses, three; soda, half a tea-spoonful; vinegar, a table-spoonful.
DIRECTIONS.—Scald the meal, add the lard, vinegar, and molasses, dissolve the soda in water, stir in briskly, make into flat biscuits an inch thick, bake in a moderate oven. Bake these cakes well. Eat hot.

### 476. Egg Meal Biscuit.

TIME.—*To bake, half an hour.*
ARTICLES.—Meal, a pint; butter or sour milk, a pint; one egg; lard, a table-spoonful; salt, a tea-spoonful; soda, a tea-spoonful.
DIRECTIONS.—Work the lard into the meal and salt; beat the egg, stir into the milk, add to the meal; then add the soda; if the milk is sweet, use two tea-spoonfuls of tartar. Bake in a moderate oven.

### 477. Indian Biscuit.

TIME.—*To bake, about forty minutes.*
ARTICLES.—Meal, a pint; butter, two ounces; two eggs; milk.
DIRECTIONS.—Wet the meal well with boiling hot water, put in the butter and a little salt, beat two eggs very light, and add when cool; stir in enough milk to make a batter, beat well, and bake in a hot oven.

### 478. Mrs. Winslow's Meal Muffins.

TIME.—*Fifteen minutes to bake.*
ARTICLES.—Corn meal, a pint; lard, two table-spoonfuls; two eggs; soda, a tea-spoonful; cream of tartar, two; milk.
DIRECTIONS.—Melt the lard, beat the eggs well, dissolve the soda, mix the tartar in the meal, stir in all, and as much sweet milk as will make a batter. Bake in tins or muffin rings in a moderate hot oven. Use half flour, if desired.

### 479. Indian-Meal Wafers.

TIME.—*Ten minutes.*
ARTICLES.—Meal, six table-spoonfuls; flour, two; lard, two; milk; salt.
DIRECTIONS.—Mix all, using enough milk to thin it to a batter, fry a light brown; always have the pans hot before frying.

### 480. Wheat and Corn Crumpets.

TIME.—*To fry, about fifteen minutes.*
ARTICLES.—Half a gill of yeast; a quart of warm milk; a tea-spoonful of salt; a teacupful of melted butter; yellow corn meal.
DIRECTIONS:—Put the yeast into a quart of warm milk, with a tea-spoonful of salt; stir in sufficient wheat flour to make a good batter, set it in a warm place to rise; in the morning add the melted butter, and a handful of yellow corn meal. Fry them on a hot griddle previously rubbed over with butter before putting on the cakes. A spoonful of butter will be sufficient for one.

### 481. Meal Fadge.

TIME.—*One hour.*
ARTICLES.—Four ounces of meal; two ounces of butter; a salt-spoonful of salt; a quarter of a pint of milk.
DIRECTIONS.—Take four ounces of meal, two ounces of butter, and a little salt; make it into a stiff paste with milk, and bake it for one hour on a griddle over the fire, turning it often. It will not do to bake it in an oven. If baked too long it gets like pie crust.

### 482. Meal Griddle Cakes.

TIME.—*To fry, a few minutes.*
ARTICLES.—Meal, a pint; salt.
DIRECTIONS.—Scald at night half a pint of meal, mix the other in cold water, add the salt, set it to rise. In the morning fry slowly. Eat with butter and syrup.

### 483. All kinds of Griddle Cakes.

TIME.—*To fry, a few minutes.*
ARTICLES.—Eggs, two; sour milk, a tumblerful; soda, a tea-spoonful; or use sweet milk, and yeast-powders, and eggs; or one tea-spoonful of soda, and two of cream of tartar, with water and eggs. INDIAN MEAL, or RYE MEAL, or Graham meal, or wheat meal, or buckwheat meal, or wheat flour, can be used, and in any proportions. Crumbs of bread can be mixed with the batter.

## INDIAN MEAL.

### 484. Meal Drop-Nuts.
TIME.—*To bake, half an hour.*
ARTICLES.—Meal, one pint; rye flour, same; syrup, three table-spoonfuls; soda, a tea-spoonful, tartar, two; milk.
DIRECTIONS.—Make as above, drop the batter into greased pans, bake in a moderate oven, eat with butter and syrup.

### 485. Meal Omelets.
Scald a cup of meal, beat up six eggs, add to the meal, fry brown. Very good for breakfast. One-half flour can be added if desired.

### 486. Meal Pound-Cake, Rich.
TIME.—*To bake, about one hour.*
ARTICLES.—Corn meal, a pound; sugar, the same; wheat flour, half a pound; butter, the same; nutmeg grated; cinnamon, a tea-spoonful; eggs, six.
DIRECTIONS.—Stir the butter and sugar to a cream, beat the eggs very light, and add to them the meal and flour first mixed, then the spices; line your pan with paper well buttered, pour in the mixture, bake it in a moderate oven.

### 487. Molasses Meal Pound Cake.
Made the same as above, with exception of molasses instead of sugar.

### 488. Corn-Meal Pudding without Eggs.
TIME.—*To bake, about two hours.*
ARTICLES.—Corn meal; four cups very strong coffee; a cup of sugar; molasses, a cup; butter, a cup; raisins, a cup; soda, a tea-spoonful; spices.
DIRECTIONS.—Make four coffee-cups of very strong coffee, scald two cups of meal, with the coffee; chop the raisins, and add the molasses, sugar, butter, and the currants, dissolve the soda in a little warm water, add. Stir all well together, and if too thin, stiffen it with flour. Use very little spice.

### 489. Meal, Fruit, and Coffee Cake.
TIME.—*Half an hour to bake.*
ARTICLES.—Seven heaped table-spoonfuls of sifted corn meal; two dessert-spoonfuls of lard or butter, heaped; a tumblerful of molasses; two tea-spoonfuls of powdered ginger; a quart of *hot boiled sweet* milk.
DIRECTIONS.—Mix well, and pour into a buttered dish, and just as it is put into the oven, stir in not quite a tumblerful of cold water; bake half an hour. Serve with a rich sauce.

### 490. Indian Suet Pudding.
TIME.—*To bake, two hours.*
ARTICLES.—Half a pint of Indian (yellow) corn meal; one quart of milk; half a tea-cup of suet; one tea-spoonful of ground ginger; two ounces of sugar; half a tea-cupful of butter; one egg; a little salt.
DIRECTIONS.—Stir the corn meal very gradually to a quart of boiling milk; when it has cooled, add a little salt and half a tea-cupful of suet chopped very fine, or the same quantity of butter; put to it half a nutmeg grated, a tea-spoonful of ground ginger, one well-beaten egg, and two ounces of pounded sugar, or sugar made into a syrup; put it into a buttered dish and bake it.

### 491. Baked Pudding.
To a quart of mush, add two well-beaten eggs, quarter of a pound of butter, sugar, and spice to taste; add a little milk; bake in an earthen dish.

### 492. English Baked Meal Pudding.
TIME.—*To bake, an hour.*
ARTICLES.—Corn meal, seven heaped table-spoonfuls; lard, two; ginger, half a table-spoonful; milk, a quart; molasses, a cup; water, a large cupful; a grated lemon peel.
DIRECTIONS.—Mix the meal in hot milk, then add the rest; pour it in a greased dish pour on top a cup of water or milk; bake in a moderate oven.

### 493. New England Pudding.
TIME.—*To bake, four hours*
ARTICLES.—Corn meal, one large cupful; molasses, half a cupful; milk, one quart.
DIRECTIONS.—Scald a little over half of the milk, stir the meal into the hot milk, then the molasses, a little salt; let cool; pour in a dish, and then pour on top the rest of the cold milk as you set it in the oven to bake.
REMARKS.—The New Englanders have this pudding for their Sunday dinners generally. They make it, as per recipe, more or less in quantity, on Saturday, set it away in a cool place, and four hours before dinner, in winter, pour on the milk, put it in the oven, and have it hot without any labor on Sunday. In summer it is generally cooked on Saturday, and eaten cold on Sunday. *See remarks on cooking for Sunday and Monday, on Saturday.*

### 494. French Baked Indian Pudding.
TIME.—*To bake, two hours.*
ARTICLES.—Meal, a coffee-cupful; milk, two quarts; molasses, one-third of a cup; sugar, same.
DIRECTIONS.—Boil the milk in the TEA-KETTLE BOILER; when boiling pour out one-half, and into the remainder stir the meal in slowly, leaving no lumps in it; pour it into a pudding dish; add the rest of the milk, the sugar, and the molasses, and bake two hours; stir once, the first half hour, but not afterward.

### 495. Steamed Plum Pudding,
One quart Indian meal; one cup molasses; one cup raisins; one quart boiling water; stir all together, and steam three hours.

### 496. Boiled Corn Meal and Cheese Pudding.

TIME.—*Two hours.*
ARTICLES.—Meal, a pound ; cheese, half a pound ; milk, a quart ; hot water ; salt.
DIRECTIONS.—Boil a quart of milk in the TEA-KETTLE BOILER; scald a pound of meal with hot water; grate or cut in thin slices, the cheese; stir all into the hot milk, then into a pan, bake or boil an hour

### 497. Boiled Corn Meal and Pork Pudding.

TIME.—*To bake, two hours.*
ARTICLES.—Salt pork, one cup chopped fine;, one egg ; milk, a pint ; soda, a teaspoonful ; cream of tartar, two teaspoonfuls ; salt to taste ; meal.
DIRECTIONS. — Mix all together, using meal enough for thickening, boil in a cloth or bake. Flour can be used instead of meal, if prepared.

### 498. Boiled Meal, Fruit, and Pork Pudding.

TIME.—*Two hours.*
ARTICLES. — Meal, four cups ; pork, chopped, one cup ; raisins, chopped, one cup; milk, hot, three cups ; molasses, one cup; soda, a tea-spoonful, salt to taste.
DIRECTIONS.—Mix all the above together, first scalding the meal with the milk ; tie in a cloth and boil two hours ; use half, or all flour for a change, instead of meal.

### 499. Boiled Meal and Dried Apple Pudding.

Scald a quart of Indian meal, add a little salt and molasses and fat ; a few hours previous, set a half a pound of dried apples to soak, chop them up and add; mix together, adding a tablespoonful of soda ; boil two hours in a cloth ; eat with sauce.

### 500. Meal and Apple Dowdy.

TIME.—*Five hours.*
ARTICLES.—Meal, a quart, flour, a pint ; apples, green, half a peck, or dried apples; molasses, two cups ; soda, a tea-spoonful ; cream of tartar, two tea-spoonfuls.
DIRECTIONS.—Scald the meal, mix the tartar with the flour and a little lard ; then stir in the soda in water ; mix all with the meal, make a paste ; line an earthen dish, put the apples in first peeled and sliced, add the molasses, the cinnamon, cover with the top crust, bake five hours in a slow oven. Very fine dish.

### 501. Freedman's Hoe-Cake.

TIME.—*To bake, half an hour.*
ARTICLES.—A quart of Indian meal ; a spoonful of fat, a little salt, and boiling water.
DIRECTIONS.—Pour hot water on the meal, add butter and salt, make a stiff dough, knead, or work it for ten minutes ; bake on a board or tin before the fire slowly.

## FLOUR, BREAD, Etc.

### WHEAT FLOUR, Etc.

THE BEST AND CHEAPEST FLOUR TO USE.

Maryland, Virginia, Georgetown, St. Louis, and Southern flours generally are much the strongest ; they cost more but are as cheap in the end, for they make the most bread, and always the whitest. California flour is good and cheap, compared with western flours ; they are not so strong as southern. A dark, sweet flour is full as healthy as any, and, of course, cheaper

### WHEAT, RYE, BARLEY, CORN, AND OAT FLOUR.

Flour is made from all the above grains, especially from wheat and rye, for general use ; one contains about as much nutriment as the other, but general use and taste has selected wheat flour, although the Germans use much rye flour. All classes, however, are rapidly learning to eat it also. Well made, of good rye, it can hardly be told from wheat. The writer has made dinner from *rye bread and cheese*, on many occasions, and at one time a party of which she was one, called at a house in the country. The German woman said all she had was some bread and cheese. Not one of the party (eight in number, all Americans) knew what kind of bread they were eating until the writer told them. She said it cost her six dollars and a half a barrel ; good wheat flour was worth sixteen dollars fifty cents at the time. I mention this fact to show that a poor German wife could make as good bread from rye as wheat flour, saving ten dollars a barrel. Flours are ground too fine ; the whiter and finer the flour the more starch, and the less nutriment and health-giving properties there are in it, and the more costly it is.

Most people are unaware how unhealthy fine flour is. In experiments made on healthy dogs with fine flour bread alone, with water, two years ago, it killed them all within forty days ; most of them died within thirty days. On Graham flour bread, which is wheat ground coarse, with the hulls or chaff in, they grew fat and healthy, and did not die. When fed on corn meal bread they were healthy and fat, and we assert that any one who should eat fine flour bread of any kind alone, without medicine, would not live sixty days. The reason of it is that its starchy nature is like a paste, clogs up the stomach and intestines; the liver refuses to act ; the result is sickness and death.

Let all enjoy nature and art, but not to excess. In many things fine flour is excellent—for cakes, pastry, and once a day for bread, biscuit, or rolls.

In making bread, in our recipes below, we give a variety of recipes for making flour bread, and biscuit. Wheat, rye, corn, Graham, and barley flours can be used in any quantity to suit the palate, or a little meal of either of the above can be put in. A pound of fine wheat flour costs as much as two pounds of rye or Graham flour, or three of corn meal, giving no more nutriment. Try a variety, for it is the spice of life. You will not regret it. You will SAVE HEALTH AND WEALTH.

## YEAST BREAD, etc.

### 502. How to make Excellent Yeast Bread, Rolls, Biscuit, Twists, etc.

Yeast is made from hops, flour, potatoes, etc. We give three of the best ways to make it. Yeast acts by fermentation, which produces gases in the dough, and is held by it, in consequence making the dough light; Heat causes the fermentation, cold prevents it. As the heat of the oven holds the dough just as the gases make it,—the more kneading the better, as it makes it fine. It is necessary, to make good bread, to understand the reasons fully why yeast makes the bread rise; therefore, to make nice bread, etc., follow these rules:

1st. FLOUR should be kept in a dry closet—if at all damp it will make the bread heavy. When about to make bread put the quantity of flour you are to use in a pan near the fire in order to have it warm and dry for use. Seven pounds of flour or meal make a good batch of bread.

2d. YEAST.—Use fresh liquid yeast, or if your own, keep it well corked in a bottle; or use the yeast cakes now for sale in the stores. The better the yeast the less you require. Too much yeast makes the bread taste of yeast and has a bad effect on the bread; it dries quick and is not so sweet as if risen slowly. Too little yeast will make it heavy. To seven pounds of flour or meal a gill of yeast.

3d. SALT.—Sift it with the flour. To seven pounds of flour or meal, a large tablespoonful.

4th. FAT.—Three table-spoonfuls of any fat kneaded into the dough after it has risen the first time, makes it flaky, rich, and short.

5th. CLEANLINESS is all-important; have the pans, hands, and arms clean.

6th. DOUGH.—Never have it half made, nor allow it get cold before it is finished; if you do, it will be heavy. After making it, cover the pan with a thick cloth.

7th. KNEADING.—Fold the fingers over the thumbs, beat and pummel the dough until it ceases to stick to your hands. Do this on making, and after it has risen. Much kneading makes it whiter and finer.

Bread can scarcely be kneaded too much; the reason is plain—the fermented yeast forms very small globules, making a dense yet light bread.

8th. SOURING.—If the dough sours, dissolve a tea-spoonful of soda in as much hot water; work it into the dough—some prefer it after this is in; it makes a different taste to it, and the bread is whiter and tenderer.

9th. HEAT.—Dough should be made in cold weather in a warm room and kept there. If it is too slow in rising, set it over a pan of hot water and keep it warm.

10th. CONSISTENCY.—If too thin, add more flour; it should not run or spread; if too thick, let it rise a little longer, or add a little warm water.

11th. TO KEEP DOUGH GOOD.—Keep in winter in the cellar, or any cool place; in summer in the refrigerator. By so doing you can have hot bread or biscuit at any time. If it sours, use the soda.

12th. BAKING.—Bake in a moderately hot oven for bread; biscuit should have a hotter oven.

13th. TO KNOW WHEN BREAD IS BAKED —When bread is brown and firm to the touch all over, it is done. We give the time of baking as near as possible, but the heat of the ovens varies very much; therefore care must be taken not to overdo or underdo the bread and biscuit.

### 503. Hop Yeast Cakes.

In justice to our readers, and for their convenience, we recommend the hop or yeast cakes to housekeepers. They are made uniform, are handy, and can be used at any time. It saves running to the baker's, or bothering making yeast.

### 504. How to use Hop Yeast Cakes.

DIRECTIONS.—Dissolve the hop-cake in a cup of blood-warm water, add flour enough to make a THICK BATTER; set in a warm place until it rises, or looks spongy—three or five hours according to warmth—before adding to flour, then proceed the same as with liquid yeast. Care must be taken to keep the dough in a warm place while rising. Should it ever occur that the bread tastes of the yeast, it will be conclusive that there has been too much used for the quantity of flour.

### 505. How to make Yeast Cakes.

Put a large handful of hops into two quarts of boiling water. Boil three large potatoes until they are tender. Mash them and add to them two pounds of flour; pour the boiling hop water over the flour through a sieve or colander, and beat it until it is quite smooth. While it is warm add two table-spoonfuls of salt, and half a tea-cupful of sugar. Before it is quite cold stir in a pint of good yeast. After the yeast has become quite light, stir in as much Indian meal as it will take to roll it out in cakes, and place them on a cloth in a dry place, taking care to turn them every day. At the end of a week, or ten days, they may be put into a bag, and should be kept in a dry place. When used, take one of these cakes, soak it in some milk-warm water, mash it up smooth, and use it as any other kind of yeast.

### 506. To make Baker's Yeast.

TIME.—*To make, two hours.*

ARTICLES.—Three table-spoonfuls of flour, two quarts of water, a quarter of a pound of brown sugar, a quarter of a pound of yeast.

DIRECTIONS.—Make three spoonfuls of flour into a smooth batter with a little cold water; then add to it nearly two quarts more water, and a quarter of a pound of brown sugar; put it over the fire; stir it occasionally, and then set it to cool; when it is only lukewarm, add two table-spoonfuls of good yeast; set it in a warm place, or near the fire, for a day to ferment; then pour off the thin liquor from the top, shake the remainder up, and put in a bottle for use, or keep it in a covered stone jar. A gill of this yeast will be sufficient for seven pounds of flour.

### 507. Potato Yeast.

Boil a quarter of a peck of potatoes, mash them fine, and thin them a little with the water in which they have been boiled; add some salt and a table-spoonful of brown sugar; when lukewarm, stir in about half a pint or more of old yeast, let it rise, then cover it closely and put it in a cool place,—it is fit for use then.

### 508. Hop Yeast.

Tie a large handful of hops in a thin bag and boil them in three quarts of water; moisten with cold water a sufficient quantity of flour, and stir in the hop yeast while boiling hot; add a handful of salt; let it stand until it is about lukewarm, and then add about a pint of old yeast; when it is light, cover it and stand it in a cool place, for use

### 509. How to make Nice and Good Cream of Tartar and Soda Bread.

It is very important to have light, sweet bread. It is not always convenient to have yeast bread, and a change is agreeable. To have the above chemicals pure and uniform is all-important; they will keep in tin cans any length of time, therefore we recommend that *cream of tartar*, *saleratus*, or *soda*, be bought in large quantities of wholesale druggists, and buy the best

*Cream of tartar* is made from the settlings of wine; *saleratus* and *soda* are made from potash.

#### THE WAY THEY WORK.

*Cream of tartar is an acid; soda* and *saleratus* are anti-acids.

When the dissolved soda is worked into the dough, it meets the acid, and they form into gases, which, trying to escape, cause the dough to rise into little minute bubbles, the heat of the oven causes them still more to ferment, and then baking the dough forms a crust which confines the gases, and that causes the bread or biscuit to be light.

1st. CREAM OF TARTAR—Two heaping tea-spoonfuls to two quarts of flour or meal; sift it with the flour or meal. *Too much tartar* makes the bread sour, and is unhealthy.

2d. SALERATUS—An even tea-spoonful, or SODA a tea-spoonful, to two quarts of flour or meal; dissolve first in half a tea-cupful of water; when dissolved, put it into the water or milk; that is to be used as soda, unless prepared in this way is apt to discolor the bread. Too much soda makes the bread yellow and offensive, and is unhealthy.

3d. SALT—A heaping tea-spoonful to two quarts of flour or meal; sift it with the flour or meal, and cream of tartar.

4th. FAT.—A table-spoonful of any kind of fat to two quarts of flour or meal; after it is sifted, work it in the dry flour or meal, that is if shortening is desired.

5th. MILK OR WATER—A pint; milk is much the best, and adds all it costs to the goodness of the bread.

6th. SOUR OR BUTTER MILK—A pint. If you have or can get either, it is best, as it saves the cream of tartar, the acid of the milk doing as well; use the soda, however, but no tartar.

7th. DOUGH.—The dough must be as thin in consistency as possible, so as to pat it out on a board half an inch thick, and cut it with a round cake cutter.

8th. THE OVEN.—Always have that ready and hot, for this bread must be baked as soon as made, in a quick oven.

9th. HEALTH. — Hot bread is not as healthy as cold bread, still a little will kill no one. As these biscuits are very good warm, the healthy can eat them. The dyspeptic and invalid had better not eat them.

### 510. Yeast Powder,

(not yeast cakes, nor hop cakes), is made of one-third soda, or one-quarter improved saleratus, or two-thirds of cream of tartar, well mixed. I prefer to use the soda and tartar separately.

## GRAHAM FLOUR BREAD AND ROLLS.

### 511. To make Good Corn Meal Yeast Bread or Biscuit.

The above rules apply to corn meal, or Graham flour, or rye meal, or brown bread, biscuit, etc., except,

1st. They must be made thinner in a thick batter, and all the work can be done with a strong spoon; no lard is needed; they are not so much trouble to make.

2d. They generally require molasses to sweeten them.

3d. They require longer baking.

4th. Corn meal soda-biscuit and bread do not require so hot an oven as flour.

5th. Except these five things the yeast and soda rules apply to the corn-meal recipes for bread, biscuit, etc.

### 512. Rye or Wheat Flour Yeast Bread.

TIME.— *One hour to bake loaves of two pounds' weight each.*

ARTICLES.—Seven pounds of flour; two quarts of warm water; a large table-spoonful of salt; half a pint of yeast; two large table-spoonfuls of fat.

DIRECTIONS.—Put the flour into a deep pan, heap it round the sides, leaving a hollow in the center, put into it a quart of warm water, the salt and yeast; have ready three pints more of warm water, and with as much of it as may be necessary, make the whole into a rather soft dough, kneading it well with both hands. When it is smooth and shining, strew a little flour on it, lay a thickly folded cloth over the pan, and set it in a warm place by the fire, for four or five hours in cold weather, or all night; then knead it again for a quarter of an hour, at the same time kneading in the fat; cover it over, and set it to rise again. Divide it into two or three loaves, and bake it in a quick oven. It will take one hour to bake it, if divided into loaves weighing two pounds each; and two hours, if the loaves weigh four pounds each. This bread can be made of rye, or wheat, or Graham flour, or any kind that may suit. Corn meal can be added.

### 513. Graham Flour Bread.

TIME.— *Bake a little longer than yeast bread.*

Made same as yeast bread, adding a cup of molasses, and baking longer. This bread is made from Graham flour. If you wish it coarse, do not sift it; if, on using it, it is found to be too coarse or opening for the bowels, the bran can be sifted out. More molasses can be added, or none, as preferred. It is better for costive persons than any medicine.

### 514. Graham and Flour Bread.

Made same as yeast bread, sifting the Graham flour, and adding one-half wheat flour. Add a cup of molasses.

### 515. Potato Bread.

TIME.—*To bake, one and a half to two hours.*

ARTICLES.—Two and a half pounds of mealy potatoes; seven pounds of flour; a gill of yeast; two ounces of salt.

DIRECTIONS.—Boil two pounds and a half of nice mealy potatoes, till floury; rub and mash them smooth; then mix them with sufficient cold water to let them pass through a coarse sieve, and any lumps that remain must be again mashed and pressed through. Mix this paste with the yeast, and then add it to the flour. Set it to rise, well-knead it, and make it into a stiff, tough dough. Bake.

### 516. Rice Bread.

TIME.—*One and a half to two hours.*

ARTICLES.—Half a pound of rice; three pints of water; six pounds of flour.

DIRECTIONS.—Boil half a pound of rice in three pints of water, till the whole is quite thick; with this, and yeast, and six pounds of flour, make the dough.

### 517. Bread without Yeast or Soda.

TIME.—*Five hours to rise.*

ARTICLES.—Milk or water, a quart; salt; flour; lard, two table-spoonfuls.

DIRECTIONS.—Make the milk or water lukewarm; stir in the salt, as much as will do for the bread; stir in flour to make a paste; do this in a kettle; set it in a pot of warm water; keep the water or milk warm. In five hours it will foam like yeast; then knead in flour and lard, put in pans, let them rise again, and bake in a quick oven.

### 518. French Rolls.

TIME.—*Half an hour.*

ARTICLES. — One pound of flour; one egg; one ounce of butter; one spoonful of yeast; a little salt, and some milk.

DIRECTIONS.—Beat well the butter into the flour, adding a little salt; beat an egg, and stir it into the flour with the yeast, and a sufficient quantity of milk, to make the dough rather stiff. Beat it well without kneading it; set it to rise, and bake it on tins. This quantity will make about six rolls.

### 519. Irish Rolls.

TIME.—*Fifteen to twenty minutes.*

ARTICLES.—Two pounds of fine flour; one tea-spoonful of fine salt; one dessert-spoonful of powdered sugar; half a tea-spoonful of best carbonate of soda; whites of eggs, and some sour buttermilk.

DIRECTIONS.—Mix with the flour, the salt, sugar, and carbonate of soda. Then beat the whites of two eggs into a strong froth, with a sufficient quantity of sour buttermilk, and mix them up the same as rolls made with yeast. Make them up at once into whatever shape you like. Wash them over with the white of an egg, and bake them in a rather quick oven, of a light brown, for about a quarter of an hour, or according to the size of your rolls. They are very light and white. The sourer the buttermilk, the lighter the rolls will be. A basin of buttermilk will keep for a week, or very sour milk will answer as well.

### 520. English Rolls.

TIME.—*Twenty minutes to bake.*

ARTICLES.—Two pounds of flour; two ounces of butter; three spoonfuls of good yeast; one pint of warm milk.

DIRECTIONS.—Take the flour; rub the butter into it; add the yeast strained, and mix all well together with a pint of warm milk. Set it before the fire to rise, make it into twelve rolls, and bake them in a moderate oven.

### 521. Bakers' Rolls.

TIME.—*Twenty minutes to bake.*

ARTICLES.—Three pounds of flour; two table-spoonfuls of yeast; one tea-spoonful of salt; half a tea-spoonful of soda.

DIRECTIONS.—Put the flour into a pan, make a hollow in the center, and put in the salt, soda, and yeast. Make it into a soft dough with some warm milk; work or knead it until it is smooth and shining, then cover it and set it in a warm place, for two hours. Work it again very smooth, let it rise, and again knead and divide it in pieces twice the size of a hen's egg; roll it between your hands to the length of your finger; lay them so as to touch each other, on baking-tins, brush them over with milk, and set them in a quick oven, for fifteen or twenty minutes, until they are a delicate brown. Break one open to see if it is done, and serve them hot for breakfast, broken open, as cutting them when hot soddens them. To make a roll in form egg-shape, then not quite half lap it over, or cut round and lap over one-third.

### 522. Bakers' Twists.

TIME.—*Nearly one hour.*

DIRECTIONS.—Let the bread be made as directed for bakers' rolls; then take three pieces as large as a half-pint bowl; strew a little flour over the paste-board; roll each piece under your hands to twelve inches, length, making it smaller in circumference at the ends than in the middle. Having rolled each piece in this way, take a baking-tin, lay one part on it, join one end of each to the other two, and braid them together the length of the roll. Join the ends by pressing them together; dip a brush in milk, and pass it over the top of your twists. After ten minutes set them in a quick oven, and bake them for nearly an hour. They can be made smaller if desired.

### 523. Velvet Biscuit.

TIME.—*Fifteen minutes.*

ARTICLES.—One pint of warm milk; two eggs; half a gill of yeast; a tea-spoonful of soft butter; a tea-spoonful of salt; sufficient flour to make a soft dough.

DIRECTIONS.—In the milk and two well-beaten eggs put the yeast, soft butter, and salt. Stir into it sufficient flour to make a soft dough; strew some flour over it; lay a warm towel over the pan, and set it in a warm place to rise (three hours in the summer, or until light in the winter). Dip your hands in flour, and work the dough down; make it into small flat cakes; lay them on a buttered tin pan, quite near each other, and bake them in a quick oven for fifteen minutes, or until done.

These cakes may be mixed at night, and baked for breakfast. Keep the dough cool for supper, if required.

### 524. Sponge Flour Biscuit.

TIME.—*About ten minutes to bake.*

ARTICLES.—Flour, a quart; sweet milk, a pint; lard, a table-spoonful; salt, a tea-spoonful; yeast, a ten-cupful.

DIRECTIONS.—Sift the flour and salt into a pan; heat the milk and lard together; pour the yeast and milk into the flour; make a stiff dough when risen; grease a pan; drop the batter on in large table-spoonfuls; let them set where they will be merely warm (no more), then bake in a quick oven; eat at once. They may be baked in cups.

### 525. Rye and Flour Tea Biscuit.

TIME.—*To make and bake, half an hour.*

ARTICLES.—Rye flour, one tumbler; wheat flour, two tumblers or large cups; cream of tartar, a tea-spoonful; soda, half a tea-spoonful; fat, a table-spoonful; milk.

DIRECTIONS.—Sift the flours and tartar together; rub in the fat and salt; add the soda and milk, or water enough to make a soft dough; roll an inch thick; cut them out, prick, and bake in a hot oven. Use all, or parts of, any flour.

### 526. Breakfast Biscuit.

TIME.—*Twenty minutes.*

ARTICLES.—A piece of risen bread dough the size of a small loaf; one egg; one table-spoonful of butter or lard; a little milk.

DIRECTIONS.—Take a piece of risen bread dough, and work into it one beaten egg and a table-spoonful of butter or lard; when it is thoroughly amalgamated, flour your hands and make it into balls the size of an egg; rub a tin over with milk, and set them in a quick oven for twenty minutes, and serve them hot for breakfast. When eaten, break them open; to cut would make them heavy.

### 527. Milk Biscuit.

TIME.—*Half an hour.*

ARTICLES.—Six handfuls of flour; half a pint of milk; a small piece of butter; half a tea-cup of yeast; one egg.

DIRECTIONS.—Put the flour in a basin, with half a pint of milk and a small piece of butter; warm the milk—in the winter increase its temperature. Mix the yeast in a little cold water; add it to the milk and batter; make a hole in the flour, and pour the mixed milk and yeast into it, stirring it around until it is a thick batter; add to it one beaten egg; cover it over, and set it before the fire, keeping it warm. When it has risen a little, mix it into a dough; knead it well; put it again to rise; and when it is risen a great deal, form your biscuit. They will take nearly half an hour to bake, or according to the size you make them. Rub them once, while hot, with a paste-brush dipped in milk.

### 528. Sour Milk Biscuit.

TIME.—*To make and bake, forty minutes.*

ARTICLES.—One pint of rye flour; one pint of wheat flour; then soda, half a tea-spoonful; sour milk; fat, table-spoonful; salt.

DIRECTIONS.—Rub the fat in the flour; dissolve the soda in hot water; add salt, to taste; wet the flour with sour milk until a soft dough is formed; make into thin biscuit; bake in a quick oven; use all of one kind of flour, if preferred.

### 529. Rye or Wheat Flour Crackers.

TIME.—*Half an hour, to make and bake.*

ARTICLES.—Rye or wheat flour, one quart; butter or fat, four ounces; soda, half a tea-spoonful; salt, same; milk.

DIRECTIONS.—Take the flour and salt, and rub the fat well into it; dissolve the soda; then add sweet milk to make a stiff dough; knead well; cut the crackers round, half an inch thick; bake in a quick oven.

### 530. Rye or Wheat Flour Drop Cakes.

TIME.—*To make and bake, half an hour.*

ARTICLES.—A pint of rye or wheat flour; two eggs; salt; sugar, a tea-spoonful; milk; soda, a third of a tea-spoonful; cream of tartar, two-thirds.

DIRECTIONS.—Sift a pint of either, or parts of the flours, and tartar, salt, and sugar; add the eggs well beaten, and the dissolved soda; lastly, drop the batter in balls on a greased pan or small pans; bake in a quick oven.

### 531. Graham Flour Mush.

This is an excellent article for infants and young children. It will do for a change, in the cases of adults, but is not equal to the coarser preparation of the grain. It is cooked like Indian mush.

### 532. Unleavened Bread.

This bread is made by the water-cure, and hygienic believers who are opposed to the use of yeast, soda, saleratus, salt, and cream of tartar. Persons with very weak stomachs will derive benefit from the use of this bread. As a change any one can use it, if they desire to. This bread requires a hot oven.

### 533. Graham Gems.

Into cold water stir Graham flour sufficient to make a batter a trifle thicker than that used for ordinary griddle cakes. Bake from one-half to three-quarters of an hour in a *hot* oven, in small tins or a tin pan. The flour should be stirred in slowly. Use soft water or part milk.

### 534. Graham Diamonds.

Pour boiling water on Graham flour, stirring rapidly till all the flour is wet. Too much stirring makes it tough. It should be about as thick as can be stirred easily with a strong iron spoon. Place the dough with plenty of flour upon the moulding board, and knead it for two or three minutes. Roll out half an inch thick, and cut in small cakes or rolls. If a large quantity is required, roll about three-fourths of an inch thick, and cut with a knife in diamond shape. Bake, in a very hot oven, forty-five minutes.

### 535. Graham Biscuit.

Make Graham mush as for the table; when cool, mix with it Graham flour sufficient to roll well. Knead for a few minutes, roll three-fourths of an inch thick, cut with a common biscuit cutter, and bake in a hot oven, from thirty to forty-five minutes.

### 536. Wheat Meal Crisps.

Make a very stiff dough of Graham flour and cold water; knead thoroughly, roll as thin as possible, and bake for twenty minutes in a hot oven.

### 537. Oat Meal Mush.

This, in Scotland, is called stirabout. It is a favorite with many persons, and makes a pleasant change of dishes. It is cooked precisely like Indian mush.

### 538. Uses for Stale Bread.

Stale bread may be cut into slices and softened by pouring a small quantity of boiling water over it. Cover the pan containing it, to prevent the escape of the steam. As soon as the bread is soft, season the slices with pepper and salt, have some hot lard, ham fat, or sausages, dripped in a pan, dust a little flour or Indian meal on each slice, and fry them a delicate brown. Boiling milk, if you have it, is better than water to soften the bread.

# OYSTERS.

In many parts of our country oysters are to be had merely by gathering them on the shore. At most places they are sold very cheap. As a healthy, nutritious, and cheap article of food we recommend oysters; many dishes can be made from them.

In cases of debility, raw oysters and the soup are very strengthening.

The American oysters are unquestionably the best that can be found. They vary in taste according to how they are treated, either after being dredged or while imbedded, and also according to the nature of the soil and water in which they have lived. It is very wrong to wash oysters; we mean by washing oysters, the abominable habit of throwing them in cold water as soon as opened, then to be sold by the measure. It is more than a pity to thus spoil such an excellent and delicate article of food.

Oysters like lobsters are not good when dead. To ascertain if they are alive as soon as opened, and when one of the shells is removed, touch gently the edge of the oyster, and if alive it will contract.

### 539. To Feed Oysters.

Wash them perfectly clean with water, then lay them bottom downwards in a deep pan, and pour over them salt water; the salt should be previously dissolved in the water, allowing about five or six ounces to each gallon of water. Change the water every day. You may fatten them by putting oat meal into the water every day.

### 540. To Keep Oysters Alive and Good.

Put them in a clean pan, cover them with pure water moderately salted, and changed every day. Keep them in a cool place.

### 541. To Open Oysters.

In opening them, try and avoid cutting them by keeping the point of the knife close to the shell. In New York they crack the point of the oyster to open them, but they can be opened without that, and it avoids the fine pieces of shell getting into the meat of the oyster.

### 542. Raw Oysters.

When well washed open them, detaching the upper shell, then detatch them from the under shell, but leave them on it; place on a dish and serve.

To eat them, sprinkle salt, pepper, and lemon juice on, and eat.

They are excellent eaten with thin slices of brown bread and butter.

### 543. Steamed Oysters (Washington Style).

TIME.—*About ten minutes.*

Put a peck of oysters in a steamer, steam them until they open their shells, open them while hot, eat with vinegar and pepper or sauce, on the half shell or on a plate.

REMARKS.—We have eaten them in this style, and consider it one of the best modes of cooking them known; in Washington it is very popular, we have seen over two hundred persons in one saloon eating them at the same time.

### 544. Roast Oysters (in the shell).

TIME.—*A few minutes.*

Wash some oysters, lay them on a gridiron over a bright coal fire, roast until the shells open, lift off the upper shell, put the lower half, with the oyster in it, on a plate; eat them with butter and any sauce.

### 545. Baked Oysters.

TIME.—*A few minutes.*

DIRECTIONS.—Wash some oysters, put them in a pan, then in a hot oven, and let them bake until the shells open; serve and eat same as roast oysters.

### 546. Boiled Oysters.

TIME.—*A few minutes.*

Let the shells be nicely cleaned, boil the oysters in them as you do lobsters, and serve them in their shells with plain melted butter.

### 547. Broiled Oysters.

TIME.—*Six or eight minutes.*

ARTICLES.—As many oysters as you require; one or two eggs; bread crumbs; a little pepper, and a small piece of butter.

DIRECTIONS.—Take the largest oysters from their own liquor, lay them on a folded napkin to dry off the moisture, then dip them into beaten eggs, and then into grated bread; place a gridiron made of coarse wire over a bright, but not a fierce fire, lay the oysters carefully on it, and when one side is done turn the other. Serve them on a folded napkin, or put a piece of butter on a hot dish, sprinkle a little pepper over it, lay the oysters on, and serve.

### 548. Fried Oysters.

TIME.—*Fifteen minutes.*

ARTICLES.—Oysters, crackers, cayenne pepper, salt, eggs, cream, and butter or lard.

DIRECTIONS.—Select the largest oysters for frying; dry them; have ready some grated crackers seasoned with cayenne pepper and salt; beat the yolks only of some eggs, and to each egg add half a tablespoonful of thick cream; dip the oysters one at a time, first in the egg, then in the cracker crumbs, and fry them in plenty of hot pork fat or butter, till they are of a light brown on both sides. Serve them hot.

### 549. Stewed Oysters Plain.

TIME.—*Twenty minutes to stew.*

ARTICLES.—Oysters, butter, pepper.

DIRECTIONS.—Stew as many oysters as wanted in their own liquor, add a little butter and pepper to taste. Eat hot.

## OYSTERS.

### 550. Stewed Oysters with Milk.

TIME.—*Half an hour.*
ARTICLES.—One quart of oysters, four ounces of butter, small table-spoonful of flour, tea-spoonful of parsley, pepper, salt, and a pint of milk.
DIRECTIONS. — Procure good and fresh oysters; set them on a fire with their liquor and a little water, and boil twenty minutes.
Put the butter in a TEA-KETTLE BOILER, set on the fire, and when melted stir into it a small table-spoonful of flour; as soon as mixed, add also the parsley chopped fine, and about a pint of milk; boil gently about ten minutes then add the oysters, salt and pepper, boil again about one minute, dish the whole, sprinkle lemon juice on, and serve. Less quantity used if desired.

### 551. Stewed Oysters with Cream.

TIME.—*To boil ten minutes.*
ARTICLES.—A dozen oysters, salt, cayenne pepper, and a very little mace, a little butter and grated cracker, with a little cream.
DIRECTIONS.—Rinse the oysters, and put them in a TEA-KETTLE BOILER with the water which adheres to them; season them with salt, cayenne pepper, and mace. As soon as they begin to boil pour in the cream, and stir in the butter rolled in a little grated cracker. Let them boil and serve hot.

### 552. Stewed Oysters with Eggs.

TIME.—*Twenty minutes.*
ARTICLES.—Oysters, butter, salt, pepper, eggs, and bread crumbs.
DIRECTIONS.—Place a chafing-dish upon the table, with the lamp burning, pour in the oyster liquor, season with butter, salt and pepper; when hot add the oysters; cover with the chafing-dish cover, and stew twenty minutes, beat the eggs in a bowl, remove the dish cover and pour the eggs in stirring rapidly. Serve from the chafing-dish immediately.

### 553. Stewed Oysters with Wine, (French Style).

TIME.—*Three quarters of an hour.*
ARTICLES.—Oysters, sweet milk, a tea-cupful of bread crumbs, salt, pepper, and a table-spoonful of butter.
DIRECTIONS.—Strain the liquor so as to remove every fragment of shell; mix in equal proportions sweet milk and the oyster liquor; add to a quart of the liquor a tea-cupful of finely pulverized bread or cracker crumbs; season with salt and pepper, and a table-spoonful of butter; boil gently in a TEA-KETTLE BOILER, stirring frequently, a quarter of an hour, then add the oysters; stew half an hour, or less time if preferred, and serve hot. Use wine and spice as seasoning. Sherry or champagne and mace is the best spice for oysters.

### 554. Boiled Oyster Chowder.

Use recipe for fish chowder, using one quart of oysters instead of fish. Made properly it is cheap and good.

### 555. Baked Oyster Chowder.

TIME.—*Three quarters of an hour.*
ARTICLES.—Sweet milk, crackers, oysters, butter, pepper, salt and celery.
DIRECTIONS.—Butter a deep earthen dish; soak in sweet milk as many crackers or slices of bread as will be needed; cover the bottom of the dish with these (soda crackers are best); strew over these bits of butter; then put in a thick layer of oysters; season with pepper and salt, a little chopped celery or parsley, if liked; then crackers, butter, oysters, and seasoning until the dish is full, always having the crackers on top with bits of butter over. Pour in enough hot oyster liquor and hot sweet milk, mixed in equal proportions, to half fill the dish; this had better be put in before adding the last layer of soaked crackers; bake three quarters of an hour; serve with pickles. Clam chowder is made in the same way.

### 556. Stuffed Oysters.

TIME.—*Twenty minutes.*
ARTICLES.—Twelve oysters, bread, yolks of two eggs, little cayenne pepper, little butter.
DIRECTIONS. — Take the meat of the oysters, no juice, mince them up fine, mix in the yolks of two eggs, then the bread crumbs to thicken, then the pepper and salt to taste, then fill the shells, rounding them, so as to hold it; brown in a quick oven. Eat hot or cold.

### 557. Minced Oysters.

TIME.—*To bake half an hour.*
ARTICLES. — Twenty-five oysters, bread crumbs or powdered crackers, a cupful of wine, sweet oil, vinegar, cayenne pepper, and salt to taste; soda crackers, ten.
DIRECTIONS. — Take some fat oysters, mince them fine in their liquor, stir in some bread crumbs, sweet oil, vinegar, pepper, and salt to taste; put alternate layers of mince and crackers, first wet in the wine, in a pudding dish to bake, or a TEA-KETTLE BOILER to boil; cook half an hour either way.

### 558. Oyster Fritters (French Style).

TIME.—*Five or six minutes.*
ARTICLES.—Two eggs, half a pint of milk, and sufficient flour to make a batter, twenty-five oysters.

DIRECTIONS.—Beat two eggs and stir in half a pint of milk, and sufficient flour to make it a nice batter; dry some fine large oysters on a napkin, put a fork through the hard part, and dip each oyster twice into the batter; fry them in boiling lard or beef-dripping, and serve.

### 559. Oysters in Marinade.

TIME.—*Six minutes.*

ARTICLES.—Oysters, pepper, salt, grated nutmeg, lemon juice, batter.

DIRECTIONS.—Pour the oysters (out of the shell) in cold water over the fire, and when it boils take them out, and throw them in cold water, and then lay them out upon a cloth to dry; spread them on a dish, sprinkle them with pepper, salt, and a little grated nutmeg, squeeze lemon juice over them, let them lie a little while, dip them in batter and fry them.

### 560. Indian Curried Oysters.

TIME.—*Twenty to twenty-five minutes.*

ARTICLES. — One hundred oysters, two small or one large onion, four dessert-spoonfuls of curry powder, three ounces of butter, one cocoanut, juice of a lemon, a large sour apple, flour, salt, and a little warm water or broth.

DIRECTIONS.—Open a hundred oysters and put them with their liquor into a basin, slice two small or one large onion as thin as possible, and put in a TEA-KETTLE BOILER with a piece of butter to fry a nice brown; then stir in a piece of butter and the curry powder, adding, as you stir it, a little warm water or broth, very gradually; set it over the fire and mix in the grated cocoanut and the apple minced fine. Thicken it with a little flour made into a paste with water, and let it simmer until the cocoanut is tender. Then put in the oysters and their liquor strained, the juice of the lemon, and the milk from the cocoanut, and let it boil until the oysters are done, stirring it frequently. Serve it on a hot dish, with boiled rice on a separate dish.

### 561. Oyster Fritters.

TIME.—*Time five or six minutes.*

ARTICLES.—One quart of oysters, half a pint of milk, two eggs, a little flour, a little dripping or butter.

DIRECTIONS.—Open a quart of oysters, strain the liquor into a basin, and add to it half a pint of milk and the eggs. Stir in by degrees flour enough to make a smooth but rather thin batter; when perfectly free from lumps put the oysters into it. Have some beef-dripping or butter made hot in a very clean frying pan and season with a little salt, and when it is boiling drop in the batter with a large spoon, putting one or more oysters in each spoonful. Hold the pan over a gentle fire until one side of the batter is a delicate brown, turn each fritter separately, and when both sides are done place them on a hot dish and serve.

### 562. Oyster Meat.

TIME.—*Ten minutes to fry.*

ARTICLES.—Half a pint of oysters, five ounces of bread crumbs, one ounce of butter, the peel of half a lemon, a sprig of parsley, salt, nutmeg, a very little cayenne pepper, and one egg.

DIRECTIONS.—Half a pint of oysters, wash them well in their own liquor and mince them very fine; mix with the peel of half a lemon chopped small, a sprig of parsley, a seasoning of salt, nutmeg, and a very little cayenne pepper, and the butter in small pieces. Stir into these ingredients five ounces of bread crumbs, and when thoroughly mixed together, bind it with the yolk of an egg and part of the oyster liquor. Fry brown.

### 563. Devilled Oysters.

TIME.—*Ten minutes.*

ARTICLES.—Some fine large oysters, one ounce and a half of butter, a little lemon juice, pepper, salt, and cayenne.

DIRECTIONS.—Open a sufficient number of oysters for the dish, leaving them in their deep shells and their liquor; add a little lemon juice, pepper, salt, and cayenne; put a small piece of butter on each, and place the shell carefully on a gridiron, over a clear, bright fire, to broil for a few minutes. Serve them with bread and butter.

### 564. Oyster Omelet.

TIME.—*Ten minutes to prepare.*

ARTICLES. — Eight oysters, six eggs, a wine-glassful of flour, a little milk, pepper, salt and butter.

DIRECTIONS.—The oysters chopped fine; eggs, flour, and milk, pepper, salt, and butter. Beat the eggs very light, add the oysters and the flour, which must be mixed to a paste with a little milk. Pepper and salt to the taste. Fry in hot butter but do not turn it. As soon as it is done slip it on a dish and serve it hot. The above is the usual mode of preparing oyster omelet; but the better way is to put your oysters in a TEA-KETTLE BOILER, set them over the fire, and the moment they begin to boil take them out, drain them and dry them in a napkin. They are not so watery when prepared in this manner, and consequently will not dilute the beaten eggs as much as the former mode. When they are cold mince them and proceed as before.

### 565. Plain Oyster Patties.

TIME.—*Altogether two hours.*

ARTICLES.—Round loaves, oysters, crumbs of bread, butter, black pepper, cayenne, cream.

DIRECTIONS.—Make little round loaves, make a hole in the top of each, and scrape out a portion of the crumbs. Put some oysters into a TEA-KETTLE BOILER with their own liquor, and add to them the crumbs of bread rubbed or grated fine, and a lump of butter. Season with black pepper, and a sprinkle of cayenne. Stew for five or six minutes, and then put in a spoonful of good cream. Fill the loaves, and cover with the bits of crust previously cut up. Set them in an oven for a few minutes to crisp.

Minced veal, lamb, poultry, game, etc., may be done in the same way as for paste patties.

### 566. Oyster Pie.

TIME.—*An hour to bake.*

ARTICLES.—One hundred oysters; one gill of cream; one ounce and a half of butter; grated cracker, salt, cayenne pepper, two eggs, bread crumbs.

DIRECTIONS.—Take the oysters and dry them perfectly. Pour off half the liquor into a TEA-KETTLE BOILER; salt it to your taste. Stir in the cream, then the butter rolled in grated cracker, and a little cayenne pepper. Boil two eggs hard, chop them up and mix them with as many bread crumbs as will cover the top of your pie. Season the bread and eggs with cayenne pepper and salt. Make a rich paste, line the sides of your pie dish, put in the oysters, pour the hot liquor over them, and strew the bread crumbs on the top; cover the whole with a lid of paste. Cut an opening in the center of the top crust, and ornament it with flowers or leaves made of the paste. As soon as the crust is done take the pie out of the oven.

### 567. Pickled Oysters.

TIME.—*Half an hour.*

ARTICLES.—Two and a half quarts of oysters, vinegar, two table-spoonfuls of salt, one table spoonful of mace; one table-spoonful of allspice; the same quantity of white pepper; and a tea-spoonful of cloves.

DIRECTIONS. — Have ready the oysters with a pint of their liquor. Put the vinegar, salt, and liquor on to boil; when it comes to a boil skim it; then add the spices, give it another boil up, and after this put in the oysters. Be careful they do not burn; to prevent this use the TEA-KETTLE BOILER. They must be cooked over a quick fire. They must be served cold.

### 568. Scalloped Oysters.

TIME.—*About fifteen minutes.*

ARTICLES.—Oysters, bread crumbs, two ounces of butter, pepper and salt.

DIRECTIONS.—Open the oysters; leave each oyster in its own deep shell; sprinkle over it a little pepper and salt, and some crumbs of bread, and lay a little piece of butter on the top. Arrange the shells in a dish and put it in the oven. When the oysters are thoroughly hot they are done.

### 569. Scalloped Oysters (French style).

TIME.—*A few minutes.*

ARTICLES.—Oysters; an ounce and a half of butter; a sprig of parsley; pepper; and a little lemon juice.

DIRECTIONS. — Throw the oysters into boiling water over the fire, and let them just bubble up, not boil. Roll them in butter, with minced parsley, pepper and lemon juice. Make some of the deep shells quite clean, arrange the oysters three or four in each, put them on the gridiron, and the moment the liquor bubbles at the side, take them up and serve them.

### 570. Oyster Ketchup.

TIME.—*One hour.*

ARTICLES.—One pint of oysters, one pint of sherry; one ounce of salt; two drachms of cayenne pepper.

DIRECTIONS.—Rinse some fine fresh oysters in their own liquor, then pound them in a mortar, and to a pint of oysters put a pint of sherry. Boil them, add the salt and the cayenne pepper,; boil the sauce up again, rub it through a sieve, and when cold put it in bottles and cork and seal them.

### 571. Oyster Cracker Salad.

TIME.—*Three minutes.*

ARTICLES.—Oyster crackers (or any other kind), cabbage, celery, or lettuce, sweet oil, vinegar, pepper, mustard and salt to taste.

DIRECTIONS.—Mix altogether, *very fine.* Good to eat with any of the above dishes.

### 572. Fish Chowder.

TIME.—*To prepare, half an hour; to cook, nearly an hour.*

ARTICLES.—Four pounds of any fresh fish; pork, half a pound; milk, a pint; potatoes, twenty; onions, eight; hard crackers, one pound; or one half of each of the above.

DIRECTIONS. — Cut the pork into small pieces, fry it out, then pour it into the pot; then strew a layer of sliced onions, then a layer of sliced peeled potatoes, then a layer of fish, then a layer of crackers; repeat until all is in; season with pepper and salt; pour on hot water until it covers the contents; then let it boil until the potatoes are cooked; while the chowder is cooking, put a pint of milk in the TEA-KETTLE BOILER to boil, and add enough flour to make it thick; let it boil until the chowder is done, then pour it over the top; *do not stir the chowder, and take it up carefully.* Clams and oysters can be used instead of fish.

REMARKS.—This chowder is the favorite dish of all men who travel on the great waters, and of New England and Canada. It is cheap, healthy, nutritious, and good.

# LOBSTERS.

Lobsters are very fine shell-fish, and are caught in abundance along the shores of the New England States and Canada. The male lobster is distinguished by the narrowness of his tail; the female or hen lobster has a broader tail and small claws. All of the lobster is good to eat, except the stomach and a small gut that runs through the lobster. The flavor of the lobster is generally considered to be superior, in both purity and delicacy, to that of the other crustaceas. Lobsters are a very agreeable and nutritive article of food; they are not appropriate substances for dyspeptics or invalids. The usual way of cooking them has been to simply boil and eat them cold, with vinegar, or as a salad, but there are many other ways, which we give, to cook these very economical fish; which, we are assured, will be most acceptable to our New England households, and to all who admire lobsters; and it may teach others to like them.

### 573. To Choose Lobster.

The heaviest are the best, and very often a good small-sized lobster will weigh heavier than a large one. The male is the best for boiling, the flesh is firmer, the shell of a brighter red. Hen lobsters are best for sauce or salad, on account of their coral. They are generally sent to market boiled; if you buy them alive, then proceed

### 574. To Boil a Lobster.

TIME.—*An hour.*

Put into a large kettle water enough to cover the lobster, with a quarter of a pound of salt to every gallon of water.

When it boils fast, put in the lobster, head first. If the head goes in first, it is killed instantly. Boil it briskly for an hour, then take it from the hot water, and lay it to drain. Wipe off all the scum from it. A lobster weighing a pound takes one hour to boil, others in like proportion, more or less. It will be a bright red, when done.

### 575. Plain Boiled Lobster.

After it is boiled and cold, break off the tail, cut it in two pieces with a sharp knife; remove the small intestine; remove the meat; break the claws up; remove the meat; then break off the small legs; open the body; take out *every* thing but the stomach (or lady); cut the inner body open; arrange it all around a dish, and serve for breakfast, dinner, or supper. Use vinegar and pepper.

### 576. To Dress Lobsters.

When sent to the table, separate the body from the tail, remove the large claws, and crack them at each joint carefully, and split the tail down the middle with a sharp knife. Place the body upright in the centre of a dish, and arrange the tail and claws on each side. Garnish it with parsley. Remove the lady and gut.

### 577. Lobster Salad.

TIME.—*Twenty minutes.*

ARTICLES.—A lobster; yolks of two eggs; a spoonful of made mustard; three table-spoonfuls of salad oil; vinegar; a little salt; some fresh lettuce.

DIRECTIONS.—Pick all the meat out of the lobster; thoroughly beat the yolks of two eggs; beat in made mustard to taste, and, continuing to beat them, drop in the sweet oil; add whatever flavoring may be preferred, and some salt; mix in the vinegar to taste, and the soft part of the lobster; moisten the remainder of the lobster with this, and lay it at the bottom of the bowl; cup up the lettuce; take care that it is well rolled over in the dressing, and put it over the lobster. Mustard can be left out if it is not liked. The above quantity is given for the proportions and can be increased according to the lobster employed, or taste.

### 578. Scalloped Lobster.

TIME.—*Fifteen minutes.*

ARTICLES.—One or two lobsters; a little pepper, salt, Cayenne, and a table-spoonful of butter, or thin-melted butter, and bread crumbs.

DIRECTIONS.—Pick out all the meat from one large or two middling-sized lobsters, and cut fine in a chopping tray, with a little pepper, salt, cayenne, and melted butter sufficient to moisten it. Split the empty shells of the tails and the bodies, and fill each of them neatly with the lobster. Cover them with grated bread, and put them into an oven.

### 579. English Way to Scallop Lobsters.

TIME.—*Twenty minutes.*

ARTICLES.—One large lobster; a tea-spoonful of anchovy sauce; three table-spoonfuls of white sauce or cream; yolks of two eggs; some bread crumbs; a little nutmeg, and cayenne, and a lump of butter.

DIRECTIONS.—Cut a large fresh lobster into halves with a sharp knife; pound the spawn, pith, and coral in a mortar, with a lump of butter; then rub it through a sieve into a TEA-KETTLE BOILER; add about three large spoonfuls of white sauce or cream, a tea-spoonful of anchovy, and a little cayenne and nutmeg; boil it for five minutes, stirring it constantly. Cut the meat of the lobster into small pieces and stir it into the sauce, with the yolks of two well-beaten eggs; make it thoroughly hot; fill the shells of the body and tail; strew over them some bread-crumbs, and brown them.

BROILED, STEWED, ROAST, AND CURRY OF LOBSTERS. 63

### 580. Broiled Lobster.
TIME.—*Twenty minutes.*

After having boiled the lobster, split it from head to tail; lay it open; put pieces of butter over the meat; sprinkle it with pepper, and set the shells on a grid-iron over the bright coals until nicely heated through. Serve in the shells.

### 581. Buttered Lobster.
TIME.—*Twenty minutes.*

ARTICLES.—One lobster; one wine-glassful of vinegar; a quarter of a pound of fresh butter; one salt-spoonful of cayenne pepper; one salt-spoonful of made mustard; three heads of lettuce; one hard-boiled egg.

DIRECTIONS.—Boil a lobster; take the meat from the shell and mince or chop it fine; put the coral and green inside, but leave out the lady; to the vinegar or hot water add the butter; add the pepper and mustard, and put it with the lobster into a TEA-KETTLE BOILER. Stir it until it is thoroughly heated through.

Cut the heads of lettuce; nicely wash them; put them at the sides of a salad bowl; lay the hot lobster in the middle; garnish with the hard-boiled egg cut in circles, and serve it hot.

### 582. To Stew Lobsters.
TIME.—*Twenty minutes.*

ARTICLES.—One large or two small hen lobsters; one pint of water; one blade of mace; some whole pepper; some melted butter; a glass of white wine; juice of half a lemon.

DIRECTIONS.—Pick the meat from one large or two small lobsters in large pieces; boil the shells in a pint of water, with a blade of mace, and some whole pepper. When all the strength is extracted from the shells and spice, strain the liquor; mix the coral and the rich part of the lobster with a few spoonfuls of melted butter, a wine-glass of white wine, and the juice of half a lemon strained; put in the picked lobster; boil it up, and serve

### 583. Miroton of Lobster.
TIME.—*One hour and twenty minutes.*

ARTICLES.—One large lobster; four eggs; one penny-roll; three table-spoonfuls of cream; pepper; salt; slices of fat ham.

DIRECTIONS.—Pick out all the meat from a large hen lobster, and pound it in a mortar with the spawn and the crumb of a penny-roll previously soaked in cream. Then stir in the yolks of three well-beaten eggs, and season it with pepper, salt, and a very little pounded mace. Beat an egg to a stiff froth, and add it to the pounded lobster. Line a pudding mould with some slices of fat ham; cut as thin as possible; fill the mould with the mixture, and boil it for an hour and twenty minutes. When done, turn it out carefully on a hot dish, and pour round it some good lobster sauce.

### 584. French Curry of Lobster.
TIME.—*One hour.*

ARTICLES.—One lobster; one onion; a table-spoonful of butter; a quarter of a lemon; a spoonful of flour; two spoonfuls of curry powder; one pint of water.

DIRECTIONS.—Pick out the meat from a large lobster; put the body into a TEA-KETTLE BOILER with the water; cut the onion in slices; add the butter and a quarter of a lemon; then stir in the curry powder and the flour. When it is thoroughly done, strain the gravy from the body of the lobster; add a little pepper, salt, and the juice of a lemon; put in the picked lobster, first cut up in small pieces; let stand for an hour by the side of the fire; then boil up again, and serve hot.

### 585. Curry of Lobsters.
TIME.—*One hour.*

ARTICLES.—Two small lobsters; half a blade of mace; four spoonfuls of meat gravy; four spoonfuls of cream; two tea-spoonfuls of curry powder; one tea-spoonful of flour; one ounce of butter; juice of half a lemon.

DIRECTIONS.—Pick the lobsters or spawns from their shells; put them into a stew-pan with the mace, gravy, and the cream; rub smooth the curry powder, one ounce of flour, and an ounce of butter. Let it simmer for one hour; add a little salt; squeeze in the juice of half a lemon, and serve.

### 586. Lobster Fricasseed.
TIME.—*Eight minutes to parboil; to each pound the same time.*

ARTICLES.—Two lobsters; a pint of milk; juice of half a lemon; pepper: salt; nutmeg.

DIRECTIONS.—Parboil two moderate-sized lobsters; take out the meat from the claws and tail, and cut it into rather small pieces; put into a stew-pan with the milk; cover the pan close, and stew it gently for the same time it has previously taken to parboil the lobsters. When on the point of boiling, stir in the juice of half a lemon quickly, just as it is removed from the fire. Serve it very hot.

### 587. To Roast a Lobster.
TIME.—*Half an hour.*

DIRECTIONS.—Parboil a lobster; take it out of the water; rub it over with butter, and put it in a dish before the fire; baste it well with butter until it has a fine froth, and serve.

### 588. Lobster Cutlets Fried in Batter.
TIME.—*Twenty minutes.*

Cook as below for cutlets, using batter instead of bread-crumbs to fry them in.

### 589. Plain Lobster Cutlets.

TIME.—*To fry, twenty minutes.*

ARTICLES.—A good-sized lobster; two eggs; crumbs of bread; cayenne; salt, and nutmeg.

DIRECTIONS.—Cut the meat out of the tail and claws; slice them up about a third of an inch thick; dip them into beaten egg, then into very fine bread crumbs, which have first been seasoned with the pepper, salt, and grated nutmeg; egg and crumb them twice; fry them quickly in butter until a light brown; serve hot.

### 590. East India Lobster Cutlets.

TIME.—*Eight minutes, to fry.*

ARTICLES.—One large hen lobster and two small ones; two ounces of fresh butter; pepper and salt; one blade of mace, nutmeg, and cayenne pepper; a dessert-spoonful of anchovy sauce; four eggs; bread crumbs. For the sauce, the coral of the lobster; a spoonful of anchovy sauce; a small cupful of melted butter.

DIRECTIONS.—Pick the meat from a fine hen lobster and two small ones, and pound it in a mortar with part of the coral and a seasoning of pepper, salt, mace, nutmeg, and cayenne pepper. Add the yolks of two well-beaten eggs, the white of one, and a spoonful of anchovy sauce; mix the above ingredients thoroughly together, and roll it out as you would paste, with a little flour, two inches thick. Cut it into cutlets; brush them over with the yolk of egg; dip them in into bread crumbs, and fry a nice brown in butter, a spoonful of anchovy sauce, and the remainder of the coral. Pour it into the center of a hot dish, and arrange the lobster cutlets round it, as you would cutlets of meat; place between each the horns of the lobster cut into short lengths.

### 591. Lobster Balls.

TIME.—*Eight or ten minutes, to fry.*

ARTICLES.—A fine hen lobster; two eggs; bread crumbs; two ounces of butter; pepper; salt, and a very little cayenne pepper.

DIRECTIONS.—Take the meat from a fine hen lobster, and pound it in a mortar with the coral and spawn. Mix with it not quite an equal quantity of bread crumbs, seasoned with pepper and salt and a little cayenne; bind the whole with two ounces of fresh butter warmed; roll the mixture into balls the size of large duck's eggs; brush them over with beaten egg; cover them with bread crumbs, and fry them lightly. Serve them hot, after draining the grease from them.

### 592. Lobster Pie.

TIME.—*One hour.*

ARTICLES.—One lobster; a spoonful of vinegar; a table-spoonful of butter; some bread crumbs; puff paste.

DIRECTIONS.—Pick all of the meat out of the lobster, spawn and green; cut all up fine in a chopping tray, or beat it in a mortar; season it with pepper, salt, and vinegar; melt the butter; stir all together with a cupful of bread crumbs; put puff paste around the pie-plate; put in the meat; cover it over with the paste; make a hole in the top; bake it in a slow oven.

### 593. Minced Lobsters.

TIME.—*Ten minutes.*

ARTICLES.—One lobster; a glass of white wine; pepper and salt; nutmeg; cayenne, and a wine-glass of vinegar; two ounces of butter; one anchovy; yolks of eggs; bread crumbs.

DIRECTIONS.—Pick the meat from a fresh lobster; mince it very well, and put it into a stew-pan with a seasoning of pepper and salt, a little cayenne, a wine glass of white wine, and one of vinegar. Set it over a clear fire to stew for about ten minutes; melt two ounces of butter, with an anchovy, and the yolks of two well-beaten eggs; stir it into the lobster, and thicken the whole with bread crumbs; place it in a dish, and garnish with the claws and double parsley.

### 594. Lobster Soup.

TIME.—*One hour and a quarter.*

ARTICLES.—One lobster; two or three plain biscuits; one quart of milk; one quart of water; one table-spoonful of salt; one tea-spoonful of pepper; a quarter of a pound of fresh butter.

DIRECTIONS.—Pick the meat from a lobster already boiled, from its shell, and cut it into small pieces; roll the biscuits to a powder; put a quart of milk and a quart of water into a TEA-KETTLE BOILER, with a table-spoonful of salt and a tea-spoonful of pepper. When the milk and water are boiling hot, add the lobster and pounded biscuit mixed to the soup with a quarter of a pound of fresh butter; let it boil closely covered for half an hour; pour it into a tureen, and serve.

### 595. Lobster Croquettes.

TIME.—*Eight minutes to fry.*

ARTICLES.—One large lobster; two table-spoonfuls of cream; some grated bread; a tea-spoonful of anchovy sauce; one egg; juice of one lemon; pepper; salt, and nutmeg.

DIRECTIONS.—Pick the meat from a large lobster; mince it up, and mix with it the bread, anchovy sauce, cream, the juice of a lemon, pepper, salt, and a little grated nutmeg. Put it over the fire and make it very hot; turn it out, and stir in the yolk of a beaten egg. When cold, make it into balls; brush them over with egg; strew bread crumbs over them, and fry them in hot fat; pile them in a dish, and garnish with fried parsley.

# FRIED PASTRY.

## CAKES, FRITTERS, CRULLERS, AND DOUGHNUTS.

We give below several of the best recipes known for frying pastry, taken from several private family books, (as are hundreds of others.) When properly made and fried, there is nothing more palatable and universally desired than those dishes; we will insure satisfaction in the use of them.

### 596. To Fry Pastry.

TIME.—*To fry six minutes.*

Use fresh sweet lard, have at least two or three inches in a deep frying pan to save burning, and to be handy use a FRYING SIEVE, which prevents the articles from touching the bottom of the pan, and also is handy to lift all in the pan out of the fat at once. In frying potatoes or small articles they can be tossed in it, instead of being turned with a fork; try your fat to see if it is hot with a small piece of dough, if it is hot enough it will rise quickly and soak no fat. Fry a delicate brown.

### 597. Raised Doughnuts.

TIME.—*To rise six hours.*

ARTICLES.—One cup of warm milk; one cup of sugar; one yeast cake; fat, size of an egg; salt and flour. Cinnamon or other spice to taste.

DIRECTIONS.—Sift the flour, add a little salt, beat the milk and fat together, prepare the yeast cake as directed in recipe 504, or use yeast. Make a stiff dough; when risen work in the spice, and cut out in any shape and fry.

### 598. Yeast Doughnuts.

TIME.—*Time to rise about six hours.*

ARTICLES.—One quarter of a pound of butter; half a pound of sugar; two tumblers full of milk; two eggs; a tea-cupful of yeast; spice to taste and flour.

DIRECTIONS.—Prepare as above, beat the eggs well with the sugar, and add. Fry; when cold sprinkle powdered sugar over them.

### 599. Fine Doughnuts.

TIME.—*Ten minutes to prepare.*

ARTICLES.—Three eggs; two cups of sugar; one table-spoonful of butter; a large cup of sweet or sour milk; one nutmeg; scant tea-spoonful of soda.

DIRECTIONS.—Beat the eggs well with the sugar and butter, spice to taste, add the milk and the soda mixed, and flour enough to roll. Fry at once.

### 600. Plain Cheap Doughnuts.

TIME.—*To prepare ten minutes.*

ARTICLES.—A pint of milk; one egg; one cup of sugar; half a tea-spoonful of soda; one tea-spoonful of cream of tartar; flour enough to roll.

DIRECTIONS.—Prepare and cook same as for fine doughnuts.

### 601. Fried Crullers.

TIME.—*A few minutes.*

ARTICLES.—Four eggs; half a pound of sugar; three ounces of butter; one gill of milk; one tea-spoonful of cinnamon, and flour and lard.

DIRECTIONS.—Prepare as for fine doughnuts; roll it out, cut the dough into stripes, twist them and drop them in boiling lard.

### 602. Fried Crackers.

Prepare same as for recipe No. 529, and fry in hot fat.

### 603. Wonders.

TIME.—*To make, an hour.*

ARTICLES.—A quarter of a pound of sugar; ten ounces of butter; one pound of flour; three eggs; a little nutmeg, and some yeast.

DIRECTIONS.—Work the sugar and butter together till quite soft, throw in the eggs that have been previously well beaten, then add the flour and a little nutmeg and yeast. Knead twenty minutes and let it rise, then roll between your hands into round balls, the size of a small potato, but do not add any more flour. Flour your pasteboard lightly, and roll each ball into a thin oval, the size of the hand; cut with a knife, three slits like bars in the center of the oval, cross the two center one with your fingers, and draw up the two sides between; put your finger through and drop it into boiling lard. Turn as they rise, and when a nice brown take them up with a fork.

### 604. Spanish Puffs.

TIME.—*To fry, twenty minutes.*

ARTICLES.—One pint of milk; one pint of flour; a little cinnamon; almond essence; four eggs, and sugar to your taste.

DIRECTIONS.—Put a pint of milk into a TEA-KETTLE BOILER and let it boil; add the same quantity of flour by degrees, a tea-spoonful at a time, stirring it together till it becomes a very stiff, smooth paste. Put it into a basin, add a little cinnamon, a little almond essence, and sugar to your taste. After you have put in all the ingredients, beat them well together for half an hour, adding, as you beat it, and by degrees, four eggs. Make some lard hot in a pan, drop into it pieces of this paste of about the size of a walnut, and fry them.

### 605. Lemon Turnovers.

TIME.—*To bake, twenty minutes.*

ARTICLES. — Three desert-spoonfuls of flour; one of powdered sugar; rind of one lemon; two ounces of butter; two eggs, and a little milk.

DIRECTIONS.—Mix the flour, sugar, and the grated rind of the lemon with a little milk to the consistency of batter; then add the eggs well beaten, and the butter melted. Fry

### 606. Snow Pancakes.

TIME.—*To fry a few minutes.*

ARTICLES.—Four ounces of flour; a quarter of a pint of milk; a little grated nutmeg; a pinch of salt; sufficient flour to make a thick batter; and three large spoonfuls of snow to each pancake.

DIRECTIONS.—Make a stiff batter with the flour and milk, a little grated nutmeg and the salt. Divide the batter into any number of pancakes, and add the snow to each. Fry them lightly, and serve quickly.

### 607. Batter Pancakes.

TIME.—*Ten minutes to make.*

ARTICLES.—Three eggs; one pint of milk; sufficient flour; a pinch of salt; and a little nutmeg.

DIRECTIONS.—Beat the eggs and stir them into the milk, add the salt and sufficient flour to make it into a thick smooth batter. Fry them in boiling fat; roll them over on each side, drain and serve them very hot, with lemon and sugar.

### 608. Rye Flour Pancakes.

TIME.—*Ten minutes to make.*

ARTICLES.—A pint of milk; two eggs; sugar; half a cup of flour to make a stiff batter; hot fat, a tea-spoonful.

DIRECTIONS.—Same as for batter pancakes.

### 609. Irish Pancakes.

TIME.—*To make ten minutes.*

ARTICLES.—Yolks of four eggs; whites of four; one pint of milk; a little grated nutmeg; two ounces of sugar; peel of a lemon grated; three ounces of fresh butter; and six ounces of flour.

DIRECTIONS.—Warm the milk in a TEA-KETTLE BOILER and strain into it the well-beaten eggs, with the sugar, a little nutmeg, and the peel of a lemon, grated; warm the butter and stir it into the milk. Then mix in the flour to form a smooth batter. Put a piece of butter at the bottom of the pan, pour in the batter, and fry the pancakes very thin. When done, place them on a hot dish, one over the other, and serve them quickly, and as hot as possible.

### 610. Fruit Fritters.

TIME.—*To fry ten minutes.*

ARTICLES. — One pound of flour; one ounce of yeast; a little milk; two ounces of loaf sugar; four eggs; three ounces of butter; the peel of half a lemon; marmalade, jam, or fruit.

DIRECTIONS.—Put the flour into a bowl, and put into the center the yeast; add sufficient milk to form a stiff dough, and set it by the fire to rise. Melt the butter, add it to the sugar, beat it all well together, add it to the dough, and again beat it until it will separate from the bowl. Roll this mixture into a number of balls, any size you prefer, fill each with marmalade, fruit, or jam, and set them to rise, with a floured paper under them. Then put them into a large pan of boiling lard and fry them nicely.

### 611. Orange Fritters.

TIME.—*A few minutes.*

ARTICLES.—Three oranges, butter, pounded sugar.

DIRECTIONS.—Peel the oranges, then cut them across into slices, pick out the seeds, and dip each slice of orange into a thick fritter batter. Fry them nicely, and serve them with sugar sifted over each. Any sliced fruit will answer as well.

### 612. Batter Fritters of all kinds.

TIME.—*To make, ten minutes.*

ARTICLES.—Eight ounces of flour; half a pint of water; two ounces of butter; whites of two eggs.

DIRECTIONS.—Mix the flour with the water into a smooth batter, dissolve the butter over a slow fire, and then stir it by degrees into the flour; then add the whites of the eggs whisked to a stiff froth, and stir them lightly in. Any cooked vegetables can be covered with this batter, and fried.

### 613. Bread Fritters.

TIME.—*A few minutes.*

ARTICLES.—Half a pound of currants; flour; half a pint of bread crumbs; a pint of milk; two ounces of butter; half a nutmeg; a quarter of a pound of sugar; a wine-glassful of brandy; and six eggs.

DIRECTIONS.—Grate the bread crumbs into the boiling milk, in which the butter and currants has been stirred, cover the pan and let it stand for an hour. Then beat the mixture thoroughly and add half a nutmeg grated, with the white powdered sugar and the brandy. Beat the eggs till very light, and stir them by degrees into the mixture. It should be brought to the consistency of a thin batter; and if it turns out too thin, add a little flour. Fry brown.

### 614. Croquettes of Rice.

TIME.—*An hour.*

ARTICLES.—Half a pound of rice; one pint and a half of milk; a quarter of a pound of butter; half a pound of sugar; one lemon; five eggs; and some bread crumbs.

DIRECTIONS.—Put the rice and the milk into a TEA-KETTLE BOILER, and let it simmer until quite tender. Rub the rind from the lemon with the sugar in the mortar, add it to the rice, and the yolks of the eggs, well beaten, stir it until the eggs thicken. When cold, form into small balls; whisk the eggs well in a basin, dip each ball into the egg, and then into the bread crumbs; smooth them with a knife, repeat the egg and crumbs, and put them into a frying sieve and place it in a stew-pan of boiling lard, and fry them lightly. When done, drain them from the fat and pile them on a dish; sift powdered sugar over them and serve hot.

### 615. Wafers.

TIME.—*A few minutes to make.*

ARTICLES.—A quarter of a pound of butter; a pound of flour; three eggs; salt; a teaspoonful of cinnamon; milk.

DIRECTIONS.—Make all into a batter, and bake same as for waffles.

### 616. Waffles.

TIME.—*A minute to bake.*

ARTICLES.—Ten ounces of flour; five of sugar; two eggs; flavor with essences; half a cup of wine; and milk.

DIRECTIONS.—Make a paste of the flour and milk, beat the sugar, eggs, and wine together, flavor to taste. Warm your waffle-irons, then grease them, fill them nearly full, close them, and place them over a fire. Turn the irons so as to bake the waffles on both sides; when done take out, butter, and sift sugar over them, and eat hot.

### 617. Yeast Waffles.

TIME.—*To bake a minute or two.*

ARTICLES.—Flour, one pound; milk, one pint; butter, one ounce; yeast; two eggs.

DIRECTIONS.—Beat the eggs, stir in the milk and, butter, add the flour, beat quite smooth, add sufficient yeast to make it rise; then bake as directed above.

### 618. Egg Waffles.

TIME.—*To make a few minutes.*

ARTICLES.—Three eggs; a cup of butter; a quart of milk; flour; a tea-spoonful of soda; two tea-spoonfuls of cream of tartar.

DIRECTIONS.—Make a batter of the eggs, milk, and as much flour as will thicken it; add the cream of tartar and soda in the usual way. Bake in the waffle-irons at once.

### 619. Nonesuch.

TIME.—*To make ten minutes.*

ARTICLES.—Yolks of five eggs; an even tea-spoonful of salt; flour.

DIRECTIONS.—Beat the eggs light, add the salt, and flour enough to form a stiff dough. Roll as thin as paper, cut out with a saucer, cut stripes in the center and fry. While hot, sprinkle sugar over them.

### 620. Yankee Marvels.

TIME.—*Half an hour.*

ARTICLES.—Four eggs; four table-spoonfuls of sugar; one table-spoonful of melted lard; flour enough to make a dough.

DIRECTIONS.—Prepare and fry as above.

### 621. Fried Pattie Paste.

TIME.—*Twenty minutes to make.*

ARTICLES.—One pound of flour; quarter of a pound of butter; half a pound of lard; a little salt.

DIRECTIONS.—Rub a little of the flour into a bowl with a pinch of salt, then rub in a little lard, add water enough to make it into a stiff paste, then flour the pasteboard and with your hands take out the paste; flour the roller, roll it out into a thin flat surface, spread over it rows of lard and butter, fold it over, then roll it out again; sprinkle a little flour, and repeat six times; it is then ready for any kind of pies, short cakes, or patties.

### 622. Patties and Pies.

TIME.—*Thirty minutes to make.*

ARTICLES.—Some of the above paste; and any kind of meat, poultry, or oysters. Fruit or vegetables may be used if desired.

DIRECTIONS.—Prepare the filling of meat, or any other article desired, to suit the taste; roll out the pattie paste the thickness of pie crust, cut it with a cake cutter, put a table-spoonful of the filling in the center, twist the edges together, and fry them a nice brown in plenty of boiling lard.

### 623. Patties and Pies.

Use the patties' paste. Line a dish with it and fill in with any meat or other articles, and bake; cut a hole in the top to let the steam out, and fill up with water.

### 623. Bread Patties.

TIME.—*A quarter of an hour.*

ARTICLES.—Cooked mince meat; slice of bread; yolk of egg; bread crumbs; cupful of milk or cream.

DIRECTIONS.—Cut some stale bread into thick slices, hollow out the center, dip each into the milk, brush them over with the yolk of a beaten egg; strew bread crumbs over them and fry a light brown, fill the center of one with the mince meat and cover with the other. Serve.

# GINGERBREAD, CAKES, PUFFS, PUDDINGS, ETC.

We give more recipes at the request of our friends, and can recommend them.

"Ginger is stimulating and aromatic, increases the secretion of the gastric juice, and removes flatulence. Used in moderation it is a very healthy and valuable condiment, and removes faintness and sickness in the stomach."—DR. JOHN KING.

Of all cakes none are more suitable for every one than ginger-bread or gingercakes; it rarely disagrees with any one. On pages 45 and 46 there are more recipes.

### 625. Rich Gingerbread.
TIME.—*Three quarters to one hour.*
ARTICLES.—Half a pound of butter; half a pound of sugar; half a pound of molasses; one pound of flour; half an ounce of ginger; one tea-spoonful of carbonate of soda; four eggs.

DIRECTIONS.—Put the butter, sugar, and molasses into a TEA-KETTLE BOILER together, and place it over the fire to melt. Then beat the eggs, and stir the melted butter, sugar, and molasses into the eggs, add the powdered ginger and carbonate of soda, then stir all together into the flour and bake.

### 626. Cheap Gingerbread.
TIME.—*Three quarters of an hour.*
ARTICLES.—One pound of flour; one pound of molasses; a quarter of a pound of butter; one egg; one ounce of ginger; a tea-spoonful of soda; a little milk.

DIRECTIONS.—Mix the ginger with the flour, warm the butter and molasses, and mix it well with the flour and ginger. Make a few spoonfuls of warm milk, dissolve a tea-spoonful of soda in it, and mix the whole up lightly with the egg well-beaten, and bake in a long buttered tin for three quarters of an hour. Just before it is removed from the oven brush it over with the yolk of an egg, well-beaten with a little milk, then put it back in the oven and finish baking. The time, of course, must be according to its size.

### 627. Gingercakes.
TIME.—*Half an hour.*
ARTICLES.—One pound of moist sugar; half a pound of butter; a cup of milk; one pound and three quarters of flour; half an ounce of ginger.

DIRECTIONS.—Put the sugar, butter, and milk into a TEA-KETTLE BOILER, let it boil until the butter is melted. Whilst it is quite hot, mix it with the flour and ginger. Roll it out thin, prick it, and cut it into any shape you like. If the paste gets stiff before you have rolled it all out, set it before the fire a little. Bake these cakes in a slack oven.

### 628. Gingerbread Loaf.
TIME.—*Three quarters of an hour to one hour.*
ARTICLES.—One pound of flour; one pound of molasses; six ounces of butter; four ounces of moist sugar; half an ounce of coriander seeds; half an ounce of caraway seeds; half a table-spoonful of soda; a quarter of a tea-cupful of cream; four eggs.

DIRECTIONS.—Melt the molasses and the butter together, add the moist sugar, the coriander and caraway seeds ground together, and ginger to your taste. Mix with the flour; mix the soda with a very little cream; mix all well together. Beat the eggs and add them to the gingerbread the very last thing. Line a tin with paper, butter it, and put the mixture in it. Bake in a slow oven.

### 629. Honeycomb Gingerbread.
TIME.—*Ten minutes.*
ARTICLES.—Half a pound of flour; half a pound of coarse sugar; a quarter of a pound of butter; one ounce of ginger; half an ounce of lemon peel; juice of one lemon; six ounces of molasses; a quarter of an ounce of butter for the tin.

DIRECTIONS.—Add the flour and sugar, rub into it the butter and the ginger, and mix it; put half an ounce of lemon peel, well grated, over it, and pour in the juice of a whole lemon. Use enough molasses to make it into a very thin paste that will spread over a sheet of tin, first having rubbed the tin with butter. Bake it in a moderate oven, and watch it carefully. When it is baked enough cut it into strips upon the tin, and roll it around your finger like a wafer.

These rolls must be kept in a tin case, if they should chance to get moist they must be renewed in the oven when wanted.

### 630. Cocoanut or Almond Gingerbread.
TIME.—*Three quarters of an hour.*
ARTICLES..—One pound of syrup; one pound of flour; one ounce of ground ginger; half a pound of butter; half a pound of moist sugar; seven ounces of grated cocoanut or pounded almonds; peel of two small lemons; one ounce and a half of candied orange peel.

DIRECTIONS.—Put the syrup into a TEA-KETTLE BOILER with the butter, and when hot pour it into the flour, previously mixed with the sugar, ginger grated, lemon peel, and sliced citron. Beat the mixture well together, and set it to become cold; then stir or beat into it the cocoanut or sweet almonds pounded, beat it for a few minutes, and then drop the mixture from a table-spoon on a buttered tin, any size you prefer the cakes to be, and bake them in a slow oven.

### 631. Orange Gingerbread.

ARTICLES.—Two pounds of flour; two pounds of molasses; eight ounces of candied orange peel; a pound of moist sugar; two ounces of ground ginger; one ounce of allspice; a pound of butter; one teacupful of milk; yolk of one egg.

DIRECTIONS.—Mix with the flour the candied orange peel cut very small, the moist sugar, the ground ginger, and allspice, and molasses; melt the butter till it is oiled, mix it well with the flour, &c., and put it in a cool place for ten or twelve hours. Roll out about half an inch thick; cut it into any form you please, or cut it into pieces rather longer than square; brush them over with milk mixed with the yolk of the egg, and bake them in a cool oven.

### 632. Gingerbread Nuts.

TIME.—*Twenty minutes to half an hour.*

ARTICLES.—One pound of sugar; two pounds of molasses; three quarters of a pound of butter; four pounds of flour; four ounces of ginger; one ounce of allspice; two spoonfuls of coriander seed; some candied orange peel; two spoonfuls of brandy; yolks of four eggs.

DIRECTIONS.—Mix the sugar, molasses, and butter, and melt all together; then stir in the flour, ground ginger, allspice, coriander seed, and the orange peel cut very small. Mix all into a paste with the eggs well beaten; add the brandy, and make them into nuts or cakes.

### 633. Sugar Ginger Crisps.

TIME.—*To bake about ten minutes.*

ARTICLES.—One cupful of sugar, two of molasses, one of butter; a teaspoonful of soda; ginger; flour.

DIRECTIONS.—Mix all the ingredients together, and add ginger to your taste, and flour enough to make a stiff dough. Roll the dough very thin and cut with a wine-glass, and bake in a quick oven.

### 634. Molasses Ginger Crisps.

TIME.—*About ten minutes.*

ARTICLES.—Two cups of molasses, one of lard; one tablespoonful of ginger; one dessertspoonful of soda; flour.

DIRECTIONS.—Mix all the above articles together; dissolve the soda in a little hot water, and add enough flour to make a stiff dough; roll thin.

### 635. Fruit Ginger Cake.

TIME.—*Nearly an hour.*

ARTICLES—One pound of flour; one cup of sugar; two of molasses; half a pound of butter; six eggs; one pound of currants; the same of raisins; half a pound of citron; one tablespoonful of ginger; one teaspoonful of cinnamon and allspice; one teaspoonful of soda and two of cream of tartar.

DIRECTIONS.—Mix all well together and bake.

### 636. Soft Ginger Cake.

TIME.—*About half an hour.*

ARTICLES.—One cup of sugar, three of molasses, one of butter, one of sweet milk; three eggs; seven cups of flour; one teaspoonful of soda beaten well into the molasses; ginger and spice to taste

DIRECTIONS.—Mix all in the usual way and bake.

### 637. Spice Ginger Cake.

TIME.—*About three quarters of an hour.*

ARTICLES.—Five eggs; two teacups of butter; four of flour; two of sugar; one teacup, not quite full, of molasses; teaspoonful of soda; a wine-glass of brandy; a tablespoonful of ginger; one of cinnamon, and one of allspice and cloves mixed.

DIRECTIONS.—Stir the soda into the molasses until it foams from the bottom; add the whites of the eggs, frothed, last; and next to the last add the molasses. Fruit may be added if desired.

### 638. Ginger Puffs.

TIME.—*Half an hour.*

ARTICLES.—Half a pound of flour; three eggs; one teaspoonful of grated ginger; a little nutmeg; a tablespoonful of loaf sugar; half a glass of white wine.

DIRECTIONS.—Add the grated ginger, pounded loaf sugar, and nutmeg, to the flour, and mix all together with the eggs, well beaten, and the wine. Bake them in cups in a quick oven, and pour a little wine sauce over them before they are sent to the table.

### 639. Ginger Pudding.

TIME.—*Three hours.*

ARTICLES.—A quarter of a pound of suet; half a pound of flour; a quarter of a pound of moist sugar; one good teaspoonful of ground ginger.

DIRECTIONS.—Chop a quarter of a pound of beef suet very fine; mix it with the flour, sugar, and ginger. Mix all dry, and put it into a well-buttered TEA-KETTLE BOILER; boil it three hours, and when done turn it out and serve with white wine sauce.

### 640. Mrs. B.'s Best Cheap Pudding.

TIME.—

ARTICLES.—Two quarts of bread, or crackers; one pound of raisins or currants; one cup of molasses; cloves, allspice, and nutmeg to taste; milk or water to soak the bread in; and salt.

DIRECTIONS.—Soak the bread in water (milk if you desire) until quite soft; mix all the articles together; put them in an earthen stone pot, then place the pot in a boiler or steamer, and steam from six to ten hours; then put in an oven and bake them slow four hours.

# FANCY DISHES FOR DESSERT.

We give below a number of fine dishes for dessert, many of which are rare, and will please those who use them. We all sometimes like to taste an odd or fancy dish, and they will be found here, with full directions how to make them.

### 641. Custard with Jelly.

TIME.—

ARTICLES.—One pint of milk, three five eggs sugar and flavor to taste, peel of half a lemon.

DIRECTIONS.—Put into a TEA-KETTLE BOILER the milk, sugar and the lemon peel cut thin; when it boils pour it out, whisk the whites and yolks of the eggs, and stir them gradually into the milk; pour it into a TEA-KETTLE BOILER, and stir it over the fire one way until it thickens; when cold pour it into custard glasses, and put a spoonful of clear jelly on some, and a dark colored jelly on the others; place the cups on a dish, and serve.

### 642. Tipsy Cake.

TIME.—*One hour to soak the cake.*

ARTICLES.—One stale sponge cake, one glass of brandy, sufficient wine to soak it, juice of half a lemon, three ounces of sweet almonds, one pint of rich custard.

DIRECTIONS.—Place a large sponge cake in the glass dish in which it is to be served, make a small hole in the centre, and pour in over the cake a sufficient quantity of sherry or raisin wine (mixed with the brandy and the juice of the lemon) to soak it thoroughly; then blanch two or three ounces of sweet almonds, cut them into long spikes, stick them all over the cake, and pour around it a pint of very rich custard.

### 643. A Cake Trifle.

TIME.—*An hour.*

ARTICLES.—A Savoy cake, or a Naples cake, a pint of milk, yolks of four eggs, whites of two, two ounces of sugar, one tea-spoonful of peach water, or any jam.

DIRECTIONS.—Take a Savoy or Naples cake, cut out the inside about an inch from the edge and bottom, leaving a shell; fill the inside with a custard made of the yolks of the eggs beaten with the milk, sweetened with the sugar, and flavored with the peach water; lay on it some strawberry, or any other jam you may prefer; beat the whites of the eggs with a little sifted sugar, until they will stand in a heap, pile it up on the cake over the preserves, and serve.

### 644. Rice and Pears.

TIME.—*One hour and a half.*

ARTICLES.—One breakfast cup and a half of rice, one pint of milk, a large table-spoonful of sugar, three eggs, a little cinnamon and nutmeg, baked pears.

DIRECTIONS.—Boil the rice till tender in the milk in a TEA-KETTLE BOILER, then put in the cinnamon, sugar, and nutmeg; take it up, let it get nearly cold, beat the eggs well, mix them with the rice, tie it down tightly in a floured cloth, and let it boil for one hour; turn it out, lay around it baked pears; garnish it with slices of lemon stuck into the rice.

### 645. Orange Sponge.

TIME.—*To make, an hour.*

ARTICLES.—One ounce of gelatine, one pint of water, juice of six or seven oranges, juice of one lemon, sugar to taste, whites of three eggs.

DIRECTIONS.—Dissolve the gelatine in the water, strain it and let it stand until nearly cold; then mix with it the juice of one lemon; add the whites of the eggs and sugar, and whisk the whole together until it looks white and like a sponge. Put it into a mould and turn it out the next day.

### 646. Apple Snow.

TIME.—*One hour and a half.*

ARTICLES.—Eight apples, half a pound of sugar, juice of one lemon, whites of three eggs.

DIRECTIONS.—Add to the pulp of the baked apples the sugar, the juice of the lemon and the whites of the eggs; whisk the whole together for one hour: put some cream or custard in a dish, and drop the whisked broth on it in large flakes; a pinch of alum makes the whisk firmer.

### 647. Apple de Par.

TIME.—

ARTICLES.—One pound of loaf sugar, half a pint of water, peel and juice of one lemon, a pound and a half of apples.

DIRECTIONS.—To the sugar add the water and the peel of the lemon cut thin, let it boil about ten or fifteen minutes in the TEA-KETTLE BOILER; take out the peel and put in the apples cut in slices, and the juice of the lemons; when they have boiled until soft enough to pulp, press them through a hair sieve, put them back into the TEA-KETTLE BOILER, and let them boil until quite stiff, stirring all the time, then put it into small moulds, or into a soup plate, and cut it in slices of any form you please for dessert. If not boiled so stiff, it may be turned out of teacups, and custard poured over it as a second course dish.

### 648. Apple Hedgehog.

ARTICLES.—Fifteen or sixteen large apples, four or five pounds of boiling apples for marmalade, three ounces of loaf sugar, whites of three eggs, some apricots or strawberry jam, half a pound of sweet almonds, half a pint of water, half a pound of sugar for the syrup.

DIRECTIONS.—Pare and core the apples, make a syrup with the water and sugar, and simmer the apples until tolerable tender in a TEA-KETTLE BOILER; drain them, and fill the part from which the core is taken with apricot or strawberry jam, then arrange them on a dish in the form of a hedgehog; stew the boiling apples down to a smooth, dry marmalade, and fill the spaces between the apples with it, covering it also entirely over them; whisk the whites of the eggs and sugar to a solid froth, spread it evenly over the hedgehog, and sift sugar over it; blanch and cut into long spikes the almonds, and stick them thickly over the surface; place the dish in a moderate oven to slightly color the almonds, and make the apples hot through.

### 649. Gooseberry Fool.

TIME.—*Two to make.*
ARTICLES.—Two quarts of gooseberries, one quart of water, sugar to taste, two quarts of new milk, yolks of four eggs, a little grated nutmeg.

DIRECTIONS.—Put two quarts of gooseberries into a TEA-KETTLE BOILER with a quart of water; when they begin to turn yellow and swell, drain the water from them and press them with the back of a spoon through a colander, sweeten them to your your taste, and set them to cool; put the milk over the fire, beaten up with the yolks of the eggs and a little grated nutmeg, stir it over the fire until it begins to simmer, then take it off and stir it gradually into the cold gooseberries; let it stand until cold and serve it. The eggs may be left out and milk only added. Half this quantity makes a good dishful.

### 650. Gateau de Pommes.

TIME.—*Three quarters of an hour.*
ARTICLES.—One pound of sugar, one pint of water, two pounds of apples, juice and peel of one large lemon, some rich custard.

DIRECTIONS.—Boil the sugar in the water in a TEA-KETTLE BOILER until the water has almost evaporated, then add the apples pared and cored, the juice of a large lemon and the peel grated; boil all together till quite stiff, then put it into a mould, and when cold turn it out and serve it.

### 651. Stewed Fruit—A Compote.

TIME.—*Twenty minutes.*
ARTICLES.—One pound and a half of fruit, three-quarters of a pound of sugar and one pint of milk.

DIRECTIONS.—The fruit should be freshly gathered. Make a syrup of the sugar in the water for each two pints and a half of fruit; let this syrup boil gently for ten or twelve minutes, and skim it thoroughly; then throw in the fruit; let it boil up quickly in a TEA-KETTLE BOILER, and afterwards simmer until quite tender, which will usually be in about fifteen minutes. Be careful that the fruit does not crack.

### 652. Iced Fruits for Dessert.

TIME.—*To dry, about three hours.*
ARTICLES.—A quarter of a pint of water, pounded loaf sugar, whites of two eggs, currants.

DIRECTIONS.—Procure some of the finest bunches of currants, well beat the whites of the eggs and mix them with the spring water, dip each bunch of currants separately into the egg and water, drain them for two minutes and roll them in some finely powdered loaf sugar, repeat the rolling in sugar, and lay them carefully on sheets of white paper to dry, when the sugar will become crystalized; arrange them on a dish with a a mixture of any other fruit; plums, grapes, or any fruit may be iced in the same manner for dessert.

### 653. Stewed Plums.

TIME.—*One hour to stew the plums separately; one hour and a half in the syrup.*
ARTICLES.—One pound and a half of plums, three-quarters of a pint of syrup, two table-spoonfuls of port wine, peel and juice of one lemon, one pound of loaf sugar.

DIRECTIONS.—Stew the plums in a little water; when tender strain them, and put to the water the sugar; boil it for one quarter of an hour in a TEA-KETTLE BOILER, skimming it carefully; when clear, add the juice, put in the plums, and let the whole simmer very slowly for about an hour and a half; when done take out the plums in a glass dish and pour the syrup over them; set them in a cold place.

### 654. Stewed Pears.

TIME.—*Three or four hours.*
ARTICLES.—Nine or ten large pears, seven ounces of loaf sugar, seven cloves, six allspice, rather more than half a pint of water, a quarter of a pint of port wine, a few drops of cochineal.

DIRECTIONS.—Pare and core nine or ten large pears, dividing them with part of the stalk on each, put them into a TEA-KETTLE BOILER, with the sugar and water, wine, cloves, allspice, and cochineal; let them stew gently over a clear fire until tender, and when done take them carefully out, and place the slices of pears in a glass dish; boil up the syrup for a few minutes, and when cool pour it over the pears and put them by to get cold; the peel of a lemon cut thin is an improvement to the flavor of the fruit.

## PRESERVES.

### JAMS, JELLIES, MARMALADE.

For making preserves a good sound fruit and good white (granulated is really the cheapest) sugar should always be used.

#### 655. The Fruit

should be sound, ripe, and good; any rind can be preserved, as well as many kinds of vegetables.

#### 656. The Sugar.

We use for all purposes white granulated sugar; it is the most economical in the end, dry and handy.

#### 657. The Preserving Kettles

Most persons use a copper or brass kettle, but we prefer, for large lots, a porcelain one; for a quart or two use the TEA-KETTLE BOILER. Never keep preserves in the kettle any longer than to cook them, as the metal will injure them.

#### 658. The Proportion of Fruit and Sugar.

A pound of fruit to a pound of sugar is generally used; a tumblerful of water to a pound of sugar to make the syrup. *Always* skim off all *the froth or scum.*

#### 659. To Keep Preserves Good.

Put them in stone jars or vessels of glass, earthen or stone; cover tightly and keep in a cool, dry place. *Look at them every month*; if they are turning, scald them and return to the jars. *Clean the jars.*

#### 660. Damson Cheese.

TIME.—*One hour and a half to boil.*
ARTICLES.—To every quart of plums allow a quarter of a pound of loaf sugar, and to every pound of pulp add half a pound of sugar.
DIRECTIONS.—Gather the plums when full ripe, put them into a jar, and to every quart of plums add the sugar. Bake them in a moderate oven until they are soft; then rub them through a hair sieve. To every pound of pulp add half a pound of loaf sugar beaten fine; boil it over a slow fire in a TEA-KETTLE BOILER, and stir it all the time; pour it into shapes, tie brandy paper over them, and keep them in a dry place. They will not be fit to use for three or four months. All cheese may be made by recipe except greengage, which does not require so much sugar.

#### 661. Green Gooseberry Jam.

TIME.—*Forty-five minutes.*
ARTICLES.—Three pounds of gooseberries; two pounds and a half of loaf sugar.
DIRECTIONS.—Pick off the stalks and buds from the gooseberries; bruise them lightly; put them into a preserving pan and boil them quickly for eight or ten minutes, stirring all the time; add the sugar pounded and sifted to the fruit, and boil it quickly for three quarters of an hour, carefully removing the scum as it rises. When done, put it into pots, cover it with brandy paper, and secure it closely down with paper moistened with the white of an egg.

#### 662. Green Gooseberry Jelly—An excellent substitute for Guava Jelly.

TIME.—*One hour and twenty-five minutes to boil the jelly.*
ARTICLES.—Six pounds of gooseberries; four pints of water; one pound of sugar to each pound of fruit.
DIRECTIONS.—Wash some green gooseberries very clean, after having taken off the tops and stalks; then to each pound of fruit pour three-quarters of a pint of spring water, and simmer them until they are well broken; turn the whole into a jelly-bag or cloth, and let the juice drain through; weigh the juice and boil it rapidly for fifteen minutes; draw it from the fire and stir into it, until entirely dissolved, an equal weight of good sugar sifted fine; then boil the jelly from fifteen minutes to twenty minutes longer, or until it jellies strongly on the spoon. It must be perfectly cleared from scum. Then pour it into small jars, moulds or glasses. It ought to be pale and transparent.

#### 663. Strawberry Jam.

TIME.—*One hour.*
ARTICLES.—To six pounds of strawberries allow three pounds of sugar.
DIRECTIONS.—Procure some fine scarlet strawberries, strip off the stalks and put them into a preserving pan over a moderate fire; boil them for half an hour, keeping them constantly stirred. Break the sugar into small pieces, and mix them with the strawberries after they have been removed from the fire; then place it again over the fire, and boil it for another half hour very quickly. Put it into pots, and when cold cover it over with brandy paper, and a piece of paper moistened with the white of an egg over the top.

#### 664. Strawberry Jelly.

TIME.—*Half an hour.*
ARTICLES.—Equal weight of sugar and strawberry juice.
DIRECTIONS.—Press some ripe strawberries through a delicately clean cloth; then strain the juice very clean, and stir into it an equal weight of sugar dried and pounded very fine. When the sugar is dissolved put into a TEA-KETTLE BOILER over a clear fire, and let it boil for half an hour, skimming it carefully as the scum rises. Put into glass jars or pots, and when cold cover it over as above directed.

#### 665. To Preserve Plums.

TIME.—*Three-quarters of an hour.*
ARTICLES.—To three pounds of plums allow three pounds of sugar.

# JAMS, JELLIES, MARMALADE.

DIRECTIONS.—Prick the plums with a fine needle to prevent their breaking, put them into a preserving pan with only sufficient water to cover them and set them over a gentle fire until the water simmers; then take them out and set them on a sieve to drain; add to the water in which the plums were boiled the above quantity of pounded sugar; boil it quickly, skimming it as the scum rises, until the syrup sticks to the spoon; then put in the greengages and let them boil until the sugar bubbles, then pour the whole into a basin and let it stand until the next day; drain the syrup from the fruit, boil it up quickly and pour it over the plums; then boil the fruit in it for five or six minutes, put them into jars, pour the syrup over them, and cover them over with brandy paper. The kernels must be blanched and boiled with the fruit.

### 666. Rhubarb Marmalade.

TIME.—*Three quarters of an hour if young rhubarb, and one hour and a half if old.*

ARTICLES.—To each pound of loaf sugar, one pound and a half of rhubarb stalks, peel of half a lemon.

DIRECTIONS.—Cut the rhubarb stalks into pieces about two inches long, and put them into a TEA-KETTLE BOILER with the loaf sugar broken small, the peel of the lemon cut thin, and the almonds blanched and divided. Boil the whole well together, put it into pots, and cover it as directed for other preserves.

### 667. Rhubarb and Orange Preserves.

TIME.—*One hour.*

ARTICLES.—Six oranges, one quart of rhubarb, one pound and a half of loaf sugar.

DIRECTIONS.—Peel the oranges carefully; take away the white rind and the pulps; slice the pulps into a TEA-KETTLE BOILER with the peel cut very small; add the rhubarb cut very fine, and sugar. Boil the whole down in the usual way with preserves.

### 668. Peach Preserves without Boiling.

TIME.—*About three quarters of an hour.*

ARTICLES.—One pound of sugar to three pounds of peaches; a quarter of a pint of water to each pound of sugar; white of an egg to every four pounds.

DIRECTIONS.—Pare and cut in halves some ripe peaches and dry them in a hot sun or warm oven for two days; then weigh them and make a syrup of the sugar, water, eggs. Stir it until it is dissolved, then set it over the fire; boil and skim it until the syrup is thick and clear; put in the kernels blanched, and when cold put a piece of paper to fit the inside of the pots, or jars, dipped in thick sugar syrup, over the top of the preserves, and close it over securely with tissue paper moistened with the white of an egg.

### 669. Fruit Preserved without Cooking.

TIME.—*About one hour.*

ARTICLES.—Any fruit and double-refined sugar.

DIRECTIONS.—Take any fruit, and put them into a deep dish; pour boiling water over to cover them, then cover the basin with a thickly folded towel, and let it remain until the water is nearly cold; take them out one by one and rub the skins off with a coarse towel; put a layer of them in a jar, cover them thickly with the best double-refined sugar pounded and sifted; then put another layer of fruit; and fruit and sugar alternately until the jar is full, the sugar being last; close and seal them down immediately, and set the jar in a cool, dry, dark place.

### 670. Fruit Jam.

TIME.—*Altogether two hours and a half.*

ARTICLES. — To every pound of fruit after being prepared three quarters of a pound of loaf sugar, juice of one small lemon, and the peel of one large one grated.

DIRECTIONS.—Pare and core the apples, cut them into very thin slices, and put them into a TEA-KETTLE BOILER, and let the fruit stew for about two hours; then put them into a preserving pan with the sugar pounded and the juice and grated peel of a lemon. Simmer the whole over a clear fire for about half an hour; after it begins to simmer all over, carefully remove the scum as it rises, and when done put the preserves into pots. When cold cover them with paper dipped into white of an egg and stretched over the top, with a piece of oiled paper next the jam.

### 671. Fruit Ginger.

TIME.—*About three quarters of an hour.*

ARTICLES.—Two pounds of apples, pears, or other fruit; one pint and a half of water; two pounds of loaf sugar; and a little ginger.

DIRECTIONS.—Put into a TEA-KETTLE BOILER the sugar pounded fine and the water; boil and skim it well, and then add the ginger; pare, core, and divide some fruit, and put them into a TEA-KETTLE BOILER with the syrup; boil them quickly until very clear, then lay them carefully on a dish; put the syrup into a jar, and when cold put in the slices of apples, and tie it closely over to exclude the air.

# PICKLING VEGETABLES AND FRUITS.

We do not consider pickles healthy for the well, and they are positively injurious to the weak and sick. No case is upon record, that we know of, of their curing the sick, but many of their killing the feeble invalid; yet a few now and then would not seriously injure the well and strong. Immense quantities are put up every year, sold, and eaten, and it is considered a necessity of civilization. As many families desire to put them up, we give a number of recipes that will aid the pickler.

### 672. The Vinegar.

Procure always the best apple, or white wine vinegar. *The success of good pickling depends upon using good vinegar. Always boil the vinegar unless stated otherwise.*

### 673. The Vegetables and Fruit

should be sound and good.

### 674. Cooking Utensils to use in Pickling.

Use saucepans or kettles lined with porcelain. If copper or tin is used to boil vinegar in, do not let it remain in them a moment longer than is necessary to boil them. Use WOODEN KNIVES AND FORKS.

### 675. The Bottles, Jars, or Vessels.

Use glass bottles for pickles. If jars are used they must be unglazed, *as the glaze,acted upon by the vinegar,* produces a strong poison. Wooden vessels for large quantities are best. Fill either of them three-quarters full of pickles, then fill with vinegar.

### 676. From July to October.

Cauliflowers, peppers, cucumbers, onions, garlic, melons, tomatoes, beans, cabbage, mushrooms, beets, artichokes, horseradish, peaches, plums, and barberries may be pickled.

### 677. Indian Pickle, to keep Ten Years.

TIME.—*Two weeks, to prepare.*
ARTICLE.—One pound of ginger root, one pound of garlic, half a pound ground mustard, quarter of a pound of mustard seed, two ounces of dry peppers, half an ounce of tumeric, same of cayenne pepper, a gallon of best vinegar.
DIRECTIONS.—Put the garlic in a strong brine for three days, soak the ginger over night, slice it, also slice the peppers and garlic, dry them, mash the mustard seed and tumeric; put all, with the vinegar, into a large stone jar stir it well every day for ten days, and cover closely; do not boil the vinegar. You can add more vinegar as it is used up. Dry any vegetable and put in this pickle, and it will keep them. USE LESS GARLIC, IF PREFERRED.

### 678. East Indian Piccalilly.

TIME.—*Three days to prepare.*
ARTICLES.—A pound each of garlic and ginger, whole black pepper and mustard seed, an ounce of tumeric, half an ounce of cayenne pepper, two quarts of vinegar.
DIRECTIONS.—Take a pound of ginger, let it lie in salt and water one night, then cut it in thin slices; take one pound of garlic, peel, divide, and salt it three days, then wash and dry it in the sun, on a sieve; take the pound of black pepper, the mustard seed and the tumeric bruised very fine, and a little cayenne pepper; put all these ingredients into a quart jar, with the vinegar boiled and poured over them, and when cold, fill the jar three parts full, and let it stand for a fortnight. Everything you wish to pickle must be salted and dried in the sun for three days. The jar must be full of liquor; and, after it is finished, for use stop it down for six weeks or two months before using it. The vinegar must be thrown over when the spices and garlic are hot.

### 679. To Pickle any Vegetables.

TIME.—*Ten days.*
ARTICLES.—Brine, vinegar, whole pepper, mustard seed, allspice, a small piece of alum and any vegetables.
DIRECTIONS.—Make a brine of salt and water which will bear an egg, let your vegetables remain in that for twenty-four hours, then take them from the brine and lay them on a pan; make a sufficient quantity of vinegar boiling hot, adding whole pepper, allspice and mustard seed; pour it over the pickles, and let them remain until the next day, then strain it off, boil it again, pour it over, and cover the pickles with a thickly-folded cloth; drain off the vinegar the next day, add a few bits of alum the size of a pea to it, make it boiling hot and again pour it over the pickles; let them remain for a day or two, then cut one across, and if it is not green through, scald the vinegar again, and pour it over them; in a few days, divide the pickles, and put those of an equal size into jars, cover them with the cold vinegar, and cover them down for use. Or they may be put into jars for immediate use, with a cloth folded over the top and a plate over the cloth.

### 680. To Pickle Plums like Olives.

TIME.—*Twenty-four hours.*
ARTICLES.—Green plums, vinegar, mustard seed and salt.
DIRECTIONS.—Make a pickle of vinegar, mustard seed and salt; make it boiling hot, then pour it over green plums gathered before they begin to turn, or before the stone is formed; let them stand all night, then drain off the vinegar, make it hot again and pour it over the plums. When cold cover them closely over.

## PICKLING VEGETABLES AND FRUITS.

### 681. To Pickle Peaches.
TIME.—*Eight or ten days.*
ARTICLES.—Half a bushel of peaches, one gallon of vinegar, four pounds of brown sugar, five or six cloves into each peach, two ounces of cinnamon.
DIRECTIONS.—Take the sound peaches, remove the down with a brush, make the vinegar hot, add to it the sugar, boil and skim it well, stick five or six cloves into each peach, then pour the vinegar boiling hot over them, cover them over, and set them in a cold place for eight or ten days; then drain off the vinegar, make it hot, skim it, and again pour it over the peaches; let them become cold, then put them into glass jars, and secure them as for preserves. The cinnamon and cloves can be added to the peaches, and the hot vinegar poured over them.

### 682. Sweet Green Tomato Piccalilly.
TIME.—*To boil, about one hour.*
ARTICLES.—A peck of green tomatoes, five table-spoonfuls of ground mustard, half a pint of mustard seed, two table-spoonfuls of ground cinnamon, one of cloves, one pound of brown sugar, three quarts of vinegar, some celery tops.
DIRECTIONS.—Peel and slice the tomatoes, boil all together until all are done.

### 683. To Pickle Whole Tomatoes.
TIME.—*To prepare, three days.*
ARTICLES.—One peck of tomatoes, a gallon of vinegar, one ounce of whole cloves, one of white pepper, one of cinnamon, three ounces of mustard.
DIRECTIONS.—Prick each tomato with a fork to allow some of the juice to exude, put them into a deep pan, sprinkle some salt between each layer, and let them remain for three days covered, then wash off the salt and cover them with a pickle of cold water which has been boiled with the spices. It will be ready for use in ten or twelve days, and is an excellent sauce for roast meat of any kind.

### 684. To Pickle Beets.
TIME —*Three quarters of an hour to one hour and a half.*
ARTICLES.—Three quarts of vinegar, half an ounce of mace, half an ounce of ginger, some horseradish, the beets.
DIRECTIONS.—Boil the beets the above time, cut them into any form you please, or gimp them in the shape of wheels and put them into a jar; boil three quarts of vinegar, with the mace, ginger, and a few slices of horseradish, and pour it while very hot over the beets; tie them over, and set them in a dry place.

### 685. To Pickle Cauliflowers.
ARTICLES.—Three ounces of coriander seed, one ounce of mustard seed, one ounce of ginger, half an ounce of mace, half an ounce of nutmegs, three quarts of water.
DIRECTIONS.—Gather on a fine day some of the whitest and closest cauliflower you can procure, break them into bunches, and scald them in salt and water, taking care they do not boil, or it would spoil their color; set them to cool, covering them over; then put them on a colander, sprinkle them with salt, and let them drain for a day and night; then place the bunches in jars, pour boiling salt and water over them, and let them remain all night; then drain them through a hair sieve, and put them into glass jars; boil the vinegar with the ginger, mustard, nutmeg, and coriander seeds, and when cold, pour it over the cauliflowers, and tie them closely over.

### 686. To Pickle Onions.
ARTICLES.—Onions, vinegar, ginger, and whole pepper.
DIRECTIONS.—Take some nice onions and throw them into a TEA-KETTLE BOILER half full of boiling water, and let them remain ten minutes. Then take them out quickly and lay them between two cloths to dry; boil some vinegar with the ginger and whole pepper, and when cold, pour it over the onions in glass jars, and tie them closely over.

### 687. To Pickle Peppers.
ARTICLES.—Some peppers, vinegar, an ounce of nutmeg, salt and water; one quart of vinegar to the above amount of spices.
DIRECTIONS.— Pick some fine peppers with the stalks on just before they turn red, and remove the seeds by opening a small place at the side; set them in strong salt and water for three days, changing it three times; then take them out and place between a thick cloth to become dry; put them into a jar and cover them with vinegar, previously boiled with the mace and grated nutmeg, and let it get cold.

### 688. To Pickle Barberries.
Take a quantity of barberries not over ripe, pick off the leaves and dead stalks, put them into jars with a large quantity of strong salt and water, and tie them down with a bladder; when you see a scum rise on the barberries, put them into fresh salt and water, cover them close, and set them by for use.

### 689. To Pickle Cabbage.
ARTICLES.—To one quart of vinegar one ounce of whole pepper.
DIRECTIONS.—Remove the coarse leaves from some cabbage, and wipe them very clean; cut them in long thin slices or shreds and put them on a large sieve, well covering them with salt, and let them drain all night, then put them into stone jars, and pour over them some boiling vinegar and whole peppers; cover them over and set them by for use.

# COFFEE.

### THE DIFFERENT KINDS—THE TRUE WAY TO BUY, ROAST, AND MAKE IT.

Recipes No. 9 and 10 gives directions how to make coffee, but this article will give more information upon the subject, which is important to every family.

We are very fond of coffee, and that of the best quality. We have used Mocha, African, Java, Rio, Maracaibo, and many others, both male and female, plain and mixed. For years we have experimented with coffee and coffee pots of every kind and quality, patented, and the old way so much used—boiling. The results of all this we now give to the public, and we assure all who will try our mode of buying, roasting, making, and preparing it to drink, that they will never use any other plan.

### 690. How to Buy Coffee.

Always buy it green (or unroasted) at wholesale, as it will keep green for a year if kept in a dry, clean place, in a good, tight box. If bought at retail buy it green, as you can see what you purchase, and are more likely to get the best article.

### 691. Mocha Coffee.

Mocha coffee is the best, but very expensive, being nearly double the price of Java; the flavor is very delicate and fine, and but few stores keep it; at times there is not a ton in New York City.

### 692. African Coffee.

This is similar in flavor to Mocha, and, like it, scarce and hard to procure. The male berry is the finest flavor.

### 693. Real Java Coffee.

For general use this is the best; it can always be had, and we like it nearly as well as Mocha. It has a fine flavor, but much that is sold for Java is not so.

### 694. Maracaibo Coffee

Stands next in order of quality, and is cheaper than the other kinds, a little stronger flavor, and does not waste so much in roasting. Many persons like it.

### 695. St. Domingo Coffee.

This is another cheap coffee, but very good for family use. It is stronger than Java.

### 696. Rio Coffee.

This is the strongest and cheapest in the market, and is used largely in the south and west. Many persons are fond of it.

### 697. Coffee made from Grain, etc.

Many substitutes have been used, such as rye, peas, corn, wheat, barley, dandelion, roots, chickory, and other articles of various kinds, yet nothing can be made that will in reality take its place. Nature intended coffee to be made into a beverage and nothing else; it is good for nothing else, but it is good for that; *and all the artificial substitutes, separately or together, will not make a good, healthy cup of coffee.*

### 698. How to Roast Coffee.

Roast once a week, and keep it in a close glass jar, tin can, or tight vessel.

Roast it until it is of a good deep uniform brown color (or buy it the same color). A cylinder, of which there are several kinds in the market, is better than a pan; spread it out on a pan to cool. Coffee swells one third after roasting, and loses about one-eighth or more in weight.

### 699. To Grind Coffee.

Never grind it until about to use it, as the flavor evaporates rapidly.

When BERNEY'S COFFEE CONE is used, grind the coffee as fine as possible; but for other vessels grind coarse. The CONE is intended to get all the strength at once, therefore the coffee must be ground to a fine powder.

### 670. To make Coffee the Right Way.

We have tried every way, and have come to the conclusion that the only way to make it is with BERNEY'S COFFEE CONE; *and it is a very simple, very easy, and a very quick way, saving nearly half the coffee, and always having it hot, fresh, clear, and strong;* saving all that fine delicate flavor which delights the palate, and is so exhilarating, refreshing and stimulating.

COFFEE SHOULD NEVER BE BOILED; it is a crude, improper way. Grind it to a fine powder, and put the quantity required in the CONE, pour on the boiling hot water, and the coffee is made; but first place the CONE in an earthen, crockery, or glass pitcher, or tea-pot. The coffee will come through as clear as brandy in a minute. Another thing, you can make it strong or weak as you may desire, as the coffee is ground to a powder, the boiling water passes through all of it and carries all the strength with it. If you wish to weaken it, add more water to the coffee. We make it very strong, and reduce it with hot milk instead of water

### 671. To make Coffee the Wrong Way.

Boil it and spoil it at once, for you drive the aroma up stairs; by using the machine coffee-pots you merely waste money, time, and coffee.

## 672. How the Coffee Cone was Invented.

The inventor, being extravagantly fond of coffee, had tried nearly all the so-called improved coffee-pots, but they all had faults. Some of these were used to boil the coffee in, some to boil and filter it, and others only to strain it,—but all of them were made of TIN. Now the cooks, in using them, would set them to boiling; and many times an hour before it was wanted. Again, they would grind the coffee coarse, and deluge it with water, and as it must be cooked and be ready for the family, they generally got slops. Again, the cook would leave the coffee grounds to remain in the pot, or wash it out with cold water, leaving some of the old coffee to remain in; this would spoil the good coffee. If any doubt it, try it and see.

The result was such as to determine Mr. Berney to invent the CONE, so that he could have it made in a minute, on his dining-table, in a pitcher; no boiling away of the strength and aroma; no spoilt coffee by dirty pots, BUT FRESH, PURE, CLEAR, AND STRONG COFFEE, WITH ALL THE DELICATE FLAVOR PRESERVED.

## MEDICINAL PROPERTIES OF COFFEE.

There are many medicinal virtues in coffee. It cures

INDIGESTION.—When taken in moderation it is a gentle stimulus to the digestive organs.

HEADACHE.—It relieves some forms of headache.

FATIGUE AND EXHAUSTION.—It is excellent when a person is fatigued or exhausted.

DRUNKENNESS.—Very strong coffee will cure drunkenness. Many fashionable bar-rooms keep it made for that purpose. It is eminently useful to cure the habitual drinker, or those who wish to cure themselves of the habit of using intoxicating liquors.

WAKEFULNESS.—It will keep any one awake, and therefore should not be drank last before going to bed.

BAD TASTE OR BREATH.—It will take away the disagreeable taste from a persons mouth, and for a time a bad breath.

DIARRHŒA, DYSENTERY.—In some persons it will check diarrhœa and dysentery.

STIMULANTS.—As a stimulant to the brain it is used by many persons. It renders it more active, and enriches the mind with ideas.

---

PROFESSOR BLOT, Founder of the New York Cooking Academy, etc., on Making Coffee:—

"There are several good filters, but the majority of people find them too complicated for daily use. *Good coffee cannot* be made in a utensil often, but wrongly, called a coffee pot, which is nothing but a pot. With such a utensil the coffee must be boiled, and as no liquor can be boiled without allowing the steam to escape, and the steam, made by boiling coffee, being its aroma, therefore, the best part of the coffee is evaporated, before it is served."

---

MRS. A. B. HILL, "Authoress of Housekeeping Made Easy," etc., remarks:—

"That after being made, coffee loses every moment some of its delightful aroma. The coffee-pot should always be kept clean, well scalded, and scoured after each boiling. It is the practice of slovenly, careless cooks, to leave the grounds from time to time in the boiler, and when the vessel is needed, empty and hastily rinse it, leaving much of the former contents adhering to the sides. The result of such management is, that the coffee, instead of being the deliciously exhilarating drink it might be, is flat, insipid, muddy, and absolutely pernicious."

And such is the case—the old coffee adhering to the sides, spoils all the good put in it.— EDITOR.

---

DR. JOHN KING, the celebrated Head of the the Eclectic Medical Fraternity in the West, says:—

"If made, or heat applied, or boiled too long, coffee becomes unpleasantly bitter. The sooner it is used after it is made, the more agreeable and stimulating it will prove, as it rapidly loses its most desirable properties by being kept.

"Taken in moderation, it is a gentle stimulus to the digestive apparatus. Strong coffee is an excellent antidote for opium or strong liquors. Coffee is useful in many cases—a valuable cordial restorative after exhaustion and fatigue, as well as to cure drunkenness. It should, however, never be used to excess."

---

DR. WARREN, of Boston, says:—

"Good coffee prevents the waste and exhaustion of the body, but it must be used as soon as made."

Coffee made by this invention (the COFFEE CONE) is clear and free from all grounds; and, by its cone shape, it fits any silver-plated or stone-china table pot, or pitcher. The cone shape also extracts all the strength from the coffee. The poorest, yet most common plan of making coffee is to boil it; yet no one who understands the nature of coffee, or any thing of the eatable or drinkable kind, would allow the odor to escape. A kitchen should be as free from odor of any kind as the parlor.

---

MR. SOYER, the great French Cook, says:—

"Filtering is the only way to make coffee."

We might fill this book with just such articles from eminent physicians and cooks, in relation to coffee.

As coffee costs so much now it is important to make it right, and we give the only true way that it can be made.

# PLEASANT AND REFRESHING DRINKS.

We all know that a cool drink in summer, and a stimulating one at any time, is delightful; to supply that want, many, too many adulterated poisonous drinks are made, to injure and destroy the body. We give a sample of them in another page; but the recipes here will enable families to make their own beverages cheap, pure, and good.

PURE WINE is strengthening and good to drink. The publisher of this work saved his life twice by the use of it. In moderation it will harm no one; but the difficulty is to get pure wine, but the recipes will enable those who desire them to do so.

### 703. Raisin Wine.

TIME.—*To stand twelve days.*

ARTICLES.—Five pounds of raisins to a gallon of water.

DIRECTIONS.—Take the raisins, pick them from the stalks, and chop them very small; then put them into a tub, and pour over them hot soft water. Let this be strained twice or thrice every day for twelve days successively, then pour the liquor into a cask, make a toast of bread, and while it is hot spread it on each side with yeast, and put it into the vessel. It will be fit to drink in four months.

### 704. Superior Ginger Wine.

TIME—*Fit to bottle in three months.*

ARTICLES.—One pound of Jamaica ginger; fifty-six pounds of loaf sugar; six dozen lemons; two bottles of brandy; eighteen gallons of water; two table-spoonfuls of new yeast.

DIRECTIONS.—Take the best Jamaica ginger, slice it very thin, and tie it in a cloth. Boil it with the sugar and the water for three quarters of an hour, skimming it all the time. Pare the lemons very thin, and pour the boiling liquor over the peels, let it stand until the next day, then stir in the juice of the lemons, and put it into the cask with the ginger and the yeast. Stir all well together and let it stand until it has done working; then add the brandy and bung it up close. It will be fit to bottle in three months.

### 705 Currant Wine.

ARTICLES.—To every gallon of currants, one gallon of water, three pounds and a half of moist sugar; and a gill of brandy.

DIRECTIONS.—To every gallon of juice, put the same quantity of cold water, and three and a half pounds of moist sugar. Put it into your cask, reserving some of the liquor for filling up. Put the cask in a warm, dry place, and the liquor will ferment of itself. When the fermentation is over, skim off the refuse, and fill up the cask with the reserved liquor. When it has ceased working pour one gill of brandy to six gallons of wine. Bung it up close for eight or nine months, then bottle it off clear. Run the sediment through a jelly bag until it is clear; bottle it and keep it twelve months before it is used.

### 706. Orange Wine.

TIME—*To stand four days.*

ARTICLES.—Seventy-five oranges,; thirty pounds of loaf sugar; one bottle of brandy; six eggs; eight gallons of water.

DIRECTIONS.—Put the sugar, water, the whites and the shells of the eggs well beaten, into a copper, and let the whole gently boil as long as any scum rises. Peel the oranges very thin, put the peels into a tub, and pour over them the boiling clarified sugar; cover it over and let it stand for four days. On the third day, squeeze the oranges and strain the juice through a hair sieve, letting it drain until the next day, then pour it into a cask and fill it up with the clarified sugar, keeping back all the peels of the oranges. If not sufficient to fill the cask, boil some water, and when cold add it; then pour in the brandy, and stop it down close. In twelve months cask it off, and return it to the cask.

If not fine add a little isinglass.

### 707. Mulled Wine.

TIME—*Five minutes.*

ARTICLES.—One quart of new milk; one stick of cinnamon; nutmeg; and sugar, to taste; yolks of six eggs; a spoonful or two of cream.

DIRECTIONS.—Boil the new milk five minutes in a TEA-KETTLE BOILER with a stick of cinnamon, nutmeg, and sugar to your taste; then take it off the fire, and let it stand to cool. Beat the eggs well, and mix them with the cream, then mix it with the wine, and pour it backwards and forwards from the saucepan to the jug several times.

### 708. Cider Wine.

Ten or more gallons of cider fresh from the press, add two pounds of good brown sugar to each gallon. When the sugar has dissolved, strain the mixture into a clean cask. Let the cask want one gallon of being full. Leave out the bung for forty-eight hours; then put in the bung, leaving a little vent until fermentation ceases; then bung up tightly. In one year it is fit for use. It needs no straining, the longer it stands upon the lees the better.

## PLEASANT AND REFRESHING DRINKS.

### 709. Tomato Wine.

Let the tomatoes be fully ripe. After mashing well let them stand twenty-four hours. Then strain, and to every quart of the juice, add one pound of good sugar. Let it ferment again, skimming frequently; when clear, bottle. To use this, sweeten a glass of water to the taste, and add the tomato wine until sufficiently acid.

### 710. Egg Wine.

TIME—*About five minutes.*

ARTICLES.—One glass of white wine; one spoonful of cold water; a few lumps of loaf sugar; a little grated nutmeg; one egg.

DIRECTIONS.—Put a glass of white wine with half a wineglass of cold water, a little sugar and grated nutmeg into a TEA-KETTLE BOILER, set it over the fire, and when it boils pour it by degrees over an egg, well beaten with a spoonful of cold water, stir it one way for a minute, and serve it with dry toast in a plate.

### 711. Elderberry Wine.

To ten quarts of berries put five quarts of water, and let stand twenty-four hours. Then skim and strain it, and to every gallon of the liquor put three pounds of sugar, half an ounce of cloves, one ounce of cinnamon, and two ounces of ginger. Boil it again, and ferment it by putting in a slice of toast covered with fresh yeast. By leaving out the spices this is said to resemble port.

### 712. Gooseberry Champagne.

Select large full-grown berries, before they begin to turn red. Allow a gallon of water to every three pounds of fruit. Put the berries in a clean tub, pour on a little water, pound and mash the fruit, then add the remainder of the water, and stir the whole well. Cover the tub with a clean cloth and let it stand four days. Stir it frequently and thoroughly; then strain the liquor through a jelly bag or coarse linen cloth, and to each gallon add four pounds of white sugar; and to every five gallons one quart of the best French brandy; mix the whole, and put it into a clean cask that will just hold it, as the cask should be full. Place the cask in a cool, dry place, and lay the bung in loosely. Secure the cask firmly, so that it cannot be shaken or moved, as the least disturbance will injure the wine. Let it work for two weeks, or more, until the fermentation is subsided. Then bottle it, and be careful to drive the corks in tightly; lay the bottles on their sides, and in six months the wine will be fit for use.

### 713. Beer.

To four gallons of water take two pounds of sugar, one quart of molasses, half a tea-cupful of ginger, one pint of sots, two spoonfuls of cream of tartar, one and a half spoonfuls of ground allspice, and three drops of oil of sassafras. Put the spices into bags, heat the water and pour it over the spices, mix the whole of the ingredients in an open vessel, let it stand over night, then skim off the top of the liquid, take out the bags of spices, and pour it carefully into jugs, bottles, or a keg. It will be fit for use in twenty-four hours.

### 714. Ginger Beer.

TIME—*One hour to boil.*

ARTICLES.—Five pounds of loaf sugar; three ounces of powdered ginger; three gallons of water; five lemons; a quarter of a tea-cupful of yeast; a slice of toasted bread.

DIRECTIONS.—Boil the sugar and ginger in three gallons of water for one hour. When it is cold add the juice and peels of five lemons, and a quarter of a tea-cupful of yeast on a slice of toasted bread. Let it stand in a tub covered with a thick cloth for two or three days. Then strain it through a thick cloth and bottle it. It will be ready to drink in four or five days after it is bottled. If wished to be very strong of ginger, more may be added.

### 715. Spruce Beer.

Pour eight gallons of cold water into a barrel, to this add eight gallons of boiling water, then put in six table-spoonfuls of essence of spruce, and sixteen pounds of molasses. When sufficiently cold add half a pint of yeast, and roll the cask about and shake it well. Keep it in a warm place for two days, with the bung open; by this time the fermentation will have subsided sufficiently for bottling. Bottle it or put it in stone jars well corked, and it will be fit for use in a week.

### 716. Cranberryade.

Pour boiling water upon bruised cranberries, let them stand for a few hours, strain off the liquor, and sweeten to the taste. This forms an agreeable and refreshing beverage.

### 717. Appleade.

Slice some apples, put them in a deep pan, and pour enough boiling water over them to cover them. Place the cover on the pan, and when cold strain the liquid; sweeten it, and flavor with a little lemon.

### 718. Lemonade.

TIME—*Two hours.*

ARTICLES.—Six lemons; one quart of boiling water; one or two ounces of clarified sugar.

DIRECTIONS. — Grate the peel of six lemons, pour a quart of boiling water on it; let it stand some time; then add the juice of the lemons (take care not to let the lemon pips fall into the liquid), sweeten it with clarified sugar, and run it through a jelly bag.

### 719. Milk Lemonade.

TIME.—*Twelve hours.*

ARTICLES.—One dry lemon; one pound of loaf sugar, powdered; one pint of white wine; one quart of quite fresh boiling milk.

DIRECTIONS. — Peel the lemons, taking care first to wash the peel quite clean; let the peel be very thin. Squeeze the juice over it, and let it lay on the peel all night. In the morning add to it the powdered sugar, and the wine, and the milk. Strain it once or twice through a jelly bag till it is perfectly clear and nice. Let it get quite cold. This is a most delicious beverage in the summer.

### 720. Christmas Bowl.

TIME.—*Three hours.*

ARTICLES.—Nine sponge cakes; half a pound of macaroons; one pint of raisin wine; half a pint of sherry; two ounces of almonds; two ounces of powdered sugar candy; one pint and a half of custard.

DIRECTIONS. — Break the sponge cakes into small pieces, and place in a deep bowl with the macaroons; add the raisin wine and sherry, leaving them to soak thoroughly; sweeten with the sugar candy, and pour over the top a very thick custard. Stick with sliced almonds. Place the bowl on a stand ornamented with Christmas evergreens.

### 721. Acorn Coffee.

Peel the husks from sound ripe acorns, divide the kernels, dry them gradually, and roast them in a close vessel. While roasting they should be stirred continually, and small pieces of butter added from time to time. Care must be taken not to burn or roast them too much. When roasted they may be ground and used as ordinary coffee.

### 722. Blackberry Cordial.

To one quart of blackberry juice add one pound of white sugar; half an ounce of grated nutmeg; and half an ounce of pulverized cinnamon. Tie the spices in a fine muslin bag, boil the whole and skim it. When no more scum rises set it away to get cold, and add one pint of the best brandy. Cloves and allspice may be added in the proportion of a quarter of an ounce of each.

### 723. Beverage from Cherries.

To one pint of cherry juice put one pound of sugar. Boil it ten minutes and skim it. When cool bottle it, and cork it tight.

### 724. Egg Flip.

ARTICLES.—Three eggs; a quarter of a pound of good moist sugar; and a pint and a half of beer.

DIRECTIONS.—Beat the eggs with the sugar, make the beer very hot, but do not let it boil; then mix it gradually with the beaten eggs and sugar, toss it to and fro from the saucepan into a jug, two or three times; grate a little nutmeg on the top and serve it.

A wine glass of spirits may be added if liked.

### 725. Strawberry Sherbet.

TIME.—*To stand three or four hours.*

ARTICLES.—One pound of strawberries; three pints of water; juice of one lemon; one table-spoonful of orange flower water; one pound of double refined sugar.

DIRECTIONS.—Take one pound of picked strawberries, crush them to a smooth mass, then add three pints of water, the juice of the lemon, and the orange flower water; let it stand for three or four hours. Put the sugar into another basin, stretch over it a large cloth or napkin, and strain the strawberries through it on the sugar; wring it to extract as much of the juice as possible; stir until the sugar is dissolved, then strain again, and set it in ice for an hour, before serving in small tumblers.

### 726. Imperial Pop.

Three ounces of cream of tartar; one ounce of bruised ginger; a pound and a half of loaf sugar; half a tumbler of lemon juice; a gallon and a half of water; and a wine-glassful of yeast. Shake well together; bottle and cork well.

### 727. Corn Beer.

Boil a quart of corn until the grains crack; put the grains into a jug, and pour in two gallons of boiling water; do not use the water it was boiled in. Add a quart of molasses, a handful of dried apples, and a large table-spoonful of ginger. It will be ready for use in two or three days. If the weather is cold set it by the fire. It may be kept up several weeks with the same corn, sweetening the water before pouring in the jug.

### 728. Cheap Beer.

Two table-spoonfuls of pulverized ginger; one pint of hop yeast; one pint of molasses; six quarts of cold water; mix well and bottle immediately. In twenty-four hours it may be used.

# BISCUITS.

 We present, on this page, the enrions monogram of L.F.E., with several biscuit recipes,sent to us by HALL & RUCKEL, WHOLESALE DRUGGISTS AND MANUFACTURERS OF LUBIN'S FLAVOR EXTRACTS, Publishers of the celebrated Metropolitan Hotel Recipes, No. 218 Greenwich Street, New York City. These celebrated extracts are excellent, and made from the fruits and nuts they represent. Families cannot be too careful in using extracts, and we would advise none to be used because they are cheap, or from unknown persons, who make imitations, which can be made from oils, vitriols, and other chemicals. The house of Hall & Ruckel is too well known for their uprightness, straightforward and honorable character, to be guilty of using any thing in their Cooking Extracts but the genuine. We have tried and used them in our recipes, and recommend others so to do. Any thing needed in the drug line will be cheerfully attended to by them.

### 729. Lemon Biscuit.
TIME.—*Fifteen minutes to bake.*
ARTICLES.—One pound of white sugar, one of flour, a little soda, milk, two ounces of suet, extract of lemon.
DIRECTIONS.—Dissolve the soda, mix all well together, using milk enough to wet the dough, cut them out, put on pans greased, and bake in a hot oven.

### 730. German Biscuits.
TIME.—*Six or eight minutes.*
ARTICLES.—Half a pound of dried flour, five ounces of butter, seven ounces of sugar, two eggs, two dessert spoonfuls of cream or condensed milk.
DIRECTIONS.—Beat the butter to a cream, and mix in the flour and the cream and well beaten eggs, to form a nice, light dough; mix all well before kneading it; roll it in thin, long, narrow strips, flavor to taste, and bake on a tin in a quick oven.

### 731. Ribbon Biscuit.
TIME.—*Twenty minutes to bake.*
ARTICLES.—One pound of flour, a quarter of a pound of butter, half a pound of sugar, two eggs, a gill of milk, flavor with nutmeg extract.
DIRECTIONS.—Mix all together, cut in ribbon shape, bake in a moderate oven.

### 732. Plain Sugar Biscuits.
TIME.—*Fifteen minutes to bake.*
ARTICLES. — Flour, two coffee cupfuls; milk, one; butter, two ounces; sugar and flavor to taste.
DIRECTIONS.—Dissolve the butter in the milk warm, stir it into the flour to make a firm paste, roll it out thin, and cut it with a tumbler, prick each biscuit and bake in a hot oven.

### 733. Orange Biscuit.
TIME.—*Five or six minutes to bake.*
ARTICLES.—Four eggs, quarter of a pound of flour, same of butter and sugar, and some orange flavoring extract.
DIRECTIONS.—Beat the butter until it is a cream, and stir into it the white sugar, then mix in the flour and stir in gradually the yolks of the eggs, beaten well; whisk the whites, and mix them with the other ingredients; fill some buttered moulds, pour in the mixture, sift some powdered sugar over, and bake them in a slow oven.

### 734. Damascus Biscuits.
TIME.—*Fifteen minutes to bake.*
ARTICLES.—Four eggs, five ounces of beef suet, half an ounce of almonds, six ounces of loaf sugar, two ounces and a half of flour, and flavor to taste.
DIRECTIONS.—Beat the whites of the eggs to a froth, chop the suet and almonds separately very fine, and beat well together; mix, with the yolks of the eggs, the loaf sugar, finely sifted; beat well, and pour into the almond mixture; shake in the flour, and add the flavor of peach; bake in small tins.

### 735. Abernethy Biscuit.
TIME.—*Twenty minutes to bake.*
ARTICLES.—Two pounds of flour, quarter of a pound of butter, same of sugar, half a pint of milk, two eggs, caraway seed.
DIRECTIONS.—Mix as usual for cake, roll, cut out in any shape, bake in a moderate oven.

### 736. Savoy Biscuits.
TIME.—*Fifteen minutes to bake.*
ARTICLES. — Sugar, two coffee-cupfuls; flour, one; six eggs. flavor.
DIRECTIONS.—Beat the eggs and sugar together, add the flour and flavor, beating all together, roll to a quarter of an inch thick, bake, sprinkle sugar on top, and set in the oven again until the sugar melts.

### 737. Hickory Nut Biscuit.
Make same as for Savoy Biscuit; shell and chop the nuts, coarse or fine, and mix in; roll out thin, and bake brown.

### 738. English Biscuit.
TIME.—*About twenty minutes.*
ARTICLES.—One pound of flour, a quarter of a pound of butter, same of sugar, half a pint of milk, half a teaspoonful of cream of tartar, half a tea-cup full of water.
DIRECTIONS.—Mix the flour with butter, make milk warm and sweeten with sugar, pour it gradually into the butter paste, dissolve the tartar in half a tea-cup full of cold water and add to the mixture, working the paste to a good consistency, roll it out, and cut into small biscuits; bake in a quick oven directly after they are made.

### 739. Extract Biscuit.
Make same as English Biscuit, adding any extract desired.

## MANIOCA.

A delicious product from the East Indies. Try it with these recipes.

### 740. Manioca Pudding.

TIME.—*Half an hour.*

ARTICLES.—Four tablespoonfuls of manioca, one quart of milk, a little salt, one tablespoonful of butter, four eggs, sugar, spice, or flavoring to the taste.

DIRECTIONS.—Mix the manioca in half the milk cold, and with the butter stir on the fire in a TEA-KETTLE BOILER, until it thickens or boils; pour it quickly into a dish. Stir in the sugar and the remaining milk, and when quite cool add the eggs, spice and wine, or other flavoring. This pudding may be varied by omitting the eggs and substituting currants, chopped raisins, or candied lemon, orange or citron sliced. Bake half an hour in a moderate oven.

### 741. Manioca Apple Pudding.

TIME.—*Bake half an hour.*

ARTICLES.—Four table-spooonfuls of manioca, table-spoonful of butter, apples, lemon juice, one quart of water, a little salt, season ing.

DIRECTIONS.—Mix the manioca in the water, and boil in a TEA-KETTLE BOILER; put a thick layer of apples with a little lemon juice, sweeten well, pour on the cooked manioca, and bake till nicely browned.

### 742. Manioca Blanc Mange.

TIME.—*About half an hour to boil.*

ARTICLES.—Four table-spoonfuls of manioca, one quart of milk, a little salt, one table-spoonful of butter, sugar and flavoring.

DIRECTIONS.—Mix all together and boil till quite thick in a TEA-KETTLE BOILER, pour into an earthen mould, turn out when cold and flavor to suit the taste. Eat with syrup, cream or jelly.

### 743. Caudle for Invalids.

TIME.—*Twenty minutes.*

ARTICLES.—Two spoonfuls of manioca, one quart of water, a bit of butter, two blades of mace, some grated lemon peel, honey or sugar, spice, and brandy or wine.

DIRECTIONS.—It is made with the manioca stirred in the water with the butter, the mace, and grated lemon peel. Boil it twenty minutes in a TEA-KETTLE BOILER, stiring that it may be smooth, sweeten with refined honey or sugar if preferred, add spice to taste, and one glass of brandy or white wine. Should the mixture become too thick, stir in a little boiling water while the mixture is yet warm.

### 744. Manioca Soup.

One or two dessert-spoonfuls of manioca (first mixed in cold water) will greatly improve soup, and render it more nourishing for children or delicate persons.

## ICE PUNCHES

Are made of any alcoholic beverage. Taken in small quantities when the system is low, weak and feverish, they will refresh, invigorate and strengthen. Smaller quantities can be used; eggs can be added and more or less water and sugar may be used. Our recipes will please.

### 745. Cider Ice Punch.

TIME.—*Five minutes to freeze.*

ARTICLES.—One quart of sweet cider, two eggs, sugar.

DIRECTIONS.—Beat the eggs well, mix with the cider, and sweeten to taste; freeze.

### 746. Claret Ice Punch.

TIME.—*Five minutes to freeze.*

ARTICLES.—A bottle of claret, sugar.

DIRECTIONS.—Mix the claret with sugar to taste, then freeze.

### 747. Champagne Ice Punch.

TIME.—*Five minutes to freeze.*

ARTICLES.—One quart of lemonade, one pint bottle of champagne, one gill of gin, sugar.

DIRECTIONS.—Make the lemonade, pour it into the freezer, then the rum; open the champagne; add sugar and freeze at once.

### 748. Cordial Ice-Cream.

TIME.—*To freeze, a few minutes.*

ARTICLES.—Any cordial, a pint; water, half a pint; juice of two lemons, sugar.

DIRECTIONS.—Mix all the above together and freeze.

### 749. Wine Ice Punch.

TIME.—*Five minutes to freeze.*

ARTICLES.—Any wine, a pint; water (or not), a pint, sugar.

DIRECTIONS.—Mix and freeze.

### 750. Liquor Ice Punch.

TIME.—*Five minutes to freeze.*

ARTICLES.—A pint of any liquor, a pint of water, sugar and lemon juice to taste.

DIRECTIONS.—Mix and freeze.

### 751. Sherbet.

TIME.—*To freeze, five minutes.*

ARTICLES.—The juice of two lemons, four oranges, three pints of water, sweeten to taste.

DIRECTIONS.—Sqeeze the juice from the fruit, add the sugar and water, free.

### 752. Ice Egg-Nogg.

TIME.—*To freeze, five minutes.*

ARTICLES.—Four eggs, a quart of milk, half a pint of whiskey or brandy, sugar.

DIRECTIONS.—Mix and freeze.

# JELLY ICE-CREAMS.

On pages 12, 13, 103, and 104 will be found many recipes for making Ice-Creams, etc. Since those were published we have experimented with various other articles of food, to cheapen and give more of a variety of these delicate and deservedly popular luxuries.

It has been the custom to improve the FREEZERS by every means possible, but no effort has been made to cheapen and improve the creams.

The closer we have examined this subject the more we see the importance of our experiments, and the result has been such as to reduce the expense of fine creams so that they can be made from ten to fifteen cents per quart.

The OLD WAY OF MAKING ICE-CREAM is with cream or milk, sugar, essence, a large number of eggs. This plan made a fair, but expensive ice-cream. If milk was used the result was a course ice-cream, full of lumps of ice. What is required is a smooth rich cream, at a small expense: in order to do this we had to reduce the water to a jelly with the aid of new and cheap foods, so that the icy granules would not be formed. By our recipes this has been accomplished, and the cheapest, richest, smoothest, finest, most nutritious and healthiest ice-creams ever made, are now given to the public.

### 753. Jelly Ice-Creams.

Are made by reducing gelatineous animal and vegetable preparations to a jelly and adding sugar, eggs, and flavoring to taste. They are superior to any other.

### 754. Light Jelly Ice-Creams.

Those wishing to have them light should eat them as soon as made.

### 755. To Improve Creams.

After they are made draw off the water from the wooden freezers, pack it full of broken ice and salt, take out the dasher if you have one in the tin part, scrape off the cream that adheres to the sides, cover it over with the cover, then pack any old blankets, or any other cloth covers, around the whole freezer, let it stand for two or three hours or longer, and it will be hard, rich, and smooth. Packed with salt and ice it will keep hard as long as desired.

We prefer condensed milk to make these creams, although common milk will do. We give the recipes for common milk. If condensed milk is used, use one part milk and three parts water.

### 756. Gold Jelly Cream.

TIME.—*To prepare, half an hour.*

ARTICLES.—Yolks of five eggs, one ounce of gelatine or isinglass, one quart of milk, one quart of ice water; sugar, quarter of a pound, or to suit the taste; essence, a tablespoonful, or to suit the taste.

DIRECTIONS.—Dissolve the gelatine in the hot milk in the TEA-KETTLE BOILER, add the ice-water, then the yolks well beaten, sweeten, flavor to taste, freeze.

### 757. Silver Jelly Cream.

TIME.—*To prepare, half an hour.*

ARTICLES.—The whites of five eggs, an ounce of gelatine or isinglass, a quart of milk, same of ice-water, sugar and spice to taste.

DIRECTIONS.—Dissolve the gelatine in boiling milk in the TEA-KETTLE BOILER; after it is all dissolved, pour in the same quantity of ice water, add the whites well beaten, sugar and flavor to taste.

### 758. Gold and Silver Creams.

Made as above and served in moulds, or in glasses, are very pretty, and flavored with different flavors, are very delightful.

### 759. Tapioca Jelly Cream.

TIME.—*To boil, four hours.*

ARTICLES.—Tapioca, four ounces; milk, one quart; water, a quart; one egg; sugar and flavor to taste.

DIRECTIONS.—Soak the tapioca from two to ten hours, then boil it in the TEA-KETTLE BOILER with the milk and water until it is in a jelly, cool it with pieces of ice, beat up the eggs, the sugar and flavor, stir altogether, freeze.

### 760. Manioca Jelly Cream.

TIME.—*To soak, all night; to boil, three hours.*

ARTICLES.—Manioca, two ounces; milk, a pint; water, a pint; one egg; sugar and flavor and taste.

DIRECTIONS.—Soak the manioca all night this softens it, then boil it in the TEA-KETTLE BOILER with the water and milk until it is a jelly; when cold add the eggs, sugar and flavor, then freeze.

### 761. Cassava Jelly Cream.

TIME.—*To prepare, four hours.*

ARTICLES.—Cassava, one ounce; milk, a pint; water, same; sugar and flavor to taste; egg, one.

DIRECTIONS.—Soak the cassava, boil it in the TEA-KETTLE BOILER until a jelly, in water and milk and flavor to taste. Freeze.

### 762. Arrow-root Jelly Cream.

TIME—*To prepare, quarter of an hour.*

ARTICLES.—Two table-spoonfuls of arrow-root, one pint of milk, one pint of water, sugar and flavor to taste.

DIRECTIONS.—Mix up the arrow-root in a little cold water, set the milk and water to boil in the TEA-KETTLE BOILER, when hot add the arrow-root and sugar, let it boil ten minutes, let it get cold, and add the flavoring, and freeze.

### 763. Sago Jelly Ice-Cream.

TIME.—*Half an hour to prepare.*

ARTICLES.—Quarter of a pound of sago, a quart of milk, same of water, three eggs, flavor, and sweeten with sugar.

DIRECTIONS.—Boil the sago in the TEA-KETTLE BOILER in the milk until it is a jelly, add the water, eggs well beaten, sweeten and flavor to taste, freeze.

### 764. Rice Jelly Ice-Cream.

TIME.—*To prepare, half an hour.*

ARTICLES.—Half a pound of rice-flour, one quart of milk, one quart of water, three eggs, sugar and flavor.

DIRECTIONS.—Boil the rice and milk to a jelly in the TEA-KETTLE BOILER, when done pour in the cold water, the eggs well beaten, sugar and flavor, freeze.

### 765. Farina Jelly Ice-Cream.

ARTICLES.—Quarter of a pound of farina, milk, a quart; water, a quart; three eggs, sugar and flavor.

DIRECTIONS.—Boil the farina to a jelly in water and milk, add the sugar, when cool add the eggs, flavor and sugar.

### 766. Maizena Jelly Ice-Cream.

TIME.—*To prepare, half an hour.*

ARTICLES.—Maizena, quarter of a pound; milk, two quarts; four eggs; sugar and flavoring to taste.

DIRECTIONS.—Mix the maizena in a little cold water, put the milk in the TEA-KETTLE BOILER when the milk is hot, stir in the maizena and sugar, and boil to a jelly, beat the eggs well, when the jelly is cold, add the eggs and flavoring, freeze.

### 767. Corn Starch Jelly Cream.

Can be made the same way, making more or less, but in the same proportions.

### 768. Calf's Feet Jelly Ice-Cream.

TIME.—*To make, ten minutes.*

ARTICLES.—A pint of calf's feet jelly, a quart of milk, a quart of water, two eggs, sugar and flavor.

DIRECTIONS.—Prepare the jelly as directed in recipes 50 and 51. Boil the milk in the TEA-KETTLE BOILER, add the jelly and sugar, beat the eggs well, when cold add them and the flavoring to the milk and the flavoring.

### 769. Cocoanut Jelly Ice-Cream.

TIME.—*To boil, four hours.*

ARTICLES.—Half a pound prepared cocoanut, four ounces of tapioca, a quart of condensed milk, a quart of water, sugar, four eggs.

DIRECTIONS.—Boil the cocoanut and tapioca in half the milk and water for four hours in the TEA KETTLE BOILER, then strain, add the rest of the milk, water and egg well beaten, freeze.

### 770. Grape Jelly Ice Cream.

TIME.—*To prepare, ten minutes.*

ARTICLES.—A quart of milk, a quart of water, four ounces of cassava or manioca, a quart of sound grapes, sugar, half a pint of port wine.

DIRECTIONS.—Boil the cassava or manioca in the TEA-KETTLE BOILER with the milk and water until it is a clear jelly, then add the sugar, and when cold add the grapes and wine, then freeze.

### 771. Banana Jelly Ice-Cream.

TIME.—*To prepare, half an hour.*

ARTICLES.—Two ounces of tapioca, a pint of milk, same of water, three large bananas, sugar.

DIRECTIONS.—Boil the tapioca, milk and water to a jelly, when icy cold add the bananas mashed to a jelly, sweetened with sugar, freeze.

### 772. Wine Jelly Ice-Cream (for Invalids).

TIME.—*To prepare, half an hour.*

ARTICLES.—Half a pint of sherry, or some other wine, half a pint of water, half a pint of milk, an ounce of isinglass or gelatine, juice of two oranges, sugar to taste.

DIRECTIONS.—Put the isinglass in the hot water in the TEA-KETTLE BOILER until it is dissolved, then stir in the juice of the oranges, the milk and wine, sweeten to taste, freeze.

### 773. Very Cheap Jelly Ice-Cream.

TIME.—*Twenty minutes to prepare.*

ARTICLES.—A pint of water, a tablespoonful of syrup, a pint of milk, corn starch, flavoring.

DIRECTIONS.—Boil a pint of water and milk together in the TEA-KETTLE BOILER, mix the corn-starch in a little cold water, put in the boiler, let it boil five minutes, then sweeten with syrup, and flavor to taste when cold. Freeze.

### 774. Irish Moss Jelly Ice-Cream.

TIME.—*An hour to boil.*

ARTICLES.—Two ounces of moss, a quart of milk, two eggs, sugar, flavor.

DIRECTIONS.—Boil the moss in the water until it is a jelly, then add the milk and sugar, when cold add the eggs well beaten, sweeten and flavor to taste.

# RICH ICE-CREAMS.

Fraser, Bell & Loughran, 213 Pearl Street, New York City, Manufacturers of Tin Ware—whose house and goods we recommend to the trade for the unsurpassed qualities of their goods, as well as their honorable and just dealings, so that those purchasing tin ware wholesale should call upon them before purchasing elsewhere—present us with an illustration of the "American Patent Freezer," also, ice-cream receipts. We have repeatedly written that ice-creams, when slowly eaten, are healthy. We have made it from two to four times a week, and have given it freely to the whole family, including four children and a babe a year old, in a hot summer, and it has never disagreed with any of them. We state this fact, as many persons are under the impression that creams and ices are unhealthy. No cheaper or better luxury can be made.

The old method of freezing involved hours of really hard work of whirling by hand the common freezer. With the modern inventions, it is but a few minutes' easy exercise, which a child can do. We shall in other issues give additional receipts for freezing; and we know of no better machine than the "American Freezer" to do it in.

To those who are compelled to remain in the city during the summer, its use is almost a necessity; even during the colder months it is a delicacy that is pleasant. Try our recipes. These recipes are rich and delicious in flavor, and, of course, cost more than the common or jelly creams; but we cater for all classes.

OBSERVATIONS ON FREEZING CREAM.

In freezing ice-cream, the substance to be frozen should always be cold before putting it in the freezer, as it saves ice.

Use any common salt— not rock salt, as rock salt settles to the bottom of the tub.

Break the ice fine; a good way is to put it in a coarse sack, and break it with a mallet or round billet of wood.

### 775. Chocolate Cream.

ARTICLES.—Half a pint of strong made chocolate, one pint of milk, yolks of eight eggs, half a pint of thick cream, half a pound of loaf sugar.

DIRECTIONS.—Make the milk very hot, sweetened with the sugar, then stir carefully into it the yolks of the eggs and the chocolate; put it into a TEA-KETTLE BOILER, and stir it one way until the eggs are set in the milk, but do not let it boil; then strain it through a fine silk, or hair sieve, and stir into it the cream, and freeze.

### 776. Coffee Cream.

ARTICLES. — One large cupful of made coffee, four ounces of sugar, three-quarters of a pint of milk, yolks of eight eggs, two ounces of gelatine.

DIRECTIONS.—Put the milk into a TEA-KETTLE BOILER with the coffee, and add the well-beaten eggs and sugar; stir the whole briskly until it begins to thicken, and strain it through a sieve on the gelatine; mix it thoroughly together, and when the gelatine is dissolved in the TEA-KETTLE BOILER, freeze.

### 777. Tea Cream.

ARTICLES. — A quarter of an ounce of hyson tea, half a pint of milk, half a pint of cream, two spoonfuls of rennet, sugar to taste.

DIRECTIONS.—Boil the tea with the milk cream, and rennet in a TEA-KETTLE BOILER; when it is thick it will be sufficiently done; freeze.

### 778. Velvet Cream.

TIME.— Until the gelatine is dissolved.

ARTICLES. — One ounce of gelatine, a breakfast cup of white wine, juice of one large lemon, the peel rubbed with sugar, one pint of cream.

DIRECTIONS. — Put the gelatine into a TEA-KETTLE BOILER, with the wine, the juice of a lemon, and sufficient sugar to sweeten it rubbed on the peel to extract the color and flavor; put it over the fire until the gelatine is dissolved, and then strain it to get cold; then mix with it the cream, and freeze.

### 779. Ratafia Cream.

ARTICLES.—Six bay leaves, one quart of new milk, a little essence of ratafia, yolks of four eggs, four spoonfuls of cream, sugar to taste.

DIRECTIONS.—Put the milk into a TEA-KETTLE BOILER, with bay leaves and a little ratafia; when it has boiled up, take out the leaves, beat up the yolks of the eggs with the cream, and add sugar to your taste; stir it into the ratafia cream to thicken it, and heat again without allowing to boil; keep stirring it all the time one way, or it may curdle, and then freeze.

### 780. Bohemian Cream.

ARTICLES.—One ounce and a half of gelatine, one pint of cream, half a pint of water, six ounces of sugar, one lemon, one pint of strawberries.

DIRECTIONS.—Rub through a sieve the strawberries, sugar, and the juice of the lemon; dissolve the gelatine in the water; mix these ingredients well together, and freeze.

### 781. Chester Cream.

ARTICLES.—One pint of rich cream, peel of one lemon, a teaspoonful of the juice, one glass of raisin wine, sugar to taste, three ounces of macaroons.

DIRECTIONS.—Mix the lemon peel very fine with the cream, squeeze in the lemon juice, loaf sugar to taste, and the wine; freeze.

## CREAMS AND ICE CREAMS.

### 782 Spanish Cream.
TIME.—*Until very thick.*
ARTICLES.—Three tablespoonfuls of sifted ground rice, yolks of three eggs, three spoonfuls of water, two of orange-flower water, one pint of cream, three spoonfuls of powdered sugar.
DIRECTIONS.—Sift the rice, add to it the sugar, and mix it smooth with the water and orange flower water; then stir gradually in the cream and boil it in a TEA-KETTLE BOILER till it is of a proper thickness; then freeze.

### 783 Burnt Cream.
TIME.—*To boil ten minutes.*
ARTICLES.—One pint of cream, peel of half a lemon, a stick of cinnamon, one ounce and a half of sugar, yolks of four eggs.
DIRECTIONS.—Boil the cream with the peel of the lemon, and the stick of cinnamon in a TEA-KETTLE BOILER; pour it very slowly on the well-beaten yolks of the eggs, stirring till half cold; add the sugar pounded and sifted; take out the spice and lemon peel, pour it into a dish, and when cold, freeze.

### 784 Imperial Cream.
TIME.—*Ten minutes, to boil the cream.*
ARTICLES.—One quart of cream, peel of one lemon, juice of three; and about eight ounces of loaf sugar.
DIRECTIONS.—Boil the cream with the thin peel of one lemon, to extract the flavor, in a TEA-KETTLE BOILER, and then stir the cream until nearly cold, adding the sugar; strain the juice of the lemons into a glass dish, and pour the cream over it; mix it with the juice of the lemons, and freeze.

### 785 Pistachio Cream.
ARTICLES.—Half a pound of pistachio nuts, one spoonful of brandy, yolks of two eggs, one pint and a half of cream, sugar to taste.
DIRECTIONS.—Blanch the pistachio nuts, and pound them to a paste with the brandy; add the paste to the cream, sweeten it to your taste, and boil it in a TEA-KETTLE BOILER until it becomes thick; freeze.

### 786 Noyeau Cream.
TIME.—*Nearly half an hour.*
ARTICLES.—Two ounces of gelatine, one quart of cream, peel of one lemon, juice of three lemons, a quarter of a pound of loaf sugar, two glasses of noyeau.
DIRECTIONS.—Dissolve the gelatine in a cupful of boiling water, with the peel of a lemon cut very thin; when the gelatine is dissolved, and the essence extracted from the peel, strain it into the cream, stirring it constantly to prevent its curdling; sweeten it with sugar, and add the noyeau; whisk the whole thoroughly together for a few minutes; then freeze.

### 787 Spring Cream.
TIME.—*About twenty minutes.*
ARTICLES.—One dozen sticks of rhubarb, peel of one lemon, two cloves, a piece of cinnamon, and as much moist sugar as will sweeten it; two ounces of gelatine.
DIRECTIONS.—Clean the rhubarb, cut it into pieces and put it into a TEA-KETTLE BOILER with the peel of a lemon grated, the cloves, a piece of cinnamon, and as much good moist sugar as will sweeten it; set it over the fire and reduce it to a marmalade; pass it through a hair sieve and add to it the cream; freeze.

### 788 German Cream.
ARTICLES.—One pint of cream, six ounces of loaf sugar, peel of half a lemon, and the juice of two, one wine-glass of brandy.
DIRECTIONS.—Boil the cream with the sugar, and the peel of the lemon cut thin, in a TEA-KETTLE BOILER. As soon as it boils take it off the fire and let it stand until nearly cold; then add the juice of two lemons and the brandy; then freeze.

### 789 Almond Cream.
ARTICLES.—Five ounces of sweet almonds, six bitter almonds, one quart of cream, three ounces of loaf sugar, juice of two large lemons.
DIRECTIONS.—Blanch and pound both the sweet and the bitter almonds, and stir the paste into the cream sweetened with sugar, mixed with the strained juice of the lemons, or use the essence; whisk the whole, then freeze.

### 790 Sicilian Cream.
ARTICLES.—One pint of cream, one glass of noyeau, two ounces of gelatin, five ounces of sugar.
DIRECTIONS.—Whip the cream, add to it the noyeau, sugar, with the gelatine; mix all, then freeze.

### 791 Snow Cream.
ARTICLES.—One quart of cream, whites of three eggs, two glasses of raisin wine, two ounces of sugar, the peel of half a lemon.
DIRECTIONS.—Beat well the whites of the eggs, and put to them the cream; stir them well together, and add the wine, sugar, and lemon peel; freeze.

### 792 Housewife's Cream.
ARTICLES.—Half a pint of cream, quarter of a pint of sherry, three ounces of sugar, peel and juice of one lemon.
DIRECTIONS.—Cut the peel of a lemon into small pieces, mix the cream, wine, powdered white sugar, peel and juice of a lemon together, whisking it until quite thick; freeze.

*Two pages more of other recipes for ice creams, etc., will be given in Number Three.*

## MAIZENA.

DURYEAS' GLEN COVE STARCH COMPANY—DEPOT AND OFFICE, 49 & 51 PARK PLACE, NEW YORK CITY.—DURYEAS' Trademark adorns this page, as well as some of their recipes. No company of men have done more to elevate American manufactures of foods than they.

*Indian corn*, or *maize*, embodies many delicacies and substantials necessary to life and happiness, and it is due to the Brothers Duryea that they should be credited, not only with medals, which they have, but with the patronage of the public. We know that much of the unwillingness of wives and cooks to use corn starch, maizena, and other farinaceous foods has been from its great liability to burn, and the constant watching necessary to prevent its scorching. Now all this is obviated by cooking in the TEA-KETTLE BOILER. If the reader desires a delicate, yet hearty food, use DURYEA'S MAIZENA and CORN STARCHES. They also make Starches for Laundry use, fine, white, and strong. They only require one trial to satisfy any one of their strength, purity, and goodness, giving a gloss to the clothes. All grocers ought to keep them. There are some grocers so prejudiced against any change, as to not keep a variety of the same goods. This is a mistake. Some families will have every kind. It is therefore the interest of storekeepers to have a variety of every thing good. And among these goods should always be kept Duryeas'. GIVE THEM ONE TRIAL: IT IS ALL THEY ASK.

### 793. Boiled Custard.

TIME.—*To prepare and boil, twenty minutes.*

ARTICLES.—Two table-spoonfuls of maizena, one quart of milk, one or two eggs, half a tea-spoonful of salt, same of butter, four spoonfuls of sugar.

DIRECTIONS.—Mix the maizena with a little cold milk, salt and butter; heat the milk in a TEA-KETTLE BOILER to near boiling, and add the maizena, let it boil; then cool, and add the eggs, well beaten with the sugar, let it boil up once or twice, stirring it briskly, and flavor according to taste.

### 794. Porridge for Infants.

TIME.—*Ten minutes to cook.*

ARTICLES.—Yolks of two eggs, three tablespoonfuls of maizena, three of cold water, a little salt.

DIRECTIONS.—Mix the yolks of eggs with the maizena, water, salt, then add one pint of boiling water, and boil it in the TEA-KETTLE BOILER. Sweeten, if desired.

### 795. Fruit Pie.

TIME.—*Half an hour to bake.*

ARTICLES.—Fruit, one quart of milk, six table-spoonfuls of maizena, sugar

DIRECTIONS.—Stew the fruit in the sugar to suit the taste, add the milk, maizena and sugar to taste, boil it a few minutes in the TEA-KETTLE BOILER, put it into a pie-dish with paste for crust, and bake.

### 796. Maizena Lemon Pie.

TIME.—*Half an hour.*

ARTICLES.—One tablespoonful of maizena, half a pint of boiling water, grated rind and juice of one lemon, one tea-cupful of white sugar, and the yolks of three eggs.

DIRECTIONS.—Mix the maizena in a little cold water, add the boiling water, the rind and juice of the lemon and sugar, the eggs well beaten together; line a pie dish with paste, put in the mixture and bake in a moderate oven ; then beat the eggs to a stiff froth, add two table-spoonfuls of white sugar, one of maizena, stir them into the eggs, spread on the pie, and place in the oven until of a light brown color.

### 797. Maizena Cakes.

TIME.—To bake half an hour.

ARTICLES. — One pound of powdered sugar, one half of a pound of butter, six eggs, one pound of maizena.

DIRECTIONS.—Bake in small patty pans. Exquisitely light cakes are produced.

### 798. Maizena, or Polenta Pudding.

TIME.—*One hour and a half.*

ARTICLES.—Eight ounces of maizena, one and a half pints of milk, one ounce of butter, a little salt.

DIRECTIONS. — Mix the maizena in the milk, let it boil till it thickens in a TEA-KETTLE BOILER, put in the butter and salt, turn it out of the dish when served. This pudding is very good with meats.

### 799. Maizena Swiss Pudding.

TIME.—*One and a half hours.*

ARTICLES.—Eight ounces of maizena, one ounce of butter, quarter of a pound of moist sugar, the same of raisins, rind of a lemon, one ounce candied peel, half a pint of milk.

DIRECTIONS.—Mix the maizena with the milk in the TEA-KETTLE BOILER. When it boils add the butter, sugar, raisins.

# PREPARED COCOANUT.

The NEW YORK DESICCATING COMPANY, OFFICE AND WAREHOUSE, No. 70 Murray street, New York city, N. Y., sends us the following recipes, by which their PREPARED COCOANUT can be made into rich, healthy, and cheap puddings, pies, cakes, etc. This article possesses all the richness and delicate flavor of the green cocoanut.

It will keep in any climate, requires no labor to prepare it, as the whole nuts do, as it is finely ground, and put up in pound and half a pound papers. This is an entirely new patent preparation. All who have used it, praise it, and continue its use. In boiling prepared cocoanut, it is liable to burn if not cooked in a water bath,

or a TEA-KETTLE BOILER.
There is nothing richer than Prepared Cocoanut that we know of. A little of it in corn starch, maizena, farina, manioca, samp, cassava, sago, rice flour, tapioca or arrowroot, imparts all that delightful flavor, which is peculiar to cocoanut to a quantity of the above articles. We hope those who have not tried Prepared Cocoanut will do so. *Be sure and take none except that advertised in this Magazine, as we recommend no man's or company's goods until we have tried them.* Health and life is too precious a boon to trifle with, by using inferior articles prepared by unscrupulous men. We wish any person who are in doubt what to use, to write to us, and we

will cheerfully inform them of the best, the names of the parties manufacturing or selling them, the prices, and where to get them. This Cocoanut can be purchased of all the grocers in the land.

### 800. Cocoanut Cream.
TIME.—*About three hours.*
ARTICLES.—One paper of cocoanut, two quarts of rich milk, essence of cinnamon and rose water.
DIRECTIONS.—Boil the milk and cocoanut until tender, flavor with cinnamon and rose-water. Strain, if desired.

### 801. Cocoanut Drops.
TIME.—*To bake, a few minutes.*
ARTICLES.—One pound of sugar, one paper of cocoanut, four eggs.
DIRECTIONS.—Mix all together, drop upon white paper and bake quickly.

### 802. Cocoanut and Cracker Pies.
TIME.—*To bake, half an hour.*
ARTICLES.—One cup of cocoanut, milk, three eggs, butter and salt, sugar, crackers, rind of one lemon.
DIRECTIONS.—Put the cocoanut to soak in the milk, add the eggs, butter and salt, sugar, powdered cracker, and the lemon peel. Bake without upper crust.

### 803. Good Family Pudding.
TIME.—*To boil, three hours.*
ARTICLES.—Two cups cocoanut, three pints of milk, five eggs.
DIRECTIONS.—Boil the cocoanut in the milk in a TEA-KETTLE BOILER, add the eggs, sweeten and flavor to taste.

### 804. Cocoanut Pies.
TIME.—*To bake, about half an hour.*
ARTICLES.—Two cups of cocoanut, three pints of milk, six eggs, one cup of sugar, grated rind of a lemon.
DIRECTIONS.—Add together the cocoanut, milk, eggs, sugar, rind of the lemon if desired. Soak the cocoanut in the milk.

### 805. Cocoanut Tarts.
TIME.—*To bake, about half an hour.*
ARTICLES.—One pint of syrup, half a pound of cocoanut, rose water.
DIRECTIONS.—Make the syrup as if for sweatmeats, stir in the cocoanut, and flavor with rose-water.

### 806. Cocoanut Pudding.
TIME.—*To bake, one hour.*
ARTICLES.—Three cups of cocoanut, one quart of milk, three eggs.
DIRECTIONS.—Put the cocoanut to soak in the milk two hours, add the eggs, sweeten to the taste, and line with paste a dish, and bake.

### 807. Plain Cocoanut Cake.
TIME.—*To bake, one hour.*
ARTICLES.—Two cups cocoanut, one cup sugar, one half cup butter, one cup milk, four cups flour, three eggs, one teaspoon soda, two teaspoons cream tartar.
DIRECTIONS.—Mix all the above ingredients together, and bake.

# TAPIOCA FARINA.

By the courtesy of E. C. Hazard, Esq., No. 69 Barclay Street, New York City, Inventor and Patentee of Tapioca Farina, and Dealer in Farinaceous Goods (especially Hominy and Samp), and Fine Foreign Groceries.—Hazard's Farina is made from the roots of the Cassava Plant of Brazil (as shown in the trade mark), and is a healthy and nutritious food. It can be made into excellent Puddings, Jellies, Blanc Manges, Ice-Creams, Souffles, and other dishes for both sick and well. The handy and convenient shape it is manufactured into, and being put up in pound and half-pound packages, render it desirable. Tapioca Farina is a cheap luxury. It swells enormously in cooking, absorbing a large amount of water, and is not costly. It is easily cooked, Its strengthening, non-heating, non-irritating properties make it valuable. Give it a trial in some of the recipes here given, and a hearty meal or dessert can be made from it. The inventor of Farina from Tapioca, deserves credit for his ingenuity in preparing it in the style he does; and every man who renders any article of food more valuable to the people than it is in a crude state, is a public benefactor.

Tapioca-Farina, when cooking, is very liable to burn; to prevent which, cook it in a Tea-kettle Boiler, and it will be very easy to prepare it for the table.

We shall in our future issues give a variety of recipes to cook this and healthy luxurious food.

Nature has been bountiful in her gifts to man, and he should improve the preparation of them as much as possible.

### 808. Cassava Souffle.

TIME.—*Bake one hour.*

ARTICLES.—One pint of milk, three tablespoonfuls of tapioca farina, yolks of four eggs, half a tea-cup of desiccated cocoanut, sugar, butter and salt, and flavor to taste.

DIRECTIONS.—Boil the milk in a TEAKETTLE BOILER, and add the farina, and the sugar, butter, and salt to taste; then add the yolks of the eggs (beat the whites separate, and add afterwards); then add the cocoanut; flavor with any flavoring to suit the taste; bake in a pan greased with butter.

### 809. Tapioca Blanc Mange.

TIME.—*To boil, an hour.*

ARTICLES.—Four table-spoonfuls of cassava, one quart of cold milk, half a tea-cup of sugar, salt, a piece of lemon peel, or cinnamon stick.

DIRECTIONS.—Dissolve the cassava in the cold milk; then take the sugar, a little salt, the lemon peel or cinnamon stick; heat to nearly boiling in a TEA-KETTLE BOILER; then add the dissolved cassava and boil; take out the lemon peel; pour into a mold and keep until cold; when turned out pour round it any kind of stewed or preserved fruits, or a sauce of milk or sugar.

### 810. Cassava Jelly.

TIME.—*To bake an hour.*

ARTICLES.—Half a tea-cup of cassava, a piece of lemon peel, lemon juice, wine, and sugar.

DIRECTIONS.—Dissolve the cassava in cold water; simmer slowly in a TEA-KETTLE BOILER, with a piece of lemon peel, until clear; then add the lemon-juice, wine, and sugar, to suit the taste. Use cold.

### 811. Cassava and Rice Pudding.

TIME.—*Four hours.*

ARTICLES.—One tea-cupful of rice and cassava, half the quantity of sugar, a little ground cinnamon, three pints of cold milk.

DIRECTIONS.—Put into a deep dish the rice and cassava, mixed with the sugar; add the milk; sprinkle the cinnamon over it; bake in a slow oven.

### 812. Baked Tapioca Farina Pudding.

TIME.—*To boil, about half an hour.*

ARTICLES.—Two quarts of milk, one cup of sugar, two eggs, salt, butter, and flavor to taste.

DIRECTIONS.—Boil the milk in the TEA-KETTLE BOILER; sprinkle and mix in the farina; add the sugar, salt, and butter; let it cool; add in the eggs, well beaten; pour into cups; place them in a dripping pan half full of boiling water, and bake until brown, or steam in a steamer. Any quantity can be made, by dividing the recipe above.

### 813. French Cassava Pudding.

TIME.—*Ten minutes to boil.*

ARTICLES.—One cup of tapioca farina, one quart of milk, one dessert-spoonful of sugar, three eggs, salt, butter, and flavor.

DIRECTIONS.—Dissolve the farina in the cold milk, boil in the TEA-KETTLE BOILER, add the sugar, flavor, salt, and butter, to suit the taste.

## CONDENSED MILK.

The New York Condensed Milk Co.: Depot, 34 & 36 Elizabeth St., and 227 and 229 E. Thirty-Fourth St., New York — Gail Borden, Esq., the successful inventor of Condensed Milk, Prest.—supplies the cities of New York, Brooklyn, and Jersey City with pure Condensed Milk, sweet and fresh, from their wagons, every day, at Forty cents per quart, and they give an honest quart, condensed at forty cents a quart. Those not accustomed to the use of Condensed Milk may think it a very high price, but we assure them it is the cheapest milk sold in the city. The common milk is sold at ten cents a quart, condensed at forty cents a quart. Add four quarts of water to one quart of Condensed Milk, and you have five quarts of better milk than is sold at ten cents a quart. The fact that over ten thousand families in the cities of New York, Brooklyn, and Jersey City are using it, ought to satisfy any person that there are some reasons why they prefer it to common milk. Milk can be purchased in the country much cheaper than it can be here. Transportation of 80 per cent. of the water Mr. Borden thought useless, and by years of patient toil he has perfected the machinery to take out the water, leaving all the substance. By adding water, it is again milk.

There is no article of diet in the whole list of them which a mother should be more particular about than milk, simply because it is the natural food of children, and one which they love. That the New York Condensed Milk Co.'s milk, and the Eagle Brand of Canned Milk is pure, we have not a doubt. That it is cheaper, purer, and better than the average of city milk, we know, and we unhesitatingly recommend its use. The prices are for the summer in New York.

*In the recipes below it is meant to use Condensed Milk without any water. If, however, plain milk is used, add a little butter.*

### 814. Milk Cakes.

Time.—*To bake fifteen minutes.*
Articles.—Flour, half a pound; white powdered sugar, three great spoonfuls; one egg, a few carroway seeds, milk.
Directions.—Rub the flour and sugar together, beat up the egg and add to the flour, use pure condensed milk, make into a paste, roll it thin, cut it into round cakes, bake on tin plates.

### 815. Milk Cup Cake.

Time.—*To bake about half an hour.*
Articles.—Two teacups of flour, one of sugar, one of condensed milk, half of a teaspoonful of soda, whites of two eggs, flavor with lemon.
Directions.—Beat the eggs up with the sugar, dissolve the soda in a little water, mix it up with the flour and milk; bake.

### 816. Mrs. B.'s Milk and Egg Rolls.

Time.—*To bake about twenty minutes.*
Articles.—Flour, one pound; milk; sugar, two teaspoonfuls; yeast, three teaspoonfuls; salt, half a teaspoonful; one egg.
Directions.—Mix all the above together, use milk enough to make a dough, put the dough in a warm place, let it rise about two hours, cut in pieces the size of eggs, roll them out, lap half way over, egg them over, bake quickly.

### 817. Milk Tea Cake.

Time.—*Bake twenty-five minutes.*
Articles.—One cup of milk, one of sugar, half a cup of melted butter, two eggs, one cup of water, two tea-spoonfuls of cream of tartar, one spoonful of soda, flour.
Directions.—Beat the eggs, add the sugar, melted butter, milk, and soda, part dissolved in the water, then the flour mixed with the tartar. Bake.

### 818. Milk Pancakes.

Time.—*A few minutes to fry.*
Articles.—Milk, six table spoonfuls of flour, four eggs, a little salt.
Directions.—Beat all up together, fry thin in butter, strew nutmeg, or cinnamon and sugar on them, serve hot.

### 819. Milk Cookies.

Time.—*To bake ten minutes.*
Articles.—One half a cup of milk, two cups of sugar, one half a cup of butter; soda, half a teaspoonful; cream of tartar, two; flour to roll.
Directions.—Beat the egg and sugar together, then add the milk and butter; dissolve the soda in a little water, mix the cream of tartar with the flour, then mix all together. Roll thin, lay out and bake, in a quick oven.

### 820. Milk Jumbles.

Time.—*Fifteen minutes to bake.*
Articles.—Two eggs; sugar, a cup; butter, half a cup; milk, half a cup; cream of tartar, half a teaspoonful; quarter of a teaspoonful of soda, in water; flour, a cup.
Directions.—Beat the eggs and sugar together, dissolve the soda in a little water, mix the milk, butter, eggs, sugar, and soda with flour, roll out the mixture, and cut in strips or rounds, and bake.

### 821. Milk and Nut Cake.

Time.—*About an hour to bake.*
Articles.—Three cups of flour, two of sugar, three eggs, half a cup of butter, same of milk, cup of shelled hickory nuts, one teaspoonful of cream of tartar, half one of soda.
Directions.—Make the cake as usual, beat in the shelled nuts. Bake in a steady oven.

# THE PEOPLE'S COOKING RECIPES.

The following recipes were sent to us. They are printed just as we received them. They are not separated, as ours are. The public can judge which is the best way. All cook-books but ours are thus printed. We cordially invite wives and housekeepers to send new recipes to us: we will print them, and give each one credit for them, besides a reward.

### 822. Virginia Corn Bread.
FROM MRS. L. R—N, PETERSBURGH, VA.

Dissolve one table-spoonful of butter in three and a half pints of boiling milk; into this scald one quart of Indian meal; when cool, add a half pint of wheat flour, a little sugar, a tea-spoonful of salt, and two eggs, well beaten; mix well together, and bake in two cakes—tins well greased or buttered.

### 823. Muffins.
FROM LELAND BROTHERS' HOTEL.

One pint of milk; sufficient flour or corn meal to make a stiff batter; a table-spoonful of yeast; a little salt; let it raise; bake in rings on a hot griddle or in a hot oven.

### 824. New Method of Making Bread.
FROM MONSIEUR M——.

Tie up one pound of rice in a thick linen bag, allowing ample room to swell; boil it three or four hours until it becomes smooth paste; mix this, while warm, with ten pounds of flour, adding the usual quantities of yeast and salt; allow the dough to work a certain time near the fire, after which divide it into loaves. The flour should be dusted in, and most vigorously kneaded. This quantity of rice and flour has produced twenty-six pounds thirteen ounces of this excellent bread, which keeps moist and sweet longer than that made by the ordinary process.

### 825. New Year's Cake.
FROM MRS. A. C., BROOKLYN, N. Y.

Seven pounds of flour, two pounds of sugar, three pounds of butter, one pint of water, caraway seeds, if you wish.

### 826. Sweetmeats.
FROM MRS. M. M. C., OF CHICAGO, ILL.

If sweetmeats are boiled too long, they lose their flavor, and become a dark color; if boiled too short a time, they will not keep well. Sweetmeats should be kept in glass jars, or in those of white queensware, in a cool place. Look at them every two weeks, as they may sour; if so, scald them.

### 827. Fine Baked Custard.—FROM MRS. M—L, OF BOSTON.

Boil together gently for five minutes a pint and a half of new milk, a few grains of salt, the very thin rind of a lemon, and six ounces of loaf sugar; stir these, boiling but very gradually, to the well beaten yolks of six fresh eggs, and the whites of four; strain the mixture, and add to it half a pint of good cream; let it cool, and then flavor it with a few spoonfuls of brandy; finish and bake it as common custard, and pour it into small, well-buttered cups, and bake it very slowly from ten to twelve minutes.

### 828. Hard Times Pudding.
FROM MISS F—C, PORTLAND, MAINE.

Half a pint of molasses or syrup, half a pint of water, one-half tea-spoonful of salt, one of soda; flour enough to make a batter; boil in a bag for three hours; eat with sauce.

### 829. A Delicious Way to Prepare Tomatoes for the Table.
FROM D. L——S, WILLIAMSBURGH, N. Y.

Scald ripe tomatoes, peel and cut them up, and sweeten with sugar to the taste, add a very little salt.

### 830. Hull Corn.
FROM MR. PICKENS, OF NEW YORK.

One quart of Indian corn, one gallon of water, and one quart of a strong lye; boil until the hulls come off; wash it in cold water; then boil till tender, and eat in milk.

### 831. Scotch Ox-head Cheese.
FROM IRON AGE OFFICE, NEW YORK CITY.

Split the head in two, and wash it clean; put it in salt and water for twelve hours; then boil till the meat comes clean off the bones; take out the meat, and chop it fine; put it back into the liquid, and boil twenty minutes; season with pepper and salt; put it into shapes, and set it off with parsley. See that there is not too much liquid in it, or it will not get solid.

### 832. Tomato Catsup.
FROM MR. PETERS, BALTIMORE, MD.

Take one bushel of tomatoes and boil them until they are soft; squeeze them through a fine wire sieve, and add three half-pints of salt; two ounces of cayenne pepper; three table-spoonfuls of black pepper, and five onions, skinned and separated; mix together, and boil about three hours, or until reduced to about one half; then bottle without straining.

# JAMES Y. WATKINS & SON,

MANUFACTURERS OF

## Tin and Sheet-Iron Ware,

### HOTEL AND HOUSE-FURNISHING GOODS.

---

**BAKERS, CONFECTIONERS, HOTELS, AND RESTAURANTS SUPPLIED WITH ALL NECESSARY UTENSILS.**

---

## NO. 16 CATHARINE STREET,
### NEW YORK.

---

**Wholesale Depots**
FOR
**BERNEY'S PATENT HOUSEHOLD WARES,**
The Quarterly Magazine,
"Mystery of Living,"
THE CELEBRATED
**TEA-KETTLE BOILERS,**
AND
**Family Coffee Cones,**
**NON-EXPLOSIVE CANS,**
HAND GAS-LAMPS.

**DUTTON & CAMPBELL,**
87 CORNHILL, BOSTON.

**DUTTON & GILBERT,**
Cor. Eighth and Vine Streets,
PHILADELPHIA.

---

## JENKINS'
PURE
## SILVER POLISH
WILL REPLATE ALL
**SILVER OR PLATED WARE**
As good as new, with pure Silver,
And warranted not to change Color by Standing or Washing.

Price 50 cents and $1 per Bottle.

Office and Depot, 1366 Broadway,
Bet. 37th & 38th Sts., N.Y.

---

**P. GRIFFING & CO.,**
MANUFACTURERS OF
**CHOCOLATE & COCOA,**
191 & 193 CHRISTIE ST.,

P. GRIFFING.
JAMES S. WETMORE.
NEW YORK.

# GREAT STOVE, RANGE,
### AND
# HOUSE-FURNISHING DEPOT.
## THOMAS M. REID,
(SUCCESSOR TO N. CORT,)
### 353 Grand Street, N.Y.,
#### OPPOSITE ESSEX MARKET,

Has all kinds of STOVES and RANGES for the Kitchen or Parlor.

## COOKING STOVES.

| | |
|---|---|
| Glad Tidings, | Novelty, |
| Favorite, | Pledge, |
| Sunshine, | Hudson, |
| Umpire, | Good Will, |
| Bird, | Success, &c. |

## RANGES.

| | | | | | |
|---|---|---|---|---|---|
| Meteor, | Lone Star, | Monitor, | Excelsior, | | Perfect, |
| Excellent, | Champion, | Real, | Superior, | | Victory, |
| Bell, | Comet, | Acorn, | Excellent, | | Rival, &c. |

## PARLOR STOVES.

| | |
|---|---|
| Oriental Base Burner, | Oval American Gas Burner, |
| Modern Gas Burner, | Favorite Oval Gas Burner, |
| Illuminating American Gas Burner, | Favorite Oval Base Burner, |
| Round American Gas Burner, | Franklins, Sunbeam, &c. |

Repairs for all of the above, also for all Stoves and Ranges in this market, constantly on hand.

### JOBBING PROMPTLY ATTENDED TO.

## HOUSE FURNISHING GOODS,

Including Ivory-Handle Knives and Forks—Ivory-Handle Carvers to Match—Bread Knives—Butcher and Cook Knives—Buck (plain and polished) Knives and Forks — Meat Slicers—Mincing Knives—Oyster Knives—Preserving Kettles—Tea and Coffee Pots of Britannia Ware, and Block Tin extra Strong—Britannia Tea and Table Spoons—Britannia Soup Ladles and Mugs—Iron Tea and Table Spoons — Knife Boxes and Baskets — Wooden Boxes in Nests, for Spices, Sugar, Flour, Starch, &c. — Window Brushes, Floor Brooms, Counter Brushes — Blacking and Stove Brushes, Stoves, Ranges, and Heaters—Coal Hods, Chamber Furniture, Oak and Cedar Pails, Chopping Trays, Watering Pots, Coffee and Tea Canisters, Cedar Tubs and Pails, Wooden Scoops and Spoons, Silver-Plated Castors, Spoons and Forks, Sad Irons, Mats, Rugs, &c., &c., and every thing used in the Dining Room and Kitchen.

**All Goods Warranted as Represented. Goods delivered in any part of the city free of charge.**

## TO THE PUBLIC.

Some months ago we determined to issue a Quarterly Magazine, full of useful knowledge, to benefit mankind, and to devote each number to a special object. The first number we designed to contain Cooking and Household Recipes. We knew that the stores were filled with cook books, varying in price from fifty cents to five dollars. We bought copies of all for sale, and, after a careful examination of them, we found that they were simply copies of each other, with a slight variation of the contents. They were also extravagant in the articles to be cooked. No arrangement of TIME, ARTICLES, DIRECTIONS, OR ADVICE AS TO WHAT GOODS WERE THE CHEAPEST TO USE. Many trials of the recipes proved them failures. But how to remedy this evil? We determined to get an old, experienced housekeeper to edit this department, to procure the tried recipes of families who knew them to be good, and to practice on those that we thought to be good until they were made perfect. This was a work of much labor and research—months of time were spent in compiling this number. It is a very simple matter to edit a common magazine of stories, songs, and news, compared with this labor, for here every recipe is sooner or later tried by thousands of families, and if not correct, not only is the book thrown aside as useless, but much food is wasted, and disappointment and vexation experienced. Over ELEVEN THOUSAND copies were sold in four weeks.

A NEW FEATURE OF THE MYSTERY is the classifying of foods and useful manufactures in one, two, or more columns, with recipes for using them, so that any person wishing to cook a dish with any article which is named in a column, can do so with ease. Also common articles of household use, such as potash, benzine, etc., have their uses explained.

We have divided No. 1 into three parts, so that all parties can be suited. Those who wish nothing but Cooking Recipes can have them; those who wish all, can be accommodated with them, or any part. We shall improve this book until it is perfect, and no household should be without it. The MEDICAL NUMBER will be issued January 1st, 1869.

TO OUR ADVERTISING PATRONS we return thanks. We know that their advertisements are not misplaced—that we give value for every dollar paid us, and that many of them appreciate our magazine as a means of advertising. Several of them continue in this and other editions, and a large firm, Duryea's Maizena and Starch Co., 49 & 51 Park Place, New York City, keep their advertisement in all the numbers of THE MYSTERY, even though it be half a million copies; which number we hope to reach, and shall, if energy and perseverance will do it. F. G. Smith & Co., manufacturers of Bradbury Pianos, have contracted to advertise in Seventy-five Thousand copies. Other firms advertise in many thousand copies.

ADVERTISERS *are cautioned against paying for any advertisement unless a printed bill is presented from this office, with our Trade-Mark on it. Likewise, as several complaints have been made to us of persons being swindled by paying for subscriptions, and orders for books and goods, without receiving them at the time, we desire to state that we sell the magazines and articles to canvassers and dealers at wholesale prices, and never, under any circumstances, give persons power to collect money for books or goods unless delivered.*

THE PUBLISHER.

# THE AMERICAN
## BUTTON-HOLE, OVERSEAMING,
### AND
## Sewing Machine Company,
### No. 483 BROADWAY, N. Y.

This Celebrated Combination Sewing Machine

IS GUARANTEED

**TO DO ALL THAT IS DONE BY THE BEST LOCK-STITCH MACHINES**

AND, IN ADDITION,

OVERSEAMS,

AND MAKES

**BEAUTIFUL BUTTON & EYELET HOLES**

IN ALL FABRICS.

---

IT IS THE

BEST AND ONLY COMPLETE

## Family Sewing Machine

EVER MANUFACTURED; DOING, IN FACT,
EVERY KIND OF SEWING, WHILE THE BUTTON-HOLE IS GENUINE,

*Making the same Stitch as by Hand, and more in an hour than can be done by hand in a day, besides being stronger and more regular.*

☞ No one should fail to examine it before purchasing elsewhere. ☜

---

PRINCIPAL OFFICES:

**1100 Chesnut Street, Philadelphia;**
**483 Broadway, New York.**

# RECOMMENDATIONS.

*New York, Oct. 20th, 1867.*
A. BERNEY, Esq.—Dear Sir: Mrs. R. has used the Tea-Kettle Boiler now two months, and desires me to say that it is the best invention ever made to assist the cook in preparing all kinds of food liable to boil over or burn—in fact, it does every thing you claim for it. Yours, truly,
R. RUSSELL.

*Bergen, New Jersey, Feb. 12th, 1868.*
A. BERNEY.—Sir: My husband brought home one of your Patent Tea-Kettle Boilers. I use it all the time, and would not be without it for ten times its cost.
MRS. HASLET.

*Greenville, New Jersey, March 8th, 1868.*
A. BERNEY.—Dear Sir: After a fair trial of your Patent Tea-Kettle Boiler, I must say it is one of the best assistants a cook can have—it cannot be beat. Yours, resp'y,
E. E. EVERETT.

*New York, March 30th, 1868.*
Mr. BERNEY.—Your Tea-Kettle Boiler is the perfection of an Anti-Burning Boiler. Beats Hecker's, and all Double Boilers.
H. A. BRAFORD.

*New York, April 2d, 1868.*
ALFRED BERNEY, Esq.—I think your Tea-Kettle Boiler ought to be in every kitchen. The wife and cook's work is hard enough, and every labor-saving machine is a blessing, and should be used. I have never seen a more complete anti-burning and boiling-over boiler than the Tea-Kettle Boiler. Its shape and size make it useful in many ways. The price is so low that it can be bought even by the poorest families. May you sell hundreds of thousands of them. Yours, very truly, MRS. S. S——R.

OFFICE OF WM. H. PEEK & Co.,
WHOLESALE BOTANIC DRUGGISTS,
No. 98 John Street.
Wm. W. Peek.   Jos. A. Velsor.   Wm. H. Peck

*New York, May 19th, 1868.*
Mr. A. BERNEY.—Dear Sir: We have used your wonderful Tea-Kettle Boiler in our family for three months, and would not be without it for ten times its value.
We find it the best invention we ever saw for Boiling Milk, Ice Cream, Farina, Oysters, and many others that would be sure to burn if exposed to the hot coals. I would recommend every family to have one in the house.
W. H. PEEK.

*Jersey City, New Jersey, May 14th, 1868.*
*No. 170 South-Sixth St.*
Mr. A. BERNEY.—Dear Sir: I have seen your Tea-Kettle Boiler in use at my boarding-house for over a year, and all the cooks that have used it pronounce it the best cooking utensil they have ever used. It saves the time they previously spent in watching those kinds of food likely to burn. In fact, the use of the Boiler proves that it does all you claim for it. O. DUTTON.

## COOK'S EVIDENCE IN FAVOR OF THE TEA-KETTLE BOILER.

*Corner Rahway Avenue and Cherry Street.*
*Elizabeth, New Jersey, May 1st, 1868.*
A. BERNEY, Esq.—Your Tea-Kettle Boiler is the very best anti-burning boiler ever invented, and every family, rich and poor, ought to use them. The one we use has, in one year, saved its cost ten times over. The poor, hard-working cooks ought to insist on the family they work for, buying one, or buy it themselves.
LOUISE KITTMAR, Cook.

No cook will use any thing else to boil Milk, Corn Starch, or any thing likely to burn. B. RUNNETT.

I would advise every cook to buy one if the family will not.    LOUISE HEINDRICKS.

The most troublesome things to cook are Milk, Corn Starch, and such food as is likely to burn. Hecker's Boilers burn out very quick, but your Boilers now make the Corn Starch, Farina, Tapioca, Hominy, Samp, Rice, etc., tho—he easiest things to cook.
BRIDGET MURPHY.

Mr. BERNEY.—Here is a dollar for one of your Tea-Kettle Boilers. I am going to get married, and must have one.    JULIA D——B.

It beats any thing to cook with in the kitchen, and every cook should refuse to work without a Tea-Kettle Boiler to aid her.    MARGARET O'BRIEN.

The blessings of all cooks will be showered down on you for inventing the Tea-Kettle Boiler. ANN McBRIDE.

I have worked in families for twenty-seven years, but have never seen in any house so complete a cooking article as your Tea-Kettle Boiler. MRS. HAND.

*New York, July 18th, 1868.*
A. BERNEY, Esq.—Dear Sir: My wife has used your Tea-Kettle Boiler and find it answers every purpose you say it does. It cooks all kinds of farinaceous foods liable to burn, without burning, or any watching; in fact, she does not see how any family can do without one, and advises her friends to use them. Yours, truly,
N. D. REDHEAD,
Of T. N. HICKCOX & Co., Machinists and Manufacturers of STAMPED BRASS GOODS. Salesroom, 280 Pearl Street, New York.

## COFFEE-CONE RECOMMENDATIONS.

*New York, July 14th, 1868.*
A. BERNEY, Esq.—Dear Sir: I have used your new Patent Coffee Cone in my family, and find it makes clear, strong Coffee, saving fully one-third of the amount we formerly used. It makes it free from all grounds, and *preserves all the aroma.* I recommend every one to use them. It is all made in a few minutes. Yours truly,
FRANK ANGEONE,
With J. C. HULL'S SON (formerly W. Hull & Son), Office 32 Park Row, STAPLE and FANCY SOAPS, CANDLES and STARCH.

118 *John Street, New York,*
*July 20th, 1868.*
A. BERNEY, Esq.—Dear Sir: I have used your Patent Coffee Cone a week. The first trial the girl put in the usual quantity. It was too strong, so much so that we could not drink it without weakening it. The next time we used two-thirds of the quantity we first used, and then it was stronger than the old way of boiling. The flavor was excellent, the coffee pure and free from grounds; in fact, I never had good coffee until I used this Cone. Yours, etc.,

## RECOMMENDATIONS OF THE MYSTERY OF LIVING.

*No. 41 Bushwick Ave., Williamsburgh,*
*July 6th, 1868.*
A. BERNEY, Esq.—Dear Sir: My wife has used some of the recipes for cooking, in the "Mystery of Living," and finds them correct, economical and good. The style of having the Time, Articles and Directions seperate, makes them handy and convenient. By the use of these recipes a family can reduce their expenses one-third. Your Tea-Kettle Boiler is the perfection of an anti-burning boiler. Nothing can burn in it, or be wasted or spoiled. Yours, truly,    JOHN GLIVES.

*No. 445 Main St., Charlestown, Mass.*
*July 3d, 1868.*
A. BERNEY, Esq.—Dear Sir: I have used the recipes in the People's Book, "Mystery of Living," for a month, and would not be without it. They are *practicable and perfect, good and useful, economical and saving, plain and sure* to produce palatable dishes from the cheapest of foods. Certainly, no family should be without one, if they would live well and save money. Yours, truly,
F. MASON.

FIFTY MORE AT 116 JOHN STREET.

OPINION OF JOHN HECKER, Esq., MANUFACTURER OF FARINA, INVENTOR OF HECKER's BOILER.—The publisher called upon Mr. Hecker, and showed him some fifty pages of the MYSTERY OF LIVING. Mr. H. looked it over carefully, and said "It is the most practical, sensible, economical work on cooking I ever saw, and is just what is wanted for the million." He insisted on paying full price for half a book, saying it was cheap at that. *He also pronounced the* TEA-KETTLE BOILER *the true boiler for cooking farinaceous foods.*

# THE ZERO REFRIGERATOR,
## WITH WATER AND WINE-COOLER COMBINED.

ALEX'R M. LESLEY,

MANUFACTURER,

**605**

6th Avenue

BETWEEN

35th and 36th Sts.,

NEW YORK.

Grand

**PRIZE**

**MEDAL,**

Awarded by the

AMERICAN

INSTITUTE,

**1867.**

### Report of the Committee on Refrigerators.

"THE ZERO REFRIGERATOR is the best, not so much by possessing novel features of great merit, as by being an extremely well devised, effective, and economical construction. The principles it involves are long tested and approved. It preserves the meat and vegetables at a low temperature, with the consumption of less ice than any other known to us.

COMMITTEE. { "THOMAS D. STETSON, "JAMES B. OGDEN, "IRA L. CADY."

☞ *The Zero Refrigerator will retain a greater degree of cold, with less ice consumed, than any other Refrigerator yet invented.*

---

*From the Cultivator and Country Gentleman, June, 1867.*

"LESLEY'S REFRIGERATOR.—After a full trial we have found this Refrigerator a valuable household convenience. The ice is preserved in the central part; and the inclosed shelves, on each side, receive articles of food, fruit, etc., which it is desired to protect from the heat of summer and the cold of winter. It is a handsome piece of furniture, painted oak color, with white porcelain knobs, and will grace the handsomest pantry or kitchen hall. The ice reservoir is a most convenient place for depositing this material, where it will keep from one to three days, according to the heat of the weather, maintaining a temperature in the adjoining apartments lower than that of the coldest cellars. We have never found anything to freeze in it in winter, and in making an experiment by placing it out of doors when the thermometer was 20° below freezing, found that a small cup of cold water required five hours for a thin film of ice to form, at the same time it froze in fifteen minutes if exposed."

JUDGE STORER, of Cincinnati, Ohio, writes: "Your Refrigerator gives perfect satisfaction. It has preserved meats, vegetables, milk, and butter during the hottest months of our variable climate."

"The Zero Refrigerator is grand! excellent."—*Prof. A. E. Thatcher.*

Dr. HALL, of "*Hall's Journal of Health,*" says: "It is certainly an improvement on all others."

"I think for cleanliness and convenience of use, it is much superior to anything of the kind made."—*G. S. Wearer, Albany, N. Y.*

"Your Zero Refrigerator was in use during the hottest months of last summer. I can safely recommend it."—*Mrs. James Brooks, Fifth Avenue.*

## ALEXANDER M. LESLEY, Manufacturer,
### No. 605 SIXTH AVENUE,
Between Thirty-fifth and Thirty-sixth Streets,      NEW YORK.

☞ *The store runs through to No. 1310 Broadway.*

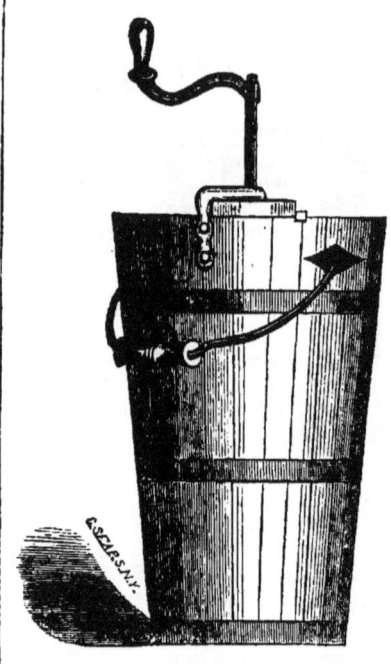 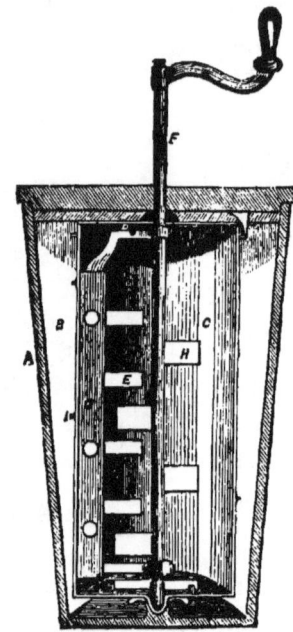

## THE AMERICAN
# ICE-CREAM FREEZER.

This Freezer surpasses all others in ease in operating, rapidity of freezing, and evenness of cream frozen. By *simply turning a crank*, three essential operations are effected at once, viz., The ice and salt is agitated, the frozen cream is scraped from the sides of the cylinder, and thoroughly mixed and beaten by the arms attached to the spindle, passing (as the crank is turned) between those on the scraper, thereby effectually preventing the formation of frozen lumps or irregularities, and producing cream unsurpassed for smoothness.

MANUFACTURED AND FOR SALE BY

## Fraser, Bell & Loughran,

Successors to **GEORGE W. ROBINS.**

MANUFACTURERS OF

PLAIN, JAPANNED, AND STAMPED

# TIN WARE,

213 PEARL STREET, NEW YORK.

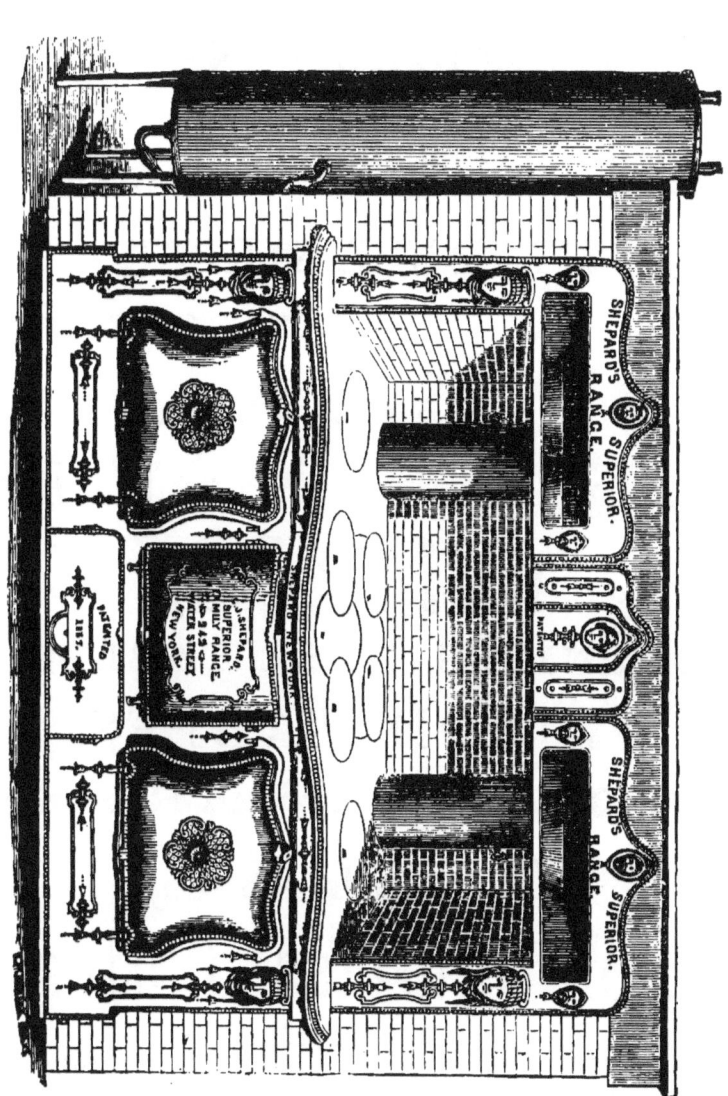

# LOOKING-GLASSES.

## W. A. WILLARD & CO.,
### 177 CANAL STREET,

W. A. WILLARD.
W. J. GRAHAM.

### NEW YORK CITY.

### ORNAMENTED
## MANTLE AND PIER
## MIRRORS,
### CORNICES, BASE TABLES,
### TRIPOD TABLES,
**Plain, Gilt, Mahogany, and Rosewood**
### LOOKING-GLASSES,
## Looking-Glass Plates,
### PICTURE GLASS, PICTURE FRAMES,
Portrait Frames, Photographic Ovals,
### GILT, WALNUT, ROSEWOOD AND GILT
## MOULDINGS,
Cord and Tassels, Screw Eyes, Glaziers' Diamonds, &c., &c.

*We invite the Public to call at our new Store, and examine our goods before buying.*

# Curran Bowering Manufacturing Co.

## TROY STOVE WAREHOUSE,
## 237 WATER STREET,
### NEW YORK.

**AGENTS FOR THE**

## CELEBRATED BARSTOW RANGE.

*A GENERAL ASSORTMENT OF*

## STOVES AND RANGES

### CONSTANTLY ON HAND.

## Brass Kettles, Coal Hods,
### AND ALL KINDS OF TIN WARE.

## HOUSE AND SHIP PLUMBING.

# KINGSFORD'S
# OSWEGO STARCH.
## THE BEST STARCH IN THE WORLD.

---

## KINGSFORD'S
# SILVER GLOSS STARCH
### GIVES A BEAUTIFUL FINISH TO THE LINEN.

---

### READ THIS!!

**Less than Half a Cent!** will pay the difference in an ordinary family washing, between the cost of *Kingsford's Celebrated Starch,* and *any of the common starches,* and the difference will be more than saved by its *extra strength.*

---

# KINGSFORD'S
# OSWEGO
# CORN STARCH.
## FOR
## CUSTARDS, JELLIES, SAUCES, PUDDINGS, BLANC MANGE, ICE CREAM, Etc.,

*Is the Original, Established in 1849, and Preserves its Reputation, as*

**PURER, STRONGER, AND MORE DELICATE**

than any other article of the kind offered, either of the same name, or with other titles.

## MR. KINGSFORD HAS PERFECTED IT!

N. B. See recipes for cooking, on pages 10–12 and 25 and 26.

# GEO. F. GANTZ & CO.,
## 136 & 138 CEDAR STREET,
### NEW YORK CITY.

## PURE WHITE ROCK
# POTASH.

Packed in cases of 48 One-pound Cans; also in Half Cases of 24 One-pound Cans.

## PRICES.

| | | |
|---|---|---|
| Single Cases | $8 50 | Per Case. |
| 5 Cases | 8 00 | " |
| 25 Cases and upwards | 7 50 | " |

Half Cases, 10 Cents each additional.

### NET CASH ONLY.

RETAILED FOR TWENTY-FIVE CENTS A CAN.

One Can is guaranteed to make 15 pounds Best White Soap.
Any housekeeper can make good Soap, as easy as a loaf of bread.
Full directions printed and sent with every Can.
Toilet Soap made as easy as Common Soap.
It makes Soap that will not injure fine fabrics.
Soap made with it will only cost Two Cents a pound.
One Can will make half a barrel of Soft Soap.
The process is easier than making bread.
It will make the very best of Soap.
No excuse for being dirty, with Soap so cheap.
Remember, Soap at Two Cents a pound.
Save the pennies, and you will soon have dollars.

## GEO. F. GANTZ & CO.,

Manufacturers of Saleratus — Paragon, Excelsior, Golden Prize, and other brands; Bi Carb. Soda, Sal Soda, Soap Powders, Andrews' Yeast Powder, West End Yeast Powder, Cream Tartar, etc.

## USE THE CONE,
## AND MAKE PURE COFFEE,
### FREE FROM GROUNDS.

We warrant every one to give satisfaction, and save ONE THIRD of the Coffee formerly used, or return the money.

Call at any hardware, house-furnishing, crockery, or tin store for one, and if they will not get it, call or write to us, and we will send it to you. No. 1, one dollar; No. 2, one dollar and twenty-five cents.

**A. BERNEY'S WHOLESALE DEPOT,**
**116 John Street, New York.**

# READ! READ!
## CALL AND SEE.
# SILVER-PLATED WARES,
OF EVERY DESCRIPTION, RETAILED AT WHOLESALE PRICES BY
# J. C. WATERS,
SUCCESSOR TO WATERS & THORP,
### 14 John St., 7 Doors from Broadway, N. Y. (up-stairs.)

The Goods offered for sale are of the best quality, plated on the finest WHITE METAL, and WARRANTED AS ABOVE.

A fine assortment of PLATED WARE of every kind constantly on hand, all of the latest Patterns and Designs.

### ANNEXED FIND ADDED A FEW OF MY PRICES.

| | |
|---|---|
| *Tea Sets*, consisting of 1 Coffee Pot, 2 Tea Pots, 1 Sugar, 1 Cream Pitcher, and 1 Slop Bowl, according to quality and design, from........ | $25.00 to 45.00 Set. |
| *Coffee Urns*, from................................... | 12.00 to 25.00 each. |
| *Cake Baskets*, from................................ | 3.00 to 12.00 " |
| *Castors*, with 6 Cut or Engraved Bottles, from.. | 4.50 to 20.00 " |
| *Small Lunch Castors*, with Salts and Spoons, from | 2.75 to 8.00 " |
| *Ice Pitchers*, from............................. | 4.50 to 14.00 " |
| *Berry Stands*, Glass Lined (different colors), from.. | 5.00 to 12.00 " |
| *Salt Stands*, Glass Lined, from................... | 2.50 to 4.50 per pair. |
| *Napkin Rings*......................................... | 2.75 to 8.00 per doz. |
| *Syrup Pitchers*, with Stands..................... | 3.00 to 6.00 each. |
| *Butter Coolers*, from ............................... | 2.75 to 8.00 " |
| *Liquor Stands*, with Cut or Engraved Bottles.... | 12.00 to 24.00 " |
| *Sugar Basket*, Glass Lined, from................. | 4.00 to 8.00 " |
| *Table Knives*, with Plated Blades and Handles.. | 12.00 per doz. |
| *Dessert Knives*....................................... | 10.00 " |

Every variety of Spoons and Forks, Soup Ladles, Gravy Ladles, Sauce Ladles, Fish Knives, Butter Knives. These are plated on finest quality of Albatta, and warranted full weight of Silver, according to their Stamp.

All kinds of old Ware Repaired and Replated in the best manner, and at the lowest possible price, and without delay.

CALL AND EXAMINE OUR GOODS BEFORE PURCHASING ELSEWHERE, AND WE WILL SATISFY YOU THAT YOU NEED NOT GO FARTHER.

# BRADBURY PIANO FORTES.

### Warerooms, 427 Broome Street, near Broadway, N. Y.

These very popular instruments are recommended as embodying all the superior qualities of a first class Piano, by the most prominent of our leading artists.

## A CARD.

Having retired from the Piano-Forte business, Messrs. FREEBORN GARRETSON SMITH & CO. will succeed me, and for them I bespeak the patronage of my friends and the public. Mr. Smith has served a regular apprenticeship in the various branches of the Piano Forte business, and has been engaged in the first manufactories in New York and Boston. I can confidently recommend him as a gentleman in all respects qualified to succeed me in the manufacture of my first class Pianos, he having had the sole charge of my manufacturing department, as Superintendent, since 1865, and having given entire satisfaction in that capacity.

NEW YORK, *July* 17, 1867.          WM. B. BRADBURY.

## TRIUMPHANT SUCCESS.

SEVEN FIRST PREMIUMS received within four weeks—Two GOLD MEDALS, ONE SILVER MEDAL, and FOUR DIPLOMAS—making in all SEVEN FIRST PREMIUMS for State Fairs, for WM. B. BRADBURY'S NEW SCALE PIANO FORTES, within the brief space of four weeks.

THE TWO GOLD MEDALS are from the FAIR OF THE AMERICAN INSTITUTE, held at the Academy of Music in September, 1868, "for the best Piano Forte," and from the New Jersey State Fair, held at Paterson, N. J., September, 1868, "for the Two BEST PIANO FORTES."

Never, in the history of trade, were so many FIRST PREMIUMS known to be given within so short a space of time.

In addition to this, we have the strongest indorsements of nearly all the well-known musicians of New York, who have personally and carefully examined our Pianos. We are also receiving similar testimonials from first class Teachers and Professors from other cities and towns.

The testimonials from GOTTSCHALK, MASON, SANDERSON, PATTISON, BERGE, ZUNDELL, HELLER, FRADELL, and others, were only given after thorough and repeated trials for several months.

R. BONNER, Esq., *Proprietor of the* "*New York Ledger,*" thus *writes in the* "*Ledger*" *of Jan.* 13, 1866.

"We bought one of Bradbury's Instruments last spring, and after using it for several months, and hearing the opinions of some of the best judges in this city—persons who have tried it—we are confident that no better Piano could be made. We do not wonder, therefore, that 'American Pianos are now at a premium in the markets of the Old World.'"

THEODORE TILTON, *Editor of the* "*Independent,*" *in a note to Mr. Bradbury:*

"MY DEAR MR. BRADBURY,—I have had the beautiful Piano so long, that now to ask me how I like it, is like asking me how I like one of my children! In fact, if you were to ask the children, I'm afraid they would say they liked it nearly as well as they like me! It speaks every day, the year round, and never loses its voice. I wish its owner could do half as well."

*We are using the* BRADBURY PIANOS *in our Families, and they give entire satisfaction.*

| | |
|---|---|
| M. SIMPSON, Bishop M. E. Church, Philadelphia. | THEODORE TILTON, Editor Independent. |
| E. S. JAMES, Bishop M. E. Church, New York. | ROBERT BONNER, Editor New York Ledger. |
| E. THOMSON, Bishop, Evanston, Ill. | A. BERNEY, Editor Mystering. |
| DANIEL WISE, Editor Sunday School Advocate. | Rev. A. COOKMAN, 2033 Vine Street, Philadelphia. |
| D. D. LORE, Editor Northern Advocate. | Rev. E. H. PATTISON, 1322 Jefferson St., " |
| DR. JAS. PORTER, Book Agent, 200 Mulberry St., N. Y. | Rev. S. W. THOMAS, 1018 Arch Street. " |
| DR. THOS. SEWELL, Pastor Pacific St. Ch., Brooklyn. | Rev. P. S. HENSON, 1330 Jefferson Street, " |
| DR. H. MATTISON, Pastor Trinity Church, Jersey City. | THOMAS HULL, Esq., 1536 N. Fifteenth Street. " |
| DR. J. P. DURBIN, Secretary of Missions, New York. | GEO. W. PERKENPINE, Esq., 56 N. Fourth St., " |
| T. S. ARTHUR, the Author, Philadelphia. | CHARLES SCOTT, Esq., 88 N. Third Street, " |

☞ *Why pay 33 per cent. by renting a Piano, when you can save from $150 to $200 by buying for cash, or pay in installments, to suit your own convenience, one of Bradbury's Celebrated Pianos. Send for Price List, or call at the Warerooms and select. We refer to the above Testimonials.*

**FREEBORN GARRETSON SMITH & CO.,** *Late Supt. and Successor to* WM. B. BRADBURY.

☞ SEND FOR ILLUSTRATED PRICE LISTS.      **427 Broome Street New York**

www.ingramcontent.com/pod-product-compliance
Lightning Source LLC
Chambersburg PA
CBHW031403160426
43196CB00007B/883